A Literature of Questions

A Literature of Questions
Nonfiction for the Critical Child

Joe Sutliff Sanders

University of Minnesota Press
Minneapolis | London

Portions of chapter 6 were previously published as "*Almost Astronauts* and the Pursuit of Reliability in Children's Nonfiction," *Children's Literature in Education* 46 (2015): 378. doi:10.1007/s10583-014-9241-z. Copyright Springer Science+Business Media New York 2014. Reprinted with permission of Springer.

Copyright 2018 by Joe Sutliff Sanders

All rights reserved. No part of this publication may be reproduced, stored in a retrieval system, or transmitted, in any form or by any means, electronic, mechanical, photocopying, recording, or otherwise, without the prior written permission of the publisher.

Published by the University of Minnesota Press
111 Third Avenue South, Suite 290
Minneapolis, MN 55401-2520
http://www.upress.umn.edu

The University of Minnesota is an equal-opportunity educator and employer.

Library of Congress Cataloging-in-Publication
Names: Sanders, Joe Sutliff author.
Title: A literature of questions : nonfiction for the critical child / Joe Sutliff Sanders.
Description: Minneapolis : University of Minnesota Press, 2017. | Includes bibliographical references and index. |
Identifiers: LCCN 2017005482 (print) | ISBN 978-1-5179-0300-8 (hc) | 978-1-5179-0301-5 (pb)
Subjects: LCSH: American prose literature–History and criticism. | Children's literature, American–History and criticism.
Classification: LCC PS493 .S36 2017 (print) | DDC 810.9/9282–dc23
LC record available at https://lccn.loc.gov/2017005482

UMP LSI

For Melendra

CONTENTS

INTRODUCTION The Literary Study of Children's Nonfiction *1*

1 Beyond Authority: Questioning the Literature of Facts *33*

2 Voice and the Seamless Narrative of Knowledge *47*

3 Nonfiction's Unfinished Characters: The People Who Are Wrong, Flawed, and Incomplete *77*

4 Inquiry at and in the Margins: How Peritexts Encourage Critical Reading *107*

5 Seeing Photographs: Breaking the Authority of Nonfiction's Favorite Medium *133*

6 The Pursuit of Reliability in *Almost Astronauts* *177*

7 The Empathy of Critical Engagement: Emotion and Sentimentality in Children's Nonfiction *199*

CONCLUSION   Critical Engagement's Moral Imperative   *223*

Acknowledgments   *233*

Notes   *237*

Bibliography   *247*

Index   *261*

INTRODUCTION
The Literary Study of Children's Nonfiction

IN THE CHILDREN'S DEPARTMENT of my local public library, the librarians hate straightening up the nonfiction section. The child patrons use the nonfiction section extensively, reading up on dinosaurs, knitting, pets, castles, celebrities, space, presidents, origami, and hundreds of other subjects for school projects as well as pleasure. The carpet on the floor tells a similar tale, worn here as nowhere else in the children's department. Yes, librarians—and, for that matter, school teachers—are reminded every time they go to straighten the shelves that nonfiction is a crucial, even exciting branch of literature for young readers, and they aren't alone. In a recent article, children's author Elizabeth Partridge rejoices at a booming interest in nonfiction for young readers. She recounts with delight the honors that nonfiction has won in direct competition with novels and picture books: a Coretta Scott King Author Award; three finalists in the children's literature category of the Los Angeles Times Book Award (including that year's winner); three finalists for the National Book Award for Young People's Literature (including the winner); a Newbery Honor; and the Margaret A. Edwards Award, a lifetime achievement award given in 2010 for the first time to an author of children's nonfiction. Children, teachers, librarians, and publishers have discovered, in what Partridge calls "this amazing, starry, silver-and-gold-stickered time," that nonfiction can provide rich reading experiences.

Literary scholars, however, have been slow to theorize the genre. Children's nonfiction has hardly been absent from the critical conversation, but its place in that conversation has generally been to articulate keen observations about children's culture more broadly. For example, one recent study of informative periodicals written by children between 1936 and 1946 tells the story of the progressive education movement in the context of which those periodicals were published (see Onion, "Writing"). Elsewhere, nonfiction serves to demonstrate the evolution of radical literature during a specific historical moment in response to unique historical stimuli (see Mickenberg, *Learning*). Specifically feminist studies explain the imperialist role played by children's nonfiction written by women during the long nineteenth century (see Norcia, *X Marks*) and how contemporary sport advice books "do more to limit, than liberate, girls" (Heinecken, "Empowering," 3). Research on a very specific period of Danish picture books includes analysis of nonfiction to demonstrate how Danish literature negotiated avant-garde Russian influence (see Christensen, "Rupture"), and other research looks at nonfiction as one aspect of how civilizations construct their own ideas of childhood and citizenship, either in eighteenth-century Britain (see Müller, *Framing*) or in America in its early stages of development (see Weikle-Mills, *Imaginary*). Nonfiction is an important part of these studies, but in each case, it primarily advances an argument about something other than itself. The results have been very useful, providing insights about culture, history, and literary history, but they have not attempted to theorize nonfiction as a genre.

The most common methodology of previous studies of nonfiction has been, as these examples show, historical, and for all its benefits, that methodology requires certain necessary strategic limitations. Most significant, at least from my perspective, is that historical approaches require us to privilege differences across time and play down significant similarities between periods. A historical approach generally has to tell a story of how things changed, not how they were fundamentally similar. The questions that historical analysis asks incline a given study to focus on discontinuity. As previous scholarship demonstrates, the results of such an approach are important and eye-opening. However, they render large-scale theorization difficult, if not impossible. My intentionally nonhistorical study hopes not precisely to recoup continuity across history but to offer a theory grounded in aesthetic analysis. This theory certainly allows historical comparisons, but such applications of the theory are best performed after the theory has been clearly established. That is the work of this book.

A Literature of Questions examines how children's nonfiction can invite or rebuff critical engagement. Specialists outside of literary studies have already begun investigating the genre's potential in this arena. Evelyn B. Freeman and Diane Goetz Person, specialists in children's literature and education, champion children's nonfiction because it provides its readers with an opportunity to "inquire and problem solve as their reading leads them to question and investigate" (*Connecting*, 5). The question of how nonfiction might ask its readers to engage in such nuanced, nonlinear thinking forms the center of my investigation. The theorization of children's nonfiction that I offer in this book is not interested in flattening the differences between historical periods but in putting aside those differences long enough to articulate an aesthetic theory of critical engagement that applies to children's nonfiction across time.

Crucially, scholarship has already demonstrated the role that literary analysis, specifically aesthetic analysis, can play in the investigation of how a text encourages the processes of inquiry, questioning, and investigation. Julie Martello, for example, has argued that drama has great potential for ideological work because of the qualities that *make it drama*. "Its teaching and learning potential," she writes, "lies in the role-taking and exploration of particular moments within the drama framework and in the guided reflection that occurs outside of the drama itself" ("Drama," 195). In other words, something in the fundamental structure of this kind of storytelling invites critical participation. Although she examines drama and I examine nonfiction, the underlying point is the same: a formal understanding of a text, indeed of an entire genre, can lead to understandings that extend beyond form. Christine H. Leland and Jerome C. Harste ("That's") make a similar argument, illustrating how semiotic reading by and with children aligns well with critical analysis to help portray a world of inequality and inhumanity in which, as their own students put it, "That's not fair!" And Peter Hollindale—a literary scholar specializing in children's literature—insists that "our priority in the world of children's books should not be to promote ideology but to understand it, and find ways of helping others to understand it, including the children themselves" ("Ideology," 10). It is this intention, of examining literature for children to enable understandings about critical engagement with ideology, that points to the heart of my study.

Paulo Freire, in his famous study of democratic education, describes a pedagogical tool that testifies to the potential for critical engagement in children's literature in general and narrative nonfiction in particular. Freire explains what he calls "codifications," which might be "sketches or photographs" or even just "a few words presenting an existential problem." It is this codification on which students are to focus as they shoulder the burdens of democracy, as they unmask the hierarchies and exploitation that the world around them struggles to mask. "Since they represent existential situations," Freire explains, "the codifications should be simple in their complexity and offer various decoding possibilities in order to avoid the brain-washing tendencies of propaganda. Codifications are not slogans; they are cognizable objects, challenges towards which the critical reflection of the decoders should be directed" (*Pedagogy*, 106–7). As such, Freire's goal in using codifications is strikingly similar to that of semiotic analysis in the classrooms that Leland and Harste describe. Codifications and their analysis also work in ways fundamentally similar to the ways in which texts and their literary analysis work. As Freire's students struggle through "various decoding possibilities" present in the isolatable, "cognizable" codifications, they take on a task very similar to the careful, generative labor that drives literary analysis. Too, because codifications are historically and culturally rooted, and because they focus on specific subjects rather than a broad swath of knowledge, they strongly resemble children's nonfiction, which increasingly, as Freeman and Person write, "explore a single topic in depth" (*Connecting*, 36). Children's nonfiction, filled with scenes and narratives that resemble Freire's codifications, lends itself well to critical reflection. To paraphrase Martello's comments about drama, an extraordinary potential for critical engagement lies in the very framework of children's nonfiction.

Although I have been careful to distinguish between historical approaches to the field and the approach of this book, the theory that I am building is directly relevant to historical readings of nonfiction, and that relevance comes mainly through the way that the genre's form creates a potential for critical engagement. Julia L. Mickenberg, for example, examines the mid-twentieth-century's burst of interest in science training for young people, a period in which nonfiction was central, and although she rarely explicates form, she routinely seeks out how the genre could be used to encourage critical engagement. Mickenberg even considers how children's nonfiction attempted to train children in scientific thinking, an evidence-based approach to understanding the world that requires critical reflection. Mickenberg's project, though, is to illuminate instances of nonfiction within historical contexts. Thus, her study carefully demonstrates how science nonfiction of the mid-century becomes more eloquent when set within the structures of the political ideologies battling at the time: "conservatives focused upon how science could be used to improve efficiency and productivity, while radicals emphasized how science could bring greater wealth for all and how its methods could be used to create critical thinkers" (*Learning*, 184). The historically specific political ideology that motivates invitations to critical engagement—rather than the techniques that nonfiction uses for doing so—is her point. Even when Mickenberg does explain such techniques, as in her study of Millicent Ellis Selsam's *Egg to Chick* (1946), her real aim is to portray a continuity between presentations of evolution in Selsam's work and in that of Friedrich Engels (193). My efforts come even closer to those of Kimberley Reynolds, especially in her very recent study of radical British children's literature in the early twentieth century. For example, she argues that early-century radical writings for children "encouraged readers to learn about, question, experiment with, disassemble, and refashion ideas, systems, and institutions." Reynolds's book, though, skillfully demonstrates how these texts both ask readers

6 ◼ *Introduction*

"to challenge the status quo" and attempt "to recruit and direct them, not just as readers but as individuals who embodied and performed the radical message" (*Left Out* 9). When Reynolds looks to the literature, her strategy is to illustrate how nonfiction of the period expressed central tenets of *and* contradictions within radical movements. She sometimes draws her evidence from how nonfiction attempts to channel critical engagement, but always as part of her narrative of radical philosophy at work in a very specific period of children's literature. Mickenberg and Reynolds, to take two of the most successful recent historical critics of the genre, are frequently interested in the place that nonfiction allows to critical engagement, an approach to which my own study's articulation of the aesthetics of critical engagement in nonfiction is immediately applicable. As *A Literature of Questions* largely skirts historical readings, it will attempt to develop a theory of the genre that is grounded in aesthetics, but its ramifications are hardly limited to form.

In 1972, Margery Fisher, a widely published reviewer of children's books and an internationally respected lecturer on the topic, released a wide-ranging survey of children's nonfiction. The vast majority of her book is given not to theorizing the genre but to explaining the joy of nonfiction and the methods by which a reader might recognize quality books. She concludes, though, with this:

> An information book must communicate facts and ideas to its readers, of whatever age or capacity, in such a way that they will develop the will and the mental equipment to assess these facts and ideas. In the broadest sense, an information book is a teacher, and the role of a teacher is to lead his pupils towards a considered independence of thought and action. Instruction is important, but freedom of thought is more important still. (*Matters of Fact,* 474)

Fisher's conclusion is a call for an approach to children's nonfiction that attends primarily to its unique qualities as well as the possibilities of the genre to provoke reflective engagement with information. It is a call that has never been answered in literary scholarship, and it has been only incompletely answered by library and education scholars. *A Literature of Questions,* therefore, attends to nonfiction, its form, and what its form tells us about the ideologies in which the genre is embedded.

Thesis and Limitations

This book proposes a method for examining children's nonfiction from a literary perspective. At its heart is formal analysis: it develops a set of hallmarks that flag places where nonfiction routinely chooses between inviting and refusing critical engagement. But this formal analysis is designed to produce observations that go beyond aesthetics: searching for where a work of nonfiction invites or refuses critical engagement reveals what ideas that text wants to normalize and what ideologies it is willing to risk by making them vulnerable to the critical attention of children. By "critical," I mean a process by which readers ask questions and test information in a pattern that I will call "punctuated plurality." By "engagement," I mean an activity that is collaborative, characterized by a sharing of authority between books and children. Attending to where books invite or refuse critical engagement offers a way of reading children's nonfiction that provides insights that begin with but extend well beyond form.

Throughout, I will use the term *children's nonfiction,* but advocates of children's literature have used various names for this field. Freeman and Person give an explanation—and complaint—that is typical for champions of the field, whatever name it uses:

> Textbooks do not create a sense of the time they are depicting but seem to teach facts in isolation. Science and mathematics texts do not portray the excitement of great discoveries and the impetus such discoveries give to other scientists, encouraging them to continue their labors. Social studies textbooks do not transmit the flavor of an era or demonstrate the impact of literature, art, science, and architecture upon political ideologies of an era. Nor is the impact of philosophical movements and major events on people and governments adequately presented. (*Connecting,* 29)

It is against this definition of textbooks that Freeman and Person define *informational children's books,* and that opposition is typical through essays originating from educational, library science, and trade perspectives. Whether the term is *informational children's book, narrative nonfiction, informational texts,* or *children's nonfiction,* these books, unlike textbooks, tend to originate from trade houses, and their market orientation has a significant influence: children's nonfiction is usually seen by its producers and consumers as different from the information-centered textbooks that are required reading, which means that children's nonfiction must be interesting and engaging in its own right. Although both textbooks and trade nonfiction focus on information, the market pressures on them create a telling distinction between the two.

It is easily possible to exaggerate the difference between textbooks and what I am calling nonfiction, but over time, those differences have become more significant as publishers specializing in each market have refined their styles and as those styles have defined their emerging markets. As Carl M. Tomlinson, Michael O. Tunnell, and Donald J. Richgels observe, history textbooks, to take one example, have increasingly come to be written for the curricula of specific grade ranges ("e.g., American History in grades five, eight, and eleven, and World History in grades six and ten") and to "cover several centuries of events (e.g., Ancient Civilizations, U.S. History, World History)." "This means," Tomlinson and his colleagues argue, "that even a rather lengthy textbook must give only shallow treatment to any topic within such a wide scope" ("Content," 55). However, writers of trade nonfiction "have the luxury of time and space to focus on a single historical event, era, or person and to treat that subject in depth. They have the freedom to present both popular and unpopular stands on controversial issues" (56). Sara L. Schwebel's study of the use of historical fiction in U.S. classrooms points to "advocates of authentic literature like [Charlotte] Huck [who] pressed for trade books—that is, literature written for children's pleasure rather than for their edification and marketed to individuals rather than to textbook committees—to be integrated throughout the curriculum" (*Child-Size History,* 1). As a result, trade nonfiction might be found in classrooms, but by the twentieth century, a strong difference in style, scope, and even subject defined the two kinds of books on which teachers relied to communicate information. The different production histories and patterns of consumption—note Schwebel's comment about "textbook committees"—have significantly added to the ability of nonfiction to address controversial subjects, especially as compared with textbooks. Mickenberg notes how, in the twentieth century, the latter "were subject to intense scrutiny at the state, local, and even national levels. The random usage of trade books made them harder to track than textbooks, which would be used by every student in a class or grade" (*Learning*, 15). Indeed, Mickenberg follows the telling case history of Mary Elting's trade book *We Are the Government* (1946), which only came under the scrutiny of red-baiting watchdogs because it was accidentally misclassified as a textbook. As a result, trade nonfiction, especially when thought of as the opposite of textbooks, is better situated to offer opportunities for critical engagement simply because it is less deeply embedded in the paranoid economy in which textbooks circulate.

Even narrowed in this way, though, "children's nonfiction" is too broad a subject for one study, so I have taken some pains to limit the instances of nonfiction that I will consider. The place and time of the texts I read, for example, are limited to American children's nonfiction dating back to books available in the late colonial period (but often published, as is true of so many other Anglophone books of the day, in Britain). U.S. texts absorb my interest because it is in America right now that enthusiasm for the field is expanding, and expanding rapidly. That burgeoning interest began when Russell Freedman's *Lincoln: A Photobiography* (1987) won the Newbery Medal in 1988, the first time a work of nonfiction had won the highest prize for American children's literature in more than forty years.[1] In recent years, the influential—and controversial—Common Core State Standards for compulsory education in the United States have made "informational" texts a primary concern, with a clear effect on the children's literature industry.[2] American children's nonfiction is also an ideal subject because archives around the country have preserved a long and well-populated history of children's nonfiction from this country, helping give historical context to the trends of the genre that have lately garnered such praise. It was while immersing myself in that history that the model of critical engagement that I describe in this book began to occur to me. I do, however, anticipate that the book will be useful to people looking closely at traditions outside the United States. For example, I suspect that Australia's long interest in linguistics, critical reading, and children's literature means that Australian readers would find parts of my theory directly applicable and quickly see how to revise and improve the theory for application to their own tradition of children's nonfiction. But for now, caught up in the extraordinary interest in children's nonfiction in the United States, this book will attempt to theorize texts that are primarily American.

Still, even that set of primary texts is so large that it threatens to make the explanation of my theory unwieldy, so although I have read broadly and deeply across the history of U.S. children's nonfiction, the examples that I present in these chapters do not aspire to historical thoroughness. In fact, entire decades receive no attention. The examples presented have been chosen not because they help fill specific historical gaps but because they seem better suited to advance the conversation about nonfiction. When deciding between examples to include, I have chosen nonfiction especially relevant to contemporary conversations in classrooms and scholarship. Thus I make a point of exploring texts favored by the awards for nonfiction granted by the American Library Association and the National Council of Teachers of English, major works (including non-award-winning titles) by authors widely discussed in scholarship and represented in award lists, and texts and authors frequently discussed in scholarship about the history of nonfiction and children's literature in general. From those works, I have chosen the textual examples that most clearly respond to the theory that I am developing. The point of the book is to articulate a theory that is useful across the history of children's nonfiction, and proving that usefulness requires application to primary texts from dramatically different periods, but it does not require representation from every decade. Just as I make no specific historical argument, I have privileged no specific set of texts or authors in illustrating my theory beyond those that are already important to the conversation about nonfiction across education, library, and literary circles.

Defining *Critical*

In adopting the word *critical* to describe the kind of engagement that nonfiction can invite, I am invoking a word that has become so widely used as to risk a lack of specificity. JoAnn Portalupi and Ralph Fletcher, for example, celebrate the growth of children in grades five through eight by explaining that the children "have become better critical readers, which can translate into making them better at rereading their own writing" (*Nonfiction,* 79). In this case, *critical* might mean something that analyzes ideology, but in practice, it means that students are able to gain some distance from their own writing in the revision process. For James A. Anderson, writing about governmental efforts to oversee children's consumption of television, the popular definition of *critical viewer* is "one who plans television viewing in advance and who evaluates the programs while watching" ("Television Literacy," 313). And for Allison Porzio, writing in "Absolute Critical Literacy for Part-Time Critical Readers," *critical reading* means imaginatively occupying other identities. At times, such an endeavor entails getting out of one's subject position to see the world from another perspective. "Critical theories," she explains, "show us the view from the sidelines; they can uncover how it feels to sit on the margins of society" (31–32). At other times, there is a hint of revolution: students who read critically can "understand and respond to power structures" (37). And in other moments, her essay praises newly popular books for young readers by claiming that they "offer us a method for teaching critical literacy; a great skill to prepare students for standardized testing and for life" (31). Although linking "critical literacy" and "life" might fit with many other uses of the word *critical,* Porzio's comment that "critical literacy" helps students prepare for "standardized testing" demonstrates that the term can be used to label a range of cognitive processes that extends very far indeed.

One valuable definition, however, weaves through Freire's thoughts on education. According to this definition, critical thinking is a process of cracking open the polished surface of the authority of texts and revealing spaces in which children (and, for that matter, adults) can ask questions, test information, and become part of the process of intellectual inquiry rather than its passive beneficiary. Where a text *resists* allowing readers into the process of inquiry, it might be said to be participating in what Freire dubs "the 'banking' concept of education, in which the scope of action allowed to the students extends only as far as receiving, filing, and storing the deposits" (*Pedagogy*, 58). In contrast, in those places where a text is willing to allow *critical* engagement, it opens itself to dialogue rather than maintaining the privilege of monologue. For Freire, critical thinking is defined by such participation:

> Banking education (for obvious reasons) attempts, by mythicizing reality, to conceal certain facts which explain the way men exist in the world; problem-posing education sets itself the task of demythologizing. Banking education resists dialogue; problem-posing education regards dialogue as indispensable to the act of cognition which unveils reality. Banking education treats students as objects of assistance; problem-posing education makes them critical thinkers. (71)

As with other writers concerned with critical thinking in the classroom, Freire sees critical engagement as an urge to focus on that which has been hidden. Dialogue, "indispensable to the act of cognition which unveils reality," exists where authority is shared and students are invited to the process of understanding and influencing reality. It is here that critical engagement can happen. The theory of nonfiction that I am illustrating is one that looks for where a text is willing to invite its readers to dialogue, to negotiation, to the testing of information, to *critical engagement,* and where it is not.

Although the popular meaning of *critical* is badly fractured, this meaning borrowed from Freire continues to find new expression in educational theory. Barbara Comber discusses "the potential of critical literacies as positive and locally negotiated practices" ("Critical Literacies," 272), a process that stakes out a claim for power on behalf of specific readers in their own networks of class, history, and privilege. James R. Carlson provides an interesting example of how a classroom dedicated to such literacies might look. In an essay on "Using Song-Poems to Teach Critically," Carlson explains that he uses the lyrics of Bob Dylan as a text in his course in part because Dylan regards his songs as a place for the continuing discovery of new meaning, even for the songwriter. Carlson asks his students to approach the lyrics in the same way. "Each time I brought in a new song," he writes, "students were given the task of 'dressing it up' for making meaning of it, but I also found that my students themselves were 'wearing new clothes,' given some autonomy as we convened in collaboration together on a text" (66). Similarly, Robert H. Ennis, in "Goals for a Critical Thinking Curriculum," defines *critical thinking* as "reflective thinking that is focused on deciding what to believe or do" (54), not focused on internalizing the information and ideology presented by the authoritative text or teacher. Finally, Christine Leland, Mitzi Lewison, and Jerome Harste open their recent book by calling for "a critical approach [that] encourages [children] to use language to question the everyday world, interrogate the relationship between language and power, analyze popular culture and media, understand how power relationships are socially constructed, and consider actions that can be taken to promote social justice" (*Teaching,* ix). In all of these definitions lies a sense of being in process, of testing and retesting. This activity is fundamentally creative and inquisitive. For Comber and Freire, the result of critical thinking is a humanizing engagement with the world that offers both an ability to pry open cracks where others have attempted to conceal the factitious nature of consensus reality and, simultaneously, an authority to define the newly exposed reality in ways that are locally useful. As Carlson demonstrates, that sort of critical engagement gives students not only authority but status as coauthor.

 I take key notions from these writers in my definition of critical engagement with nonfiction. *Critical engagement* is characterized by a sharing of authority between reader and text, allowing for a form of active dialogue between text and reader rather than the reader's passive receipt of information from the authoritative text. Although dialogue between fixed text and living reader is difficult, critical engagement allows for a form of dialogue in which readers can see the process of generating knowledge, vulnerabilities in that knowledge and the people who created it, venues for resisting or redirecting conclusions drawn from that knowledge, and avenues for performing new inquiry.

The Dialogue of Critical Engagement

In resting my definition on dialogue as opposed to monologue, I am inevitably invoking Mikhail Bakhtin, whose theories on dialogical and monological texts have influenced critical discourse analysis (CDA), literary theory, and educational theory. In a remarkable contribution to *Negotiating Critical Literacies in Classrooms*, Anne Haas Dyson elegantly combines Bakhtin with Freire to explain the success of a series of classroom exercises involving seven- to nine-year-old children, and her explanation provides compelling evidence to include Bakhtin in a theory of critical engagement and children's literature. In the class Dyson visited, the children wrote and performed a play that they chose to base loosely on a children's film about ninjas that was popular at the time. As they worked and revised, the children found themselves disappointed in the role of Emily, the only central female character offered by the film, who did little more than wait to be rescued. The students, Dyson reports, concluded on their own that this limited role was a problem, and their struggle over how to provide legitimate roles for the girls of the class forced powerful, personally relevant arguments that reached to the heart of issues of inequality. Dyson's thesis explains what happened in the classroom in terms that acknowledge Bakhtin but that fit easily into a Freirean model of education:

> Emily became a useful meditational tool for children's critical reflections in part because of that rootedness in the children's unofficial (child-governed) social world, as well as the official world of school literacy practices. Through those practices, Emily was dialogized, to use a key concept of the language theorist Bakhtin (1981); that is, she was rendered a reflexive symbol whom the children could use both to reflect on and, through writing, to take action within their world. (4)

What Dyson proposes is that the teacher gave the children a space in which to choose a moment of creative analysis. The children chose as their subject this film, and from the film, they developed a focus on a character. That focus generated multiple readings and rewritings of the character; as Dyson puts it, the character became "dialogized." Therefore, the children in Dyson's example chose the codification[3] and developed a useful, reflective meaning out of it. Necessary to dialogizing the character, to engaging generatively with the text of the film, was the step of negotiating as a coauthority with the text. Such negotiation allowed the students to develop a satisfactory answer to the problem of inequality that they found in the codification. In this way, Bakhtin and Freire dovetail beautifully, as Bakhtin provides the theoretical explanation for what a critical reader can do with material found in the Freirean codification.

To an extent, what Dyson details is beyond the scope of my study, but the link between Bakhtin and Freire is immensely valuable. Because I am writing about what books do rather than how readers respond to them, I can only attend to the codifications, to the works of nonfiction that can be approached by critical readers, not to the readers themselves. However, Dyson's account provides an example of how cracks in authority, which come through the dialogue imagined by Freire, can provide space and material with which readers can critically engage, the dialogization imagined by Bakhtin. In Dyson's essay, children engaged and forced a negotiation with the text in their pursuit of a question of inequality. In my study, the guiding question is not what children can do but where a text makes itself vulnerable to critical engagement—or where it refuses to do so. Dyson points to how the children enter into "gaps, dialogic space," where they "consider new ways of authoring Emily's relationships and, thus, new ways of authoring their own" (16). My study cannot ask whether children enter those gaps or what they do within them. It can, however, ask where a text invites readers into—or shields from them—those gaps.

Negotiating with Theory

I am neither the first to bring Bakhtin to the study of children's literature nor the first to attempt to do so in a way that illuminates the critical potential of children's literature, but in combining Bakhtin with Freire, I hope to solve a problem that has dogged an influential train of thought regarding critical thinking in children's literature. In his *Language and Ideology in Children's Fiction,* a crucial entry in the literary conversation about children's books, John Stephens examines texts from a position strongly informed by CDA and, consequently, Bakhtin. Throughout, his complaints about conservative texts are given weight by CDA's observation that we are swamped in language and those things that language takes for granted. We are, according to this perspective, overcome and carried away within the traps of language and the hegemony with which it is hopelessly bound up. As a result, Stephens's analysis is intent on revealing how we are trapped or liberated by specific speech acts, such as books.[4] Stephens, working from CDA and its roots in Bakhtin, frequently takes as his project the unveiling of the subject positions allowed to readers, implying along the way that a bad book is one that traps readers in odious positions and a good book is one that places readers in more progressive positions. Stephens arrives at this conclusion in part through a strain of thought that flows from Marx to Russian formalism to Bakhtin and Vološinov and finally on to influential contemporary Marxists such as Terry Eagleton. Eagleton's "The Subject of Literature," for example, opens with a pessimistic summary of Louis Althusser's theory of ideological state apparatuses, in which people are required to think in ways that flatter the fundamental assumptions of the state, and then goes on to explain the multiple ways that literature corrupts subjectivity, a corruption from which it is—and this is one of the reasons that I call Eagleton's summary of Althusser pessimistic—impossible to recover. This logic leads to sweeping statements about subjectivities across the ages. "The task of the moral technology of Literature," he explains, "is to produce an historically peculiar form of human subject who is sensitive, receptive, imaginative and so on . . . *about nothing in particular*" (98). Elsewhere, he explains a certain subject position and then claims that "in the middle ages, for example, it would be inconceivable to think of subjectivity outside such well-defined terms" (99). This strain of Marxist criticism, indebted to Bakhtin and prominent in the work of children's literature scholars such as Stephens, is wary of retrograde ideology, guarding against its potential to mold subjectivity.

But when laced with Freire, the bleak conclusions about subjectivity under the boot of culture implicit in Bakhtin can be leavened with some optimism. Dyson's essay about children who rewrote the role of Emily is an excellent reminder of the legitimacy of such optimism.[5] In her research, she reports on children who watched what could perhaps most charitably be described as a typical Hollywood film: an eminently forgettable, grotesquely puerile recycling of clichés marked by a gleeful rejection of historical accuracy and a confident pilfering from other cultures. The film presented a subject position in which the target child audience was to recline comfortably, glibly complicit with a sexist structure of heroism that wrote girls—when it wrote them at all—into passivity. The children who enjoyed the movie seemed to have been quite comfortable in that prescribed subject position at first, but when they began working out their own version of the story, when they engaged with the film critically, that position immediately lost its normalized, invisible status. Even the children who endorsed that position found themselves having to argue for its validity, an activity that hardly fits with the glibly complicit version of subjective agency that Eagleton imagines. Stephens never goes to the lengths that Eagleton does in his warnings about the traps awaiting subjectivity in literature, but even his concern about the corrupting potential of complicit children's literature seems less dire in the light of the students about whom Dyson writes. Indeed, from the story Dyson tells of critical engagement and dialogization, even books offering only subject positions grounded in genuinely abhorrent ideology seem remarkably less dire; even *being seduced into those positions* seems less dangerous. I wonder, in fact, if it might not be frequently useful to be corrupted by an ideology against which one is later invited to struggle. Perhaps starting a discussion with a wrong or morally reprehensible idea (or a right or morally salubrious idea), even calling on people to agree with that idea, might not be bad. It is here that the real value of combining Freire and Bakhtin becomes clear. The job of analysis is no longer to highlight what is morally suitable or to raise the alarm against that which is not. Because human beings are capable at all points of reexamining, dialogizing, and engaging critically with texts, subject positions, and ideologies, even morally reprehensible movies about ninjas seem considerably less irresistible.[6]

But for all that, Stephens is one of a handful of scholars with whom my argument will inevitably intersect. Although Stephens's interest in children's literature as a whole is much wider than my own interest in American children's nonfiction, my book is in key ways descended from his. Despite our different conclusions over the power that books have to dictate subjectivity, my arguments about how parts of a book close themselves to critical engagement is strikingly similar to Stephens's attempts to illustrate how a book presents ideology in a way that prevents its readers from arguing with or even perceiving that ideology. I am especially interested in where books will allow their own authority to be questioned, but both of us, in fact, frequently examine how books create, maintain, and project their authority. Too, Stephens's mode is characterized by close readings that generate insights about ideology, and he is similarly nervous about drawing conclusions about how real readers react (48). Even Stephens's term for the kind of book that he privileges—"interrogative text"—anticipates my search for places in which texts are more or less open to dialogue with their readers. This similarity becomes more striking late in Stephens's study as he uses another tool from Bakhtin—the notion of "carnival" in a text, during which authority is suspended—to explain how a children's book can cast doubt on the larger authority bound up with the subjectivity that the book offers. Stephens's conclusions are often nothing short of delicious, as when he examines carnivalesque language, which he claims "is used to disclose ways in which adult incompetence masks itself as adult authority, and more generally to construct subject positions in opposition to society's official structures of authority." Noting the metafictional qualities of interrogative texts, especially those making use of carnivalesque scenes or characters, Stephens observes that "such figures also contribute to the self-conscious textuality of interrogative texts, since by drawing attention to roles and role-playing they draw attention to the text itself as a construct" (122). In moments such as these, Stephens describes how a text can draw attention to or even create cracks in its own authority, and I will frequently do the same. He even notes that carnivalesque elements in a book are "not necessarily interrogative" (156), neatly derailing any attempt to simplify his thoughtful theoretical model into something mechanical, a repurposing of theory that I fear for my own model. Our conclusions are routinely different, but the questions that we ask are similar as we search out opportunities for readers to resist textual authority.

Nowhere is a gleeful intransigence in the face of textual authority more evident than in the work of Roland Barthes, especially in his theory of writerly and readerly texts, developed in the pages of *S/Z*. It is in *S/Z* that Barthes sketches out a process for the mode of evaluation he championed in "The Death of the Author," a mode that refuses to give primary weight to the intentions of the writer behind a text. Barthes's efforts to dethrone the author are fundamentally similar to Freire's efforts to decentralize learning. When Barthes characterizes his mode of evaluation as a break from the traditional search for the revelation from the "Author-God" (146), he anticipates Freire's characterization of his problem-posing education as a mode that "breaks with the vertical patterns characteristic of banking education" (*Pedagogy*, 67). Barthes *and* Freire, then, are dedicated to opposing the centralization of meaning in a uniquely authoritative source of true knowledge. What Barthes calls the "writerly text," which he opposes to the "readerly text," will invite readers to coauthor meaning, resulting in a plurality of meanings through dialogue with readers. Again, this idea echoes in the works of Freire, who argues that "the methodology proposed requires that the investigators and the people . . . should act as *co-investigators*. The more active an attitude [that people] take in regard to the exploration of their thematic, the more they deepen their critical awareness of reality and, in spelling out those thematics, take possession of that reality" (97, emphasis original). As I search for places where books are more or less vulnerable to critical engagement, it is legitimate to see similarities with places that fit Barthes's description of writerly or readerly texts.

The methodology Barthes develops in *S/Z* to carry out the evaluation he champions in "Death of the Author," too, has similarities with my own methodology, as I will be isolating specific aspects of texts, small moments and movements, with little regard for whether these aspects break away from their surrounding text along lines that flatter the aesthetic principles of the author. Barthes models that procedure, dividing a text into what he calls "lexias"—Barthes, too, is deeply influenced by linguistics—a tool that, he claims, "stars the text, instead of assembling it." These new units of text are developed by "separating, in the manner of a minor earthquake, the blocks of signification of which reading grasps only the smooth surface, imperceptibly soldered by the movement of sentences, the flowing discourse of narration, the 'naturalness' of ordinary language" (*S/Z* 1974, 13). By insisting on decentered, multiplied meanings, the evaluation Barthes practices does not

> work with "respect" to the text; the tutor text will ceaselessly be broken, interrupted without any regard for its natural divisions (syntactical, rhetorical, anecdotic); inventory, explanation, and digression may deter any observation of suspense, may even separate verb and complement, noun and attribute; the work of the commentary, once it is separated from any ideology of totality, consists precisely in *manhandling* the text, *interrupting* it. What is thereby denied is not the *quality* of the text (here incomparable) but its "naturalness." (1974, 15, emphasis original)

I, less courageous than Barthes, will rarely take full advantage of this liberated[7] strategy of reading, but I will certainly take license from Barthes both to give priority to meanings that have little to do with authorial intention and to use textual pieces of varying degrees of wholeness to expose the codes of texts. This technique is especially useful with places where texts struggle to conceal the gaps in their authority, because skillfully written texts frequently make use of aesthetic strategies to execute that concealment. My strategy hopes to disrupt the naturalness of a text's communicated meaning to examine where it is or is not willing to let readers question the validity of what it holds true.

Barthes's multiplication of meaning, though, tends toward a product that has limited usefulness in my model. The "interpretation" of literature for Barthes should not be "to give it a (more or less justified, more or less free) meaning" but to "appreciate what *plural* constitutes it." Barthes asks his reader to imagine a perfectly plural text:

> In this ideal text, the networks are many and interact, without any one of them being able to surpass the rest; this text is a

> galaxy of signifiers, not a structure of signifieds; it has no beginning; it is reversible; we gain access to it by several entrances, none of which can be authoritatively declared to be the main one; the codes it mobilizes extend *as far as the eye can reach*, they are indeterminable (meaning here is never subject to a principle of determination, unless by throwing dice); the systems of meaning can take over this absolutely plural text, but their number is never closed, based as it is on the infinity of language. (*S/Z* 1974, 5–6, emphasis original)

Barthes does not claim that such a text exists, but the kind of text that he prefers, the kind of text that responds best to his mode of evaluation, is a text that tends toward this plurality, and the correct reading of a text will look for opportunities not to settle on meaning but to extend the meanings of texts forever. The dialogization at the heart of my theory, which looks for places where a text weakens its authority, will almost inevitably multiply meaning as it invites readers to the work of inquiry, but the horizonless plurality of Barthes's ideal text would not be useful to what I am calling critical engagement. Nonfiction presents information and makes an argument about it, even if simply by virtue of having selected that piece of information as worthy of learning. My study will search extensively for places where nonfiction performs its work in ways that divide or protect authority. It will not, however, and indeed cannot, imagine the possible meanings of information as infinite. If meaning is endlessly plural, then there is no point at which to test it. I am not looking for texts that refuse to say anything or whose arguments are so self-effacing that they cannot be recognized. To hope for a sort of text that will only multiply meaning, to devise a theory of reading that will only set meaning free and never hold it still, is to search for texts and ways of meaning in which ideas cannot be tested. Critical engagement cannot exist there.

What I am proposing, then, is neither the complacent acceptance of a text's authority nor the infinite deferral of meaning but something more tangible, more ready for argument, more actionable. Insisting on endless plurality heads off action; declining to resolve a position prevents debate over that position. I am not arguing that we have to swear allegiance to a position forever—in fact, I am arguing the opposite. But we need a consensus of an idea, however limited and imperfectly understood, before we can test it, revise it, argue over it again, arrive at a new consensus, agitate, test it again, and so on and on. In this sense, what I am arguing for has similarities with Barthes's plurality, especially in his rejection of a teleological inquiry that searches for a definitive answer. The position that I am championing, though, might better be explained as a *punctuated plurality,* as a process of multiplying meanings, drawing to a consensus, testing that consensus, and then allowing the entire process to repeat from the beginning, again and again. It seems foolish to me to forbid ourselves the solidity of conclusions, even as it seems to me antidemocratic to centralize the authority of knowledge. Although this position likely requires the narrowing of meaning that Barthes condemns in readerly texts and outmoded evaluations of literature, punctuated plurality is necessary for critical engagement as I am defining it.

Sections of Books, Not Books as a Whole

As is probably already clear from my treatment of Barthes, the theory I am proposing is also different from other models because it focuses not on entire books but on moments within a book. For me, a book can include moments in which it invites critical engagement *as well as* moments in which it refuses such engagement. That opinion is certainly at odds with Barthes's explanation of readerly and writerly texts, which seems to take for granted that texts as a whole will be either readerly or writerly, and it is also at odds with some of the best scholarship on children's nonfiction written from the perspective of educational theory. Myra Zarnowski, for example, has explored the potential of the best of children's nonfiction to model critical engagement. Indeed, if Stephens is my closest spirit in the world of literary scholarship, Zarnowski is my closest spirit in the world of educational theory, as she praises what she calls books that use a *"questioning approach"* (History, 3, emphasis original). However, although she frequently asks whether a book—that is to say, a book as a whole—introduces doubt, she never explores the patterns of *in what local instances* books allow doubt and, more importantly, what the space for such doubt signifies. In her valorization of a literary technique called the "visible author," a technique I will explore at length in chapter 2, Zarnowski explains that "the immensely important benefit of reading books by visible authors is that they shift our attention to the process of historical interpretation" (*History,* 51). Obviously that shift of attention is directly relevant to the decentered, denaturalized flagging of an invitation to critical engagement in which I am so interested, but for Zarnowski, the evidence is not a moment in a book but "books" in the plural. For Zarnowski, the presence of, for example, a visible author marks a text *as a whole* as a questioning text.

I, on the other hand, am emphatically not presenting a framework in which to position an entire book but rather one in which to position individual moments in a book. Zarnowski's strategy has a tempting efficiency, but in categorizing an entire book at once, she misses opportunities to ask provocative questions. Consider for example her analysis of the author's note to Kathryn Lasky's *Vision of Beauty: The Story of Sarah Breedlove Walker* (2000). Zarnowski points out that in this note, "Lasky boldly states that there are gaps in the story." Zarnowski then goes on to celebrate a kind of authority that Lasky's honesty lends to the book. "Lasky reassures readers," Zarnowski explains, "that she has not fabricated any dialogue. And while the author admits to filling the gaps by 'responsibly imagining,' she also claims that whenever quotes appear, they are the actual words of Madam Walker. Readers find no fabricated dialogue here" (*History,* 54). But in this analysis, Zarnowski's strategy disallows generative distinctions. For instance, Lasky makes plain the gaps in the story she has studied, but she also asks readers to believe unreflectively in the authority of the quoted dialogue. While the first gesture declines authority, the second invokes it. Distinguishing between the two gestures and the evidence that they treat could reveal something important about Lasky's project, but such investigation is not possible because the book is taken as a whole. Too, the location of Lasky's honesty about the gaps in her story might be significant: what does it mean that this honesty comes in the author's note rather than in the narrative itself? Are there different audiences for an author's note and the main text of a children's book? Are there different tasks for the peritexts than for the main text? If we allow ourselves to say that a book has *moments* in which it divests itself of its authority, we can look more clearly at the project of nonfiction, in terms of genre as well as individual works.

A consequence of the decision to look at moments in books rather than books as a whole is that I am also not attempting to argue that any given book is good or bad, although I recognize that literary as well as educational theorists frequently shoulder that burden, especially when talking about children's literature. Stephens, for example, argues that "texts which offer what I have here called estranged subject positions need to be explored and their reading encouraged" (*Language*, 82). This conclusion is probably inevitable from the CDA perspective that I have outlined above: if some books offer oppressive subject positions and others offer libratory positions, the job of the scholar *must* be to label the good and the bad. Zarnowski, as we can see in her praise of Lasky's biography of Sarah Breedlove Walker, feels a similar obligation. And again, this mission is probably inevitable considering her perspective: she is an education specialist writing to other teachers with the aim of giving them ideas on how—and what—to teach better. Consequently, one piece of advice explains that nonfiction that creates a sense of puzzlement is similar to good teaching: "Creating a puzzling question is especially useful when teaching history. It's what good history teachers report doing when they design challenging activities" (*History*, 106). Even Barthes, whose writings are famous for their iconoclasm, makes plain the superiority of writerly books to readerly books and one kind of scholarship to another. In explaining the stage of evaluation in which texts accrue meanings, he twice mentions appreciation (*S/Z* 1974, 5).[8] Here and elsewhere in *S/Z*, Barthes reveals his preference for a kind of text—one that can be categorized as readerly or writerly as a whole—and Barthes is happy to use that preference to justify a hierarchy in which some books should, and others should not, be "appreciated." By examining pieces of books in order to discover where they are and are not willing to accept challenge, I will be able to put together a picture of ideological patterns I admire, sometimes in books I dislike. I will also be able to uncover patterns that disappoint me, sometimes even in books I enjoy. Thus the range of texts for which my theory is useful is broader because it refuses to label some books as good and others as bad. It would be silly of me to pretend that I *don't* prefer books that tend toward the kind of engagement that I am describing: it was, after all, my delighted discovery of invitations to such engagement that first prompted me to develop the theory. Still, it will never be my point to praise or condemn a book as being good or bad. I am too interested in moments of a book to place entire books in one category or the other.

Evaluating moments in books instead of books as a whole will also help correct an understanding of how children's nonfiction is different today from how it has been in the past. In general, the dramatic increase in the visibility of children's nonfiction in recent decades has led to an assumption that the hallmarks of today's award-winning nonfiction are unique to the current age. Sylvia Vardell, in her essay on one of the awards that marked that increase, highlights the importance of the award in part through emphasizing what she sees as new in the field:

> Today nonfiction books for children offer content that is relevant and well-researched, on an incredible variety of subjects, combined with clear and interesting style and language. Books today reflect a greater respect for the child reader, with more detail and more focus (not necessarily *everything* you *ever* wanted to know); more citation of references; sources and books for additional reading; and new honesty and objectivity—*how* to think, not *what* to think. ("New 'Picture,'" 474)

In many similar moments, Vardell praises the new nonfiction for traits that are vital to the issues of critical engagement that interest me. "Perhaps the greatest value of the new outstanding nonfiction for children," she continues in language that indicates that an interest in critical engagement is new, "is in its power to stimulate thinking, to inspire wonder, to urge questioning, to probe responses, to promote discussion, to tempt curiosity, and to generate enthusiasm" (475). Barbara Bader disagrees with the notion that recent nonfiction is inherently better than older nonfiction, but she finds acceptable the idea that they are different: "One way or another," she concludes, "the books are different—not better or worse than their predecessors, but interestingly different. Different books for different times" ("Nonfiction," 46). One of the major projects of my book will be to argue that neither of these descriptions is entirely accurate or, ultimately, as interesting as it could be. Many of the qualities that Vardell lists—relevance, research, variety, detail, focus, and even attempts to achieve objectivity with a compelling style—have been present in children's nonfiction since before the current literary marketplace emerged. Again, my goal will not be to flatten the historical differences for which others have argued. More accurately, I am attempting to nuance the history. The categorical differences between older and newer nonfiction are few and far between, and often the things that writers take to be typical of new nonfiction were already present, and in revealing ways, in older nonfiction.

Ignoring Reading Levels

In the chapters that follow, I will routinely ignore one common structuring factor of children's literature: reading levels. Throughout, I will rarely even note the recommended age level for any book, choosing instead to slip back and forth between books for middle-grade readers and high school readers, to compare informational picture books intended for preadolescent readers with monograph-style single-subject informational books intended for teenagers, and so on. Much of the conversation about children's literature, though, is guided by attention to reading levels, and there are clear reasons why. First, educators, who generally earn credentials that certify them to teach children within a specific range of ages, are required by the nature of their profession to regard material for class discussions according to the age breaks signified by grades as well as the divisions between preschool, kindergarten, elementary school, middle school, and high school. Second, the children's literature industry has been committed to a structure of age ranges that guides adoption, review, and retail policies. In fact, the production of nonfiction is often *more* susceptible to this treatment than are other aspects of the industry. Russell Freedman, a pivotal figure in the history of

American children's nonfiction, makes this susceptibility clear in a conversation about the audiences for whom he writes:

> Anyone writing a picture-book biography of Lincoln has a different set of responsibilities from someone writing a biography for sixth-graders, say, or from a Lincoln scholar writing an academic book on Lincoln. Each of these writers has a different audience and different goals. That's obvious. A picture-book biography can't deal with the same complexities and nuances as a 150-page biography for older kids. You can't use the picture-book format if you want to go into all those complications. (qtd. in Sutton, "Interview," 700–701)

Freedman is a typical example: in interviews and panel discussions, nonfiction writers routinely show a keen sense of the divisions between reading levels and how those divisions impact the formal and aesthetic qualities of their books. From conception through publication and review, children's nonfiction is often judged, at least by adults, according to the age range for which it claims to have been written.

However, I have always been reluctant to structure my analysis of children's literature by anything other than the most tentative awareness of age ranges. As I often tell my students when the subject inevitably comes up, I distrust such structures because when I was a child, I read books for adolescents; when I was an adolescent, I read books for adults; now that I am an adult, I read books for children, adolescents, and adults for both pleasure and work. Therefore, my personal path through children's literature makes me distrustful of reading levels. Furthermore, the history of children's literature quickly reveals reading levels to be as historically bounded as any other aspect of the construction of childhood. Nathalie op de Beeck's work on children's picture books gives perhaps the most damning evidence. Although contemporary adults tend to regard reading levels as an impartial reflection of natural cognitive levels, op de Beeck traces their invention to the first half of the twentieth century and links their proliferation not to nature but to efforts "to construct the modern citizen." "What appears to be an empirical calculation of age appropriateness, based on actual children's developmental needs," she argues, "is also a system for instilling a social order and consumerism" (*Suspended Animation*, 20). In other words, although reading levels purport to be child-centered tools of support for growing readers, historical evidence indicates that they are more accurately viewed as tools of marketing that reify arbitrary definitions of childhood.

Whatever one's opinion of reading levels for children in general, they are especially suspect in the world of children's nonfiction. Patricia J. Cianciolo has observed that in most cases, a child's "reading achievement level" (determined by reading achievement scores or grade placement) or even the "readability level" of a specific book (determined by a readability formula or recommendation by the publisher, a curriculum specialist, or a book reviewer) has little or no bearing on whether a particular book will be interesting or appealing to children (*Informational Picture Books*, 8). What she is explaining, based on her own experience with children and nonfiction, is that children—like adults—frequently accept the struggle of difficult reading material if their interest in the subject is strong enough. Portalupi and Fletcher also write about using nonfiction in elementary classrooms, and while they recommend providing some simple books well within the reading abilities of the students, they also argue that teachers "should give them plenty of access to more complex books . . . for their own research" (*Nonfiction*, 20). Portalupi and Fletcher supplement Cianciolo's point: children can both be interested in and draw useful knowledge from nonfiction that is written for children in higher reading levels.

Therefore, I do recognize that reading levels have an impact on formal choices that authors make in writing nonfiction for children, but reading levels will play almost no role in my analysis. As these literary and educational scholars help demonstrate, nonfiction is a field in which reading levels are especially suspect. Reading levels are a mode adults use to talk to each other about what children of certain ages should be interested in and capable of. To put it another way, reading levels help normalize the ideology behind children's literature, and because my project is to make that ideology visible, guiding my study according to the dictates of reading levels would do much more harm than good.

Chapter Outline

Chapter 1 reflects on the consequences of the common argument that nonfiction must be a literature of authority. In this chapter, I consider the idea of childhood in the context of education defined by the memorization of facts, and I build a case for structuring information about science, biography, art, mathematics, and history, not around a vain pursuit of authority, but according to what Sam Wineburg has called "a humility before the narrowness of our contemporary experience" (*Historical Thinking*, 22). The standard definition of nonfiction is that it is a literature of answers, but this chapter argues that the genre and the children for whom it is written are better served if we think of it as a literature of questions.

The next two chapters lay out the rhetorical hallmarks that enable the application of my theory. Chapter 2 examines how the voice of a book—in its use of hedges and a visible author (terms coined by Avon Crismore) as well as its dramatization of debate between sources (as theorized by Wineburg)—can attempt to invite or close off critical engagement. Hedges, words and phrases such as "perhaps" and "to a certain extent," rupture a text's authority, accentuating, even modeling, doubt rather than assurance. Similarly, research demonstrates that when the narrator of an informational text speaks in third person, readers tend to believe what is said, but when the narrator speaks in first person, readers are much more likely to challenge what they have been told. The first chapter demonstrates how these techniques, as well as the foregrounding of disagreement between external authorities, can serve to prompt questions rather than unreflective memorization of data. Chapter 3 develops theories posited by Cianciolo and Fisher to demonstrate how nonfiction texts humanize the production of knowledge, especially through their attention to the strategies that historical figures have used to pursue inquiry. Children's nonfiction has often relied on strong characters, from the heroes of biographies to the adults lecturing about scientific principles, but this chapter examines places where nonfiction points to the flaws in its characters, the times they have made mistakes, failed, or simply looked foolish. In these instances, as well as moments in which the characters of nonfiction are shown in the process of testing or even finishing one line of inquiry only to find new questions that remain unanswered, the genre demonstrates an ability to convey information while simultaneously making room for critical engagement with the people who produce knowledge. These opening chapters introduce, define, and demonstrate the terms central to the theory of nonfiction that *A Literature of Questions* constructs.

With these terms in hand, the next two chapters approach aspects of this literature that are bound up with the contemporary form of children's nonfiction: peritexts and photography. Chapter 4 extends and complicates Gérard Genette's idea of the peritext—the sidebars, captions, footnotes, introduction, notes for teachers, and other aspects of textual apparatuses—to look at how nonfiction employs these devices to centralize debate or push it to the margins. Peritexts exist in other forms of literature, but they are especially prominent in children's nonfiction, and the nonlinear reading that they encourage is simultaneously common to the genre and an especially promising venue for self-directed, critical engagement with ideas. Chapter 5 argues that children's nonfiction has both accepted and resisted an anticritical inclination that is all but endemic to photography, and it teases out the social construction of childhood reinforced by the two positions. Through extended attention to Russell Freedman's influential "photobiography" of Lincoln, this chapter examines how photography disingenuously claims to be a transparent window to truth, an authority so reliable as to require no critical engagement. Freedman's book achieved success at a key moment in the rebirth of children's nonfiction and, virtually overnight, cemented the centrality of photography in nonfiction. These explorations of peritexts and photography open up the potential for critical engagement in two aspects of children's nonfiction that are today among its most recognizable traits.

The final chapters demonstrate how nonfiction characterized by humility offers information that is truer, both intellectually and emotionally. Chapter 6 applies the observations of the previous chapters to a case study of *Almost Astronauts* (2009), which won the American Library Association's highest award for nonfiction in 2010. This reading examines how the pursuit of authority and an understanding of children as vulnerable recipients of data require the sacrifice of critical engagement and, ironically, result in a less honest book. This chapter also illustrates a point that is implicit throughout much of my study: the hallmarks that I develop in the earlier chapters are best understood as places where nonfiction chooses between inviting and refusing critical engagement, not places where we can unreflectively assume that a book has shed its authority. Chapter 7 begins with the sentimentality that drives much of *Almost Astronauts* to argue that emotional engagement can and has dovetailed with critical engagement. In these pages, I use feminist theory to index the link between emotion and intellect, between the passion of civic engagement and the objectivity of inquiry. Together, these chapters attempt to put to rest the theory of nonfiction as authoritative, animate the theory of nonfiction as capable of humble truth, and illustrate the counterintuitive implications of the shift from one to the other.

The Conclusion anticipates the argument that children are not capable of the critical engagement to which my theory argues that they are being invited. The final pages of *A Literature of Questions* offer evidence from across many countries and disciplines that children are more than capable of the kind of nuanced, careful engagement to which contemporary children's nonfiction increasingly invites them. I end by pointing out how adults—authors, teachers, parents, librarians, scholars, and caregivers—can see to it that children's books invite that sort of engagement, and I make an argument that we should.

Paulo Freire repeatedly emphasizes the importance, first, of dialogue to education and, second, of humility to dialogue. "Dialogue," he writes, "cannot exist without humility." For him, dialogue is the activity of people who are "addressed to the common task of learning and acting," and it "is broken if the parties (or one of them) lack humility. How can I dialogue if I always project ignorance onto others and never perceive my own?" (*Pedagogy*, 78). Nonfiction can never be perfectly truthful, and yet, in its best moments, it strives to share what it understands as truth with its readers. That sharing is more honest, and that honesty is more truthful, when it is humble. Humble truths show their humility not by pretending that things cannot be known or that conclusions cannot be drawn but by inviting readers to engage in the processes by which information is generated, tested, applied, and tested again. *A Literature of Questions* searches for places where nonfiction makes plain its vulnerabilities in order to spur dialogue with its readers.

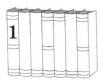

1 BEYOND AUTHORITY
Questioning the Literature of Facts

> *In the social climate of the public classroom, there often is an equation between "serious" school work and literal-mindedness, mostly because the primary business of the school is the acquisition of facts and student control.*
> —Joe L. Kincheloe, *Getting beyond the Facts*

"TRADITIONAL EXPOSITION IS STILL IN USE," writes Kathleen T. Isaacs, "but both recognition and readership go to writers who attempt to engage their readers with story—while still sticking to the facts" ("Facts," 16). A teacher, a librarian, and chair of the American Library Association/Association for Library Service to Children's Committee on Notable Children's Books, Isaacs expresses in these lines an enthusiasm for children's nonfiction that is typical for its two-step logic. First, nonfiction at the turn into the twenty-first century is lauded for its increasing use of excellent storytelling techniques. But second, nonfiction is assumed to be grounded in facts. Myra Zarnowski's book on children's nonfiction takes a similar approach, arguing that "truth-telling does not prevent an author from writing artful, well-crafted prose" (*History*, 31). This assertion comes at the end of a section titled "Telling the Truth," and it precedes a paragraph on the literary techniques that a good writer of nonfiction can use. Her point is that good nonfiction must of course be built on facts, but it can *also* be well written. In Penny Peck's advice on evaluating biographies, she explains that one must "consider several criteria," and the first of those is the factual nature of the books: "Of course," she says, rightly assuming that what she is about to say hardly needs to be said, "look for authenticity" (*Readers' Advisory,* 119). The same idea, replicated in the title of Barbara Moss's *Exploring the Literature of Fact: Children's Nonfiction Trade Books in the Elementary Classroom,* surfaces throughout the dominant discourse on children's nonfiction.[1] Children's nonfiction can and does borrow from the toolbox of fiction writers, but the prevalent perception is that it will, of course, be about facts.

Such a consensus is, unavoidably, a problem for me. If nonfiction is, as so many voices insist, primarily a genre characterized by authenticity, truth telling, and sticking to the facts, then its ability to invite critical engagement is necessarily limited. An emphasis on facts is an emphasis on teleology, and in the rush to the conclusion of inquiry that comes with the prioritization of fixed, known facts, critical engagement can only end. For that reason, the dominant perception of children's nonfiction indicates that this is a genre not only poorly suited to a search for invitations to critical engagement but diametrically opposed to them. Although the other chapters in this book explore the different ways that children's nonfiction can invite critical engagement, this chapter must first answer the obvious problem that nonfiction might be *exactly* the wrong place to look for such invitations. This chapter, then, makes an argument that is crucial to the project of the book: despite consistent—though not unanimous—observations to the contrary, nonfiction doesn't have to be a literature of facts; indeed, it shouldn't be.

I want to begin by questioning not the value of a nonfiction primarily dedicated to teaching fact but its ability to do so. Despite the conventional wisdom that good nonfiction will serve the transmission of facts from adults to children, there is evidence that children's nonfiction artfully told is a poor means to communicate facts to children. Tamara L. Jetton's study suggests that "the inclusion of biographical information in the text," for example, "tends to distract the readers from the content-specific details present in the text" ("Information-Driven," 112). Therefore, the strong sense of character featured in narrative nonfiction, one of the artistic virtues that distinguishes narrative nonfiction from textbooks, might actually work *against* the consumption of pure knowledge. Jetton found that in a group of students learning about whales through nonfiction, the children "responded more to the story events than the information about whales," which will shock no one, but she goes on to explain that the findings are "of educational importance because if these texts are to be used in a science class, which seems appropriate for this particular text, students may not respond to or remember the informational units related to that particular content area, namely subject-matter facts" (127). These findings are a real problem for educators and writers who want to insist that children's nonfiction, especially nonfiction of high literary quality, is primarily a genre of facts.

Even if, for the sake of argument, we ignore Jetton's conclusion that narrative nonfiction is a poor genre for the transmission of fact, a larger problem with the standard definition of the field is that privileging facts might actually interfere with the pursuit of other goals. Specifically, an emphasis on communicating facts may conflict with critical engagement. Evelyn B. Freeman and Diane Goetz Person, for example, report criticism of textbooks "for stressing correct answers rather than encouraging exploration and discussion of concepts." In making this choice, the writers argue, textbooks encourage students to go about "memorizing bits of information rather than using critical-thinking skills to understand ideas in context" (*Connecting,* 34). And Paulo Freire, whose experience teaching literacy to hundreds of adult manual laborers made his educational theories widely influential, explicitly rejects the data-centered, fact-based style of teaching that has characterized definitions of children's nonfiction and continues to characterize education "reform" up through today. Focusing on content, on the true and valid materials communicated by an authority figure, Friere says, transforms students "into 'containers,' into 'receptacles' to be 'filled' by the teacher. The more completely he fills the receptacles, the better a teacher he is. The more meekly the receptacles permit themselves to be filled, the better students they are." And in a turn of phrase with obvious relevance to narrative nonfiction,

Freire likens education with a focus on content to "Narration (with the teacher as narrator)," which "leads the students to memorize mechanically the narrated content" (*Pedagogy*, 58). In what has since become one of his most famous turns of phrase, Freire labels this sort of education "the 'banking' concept of education, in which the scope of action allowed to the students extends only as far as receiving, filing, and storing the deposits" (58).[2] Freire repeatedly condemns such teaching as dehumanizing, as it requires human students to understand themselves as objects that receive, contain, and surrender information on demand. To the banking model, Freire opposes a "liberating education" that focuses on "problems" rather than discrete bits of data, one that "consists in acts of cognition, not transferrals of information" (67). A theory of nonfiction that insists on the centrality of facts is only valuable in a model that takes for granted the importance of data treated as capital that moves from authority figure to reader in a linear, hierarchical relationship.

Freire's ideas about literacy have spread to other areas of education in the humanities, especially humanities education for children. Joe L. Kincheloe, for example, is a pivotal character in the story of how Freire's ideas came to be embraced in a broad swath of humanities teaching in high schools. He writes that "a study of social studies," in which Kincheloe includes at least history, sociology, and geography, "with students viewed as participants in the lived world is quite different from social studies that sees students as passive receptors in a fact-based, memory game" (*Getting* 2001, 30). He frequently identifies his approach to social studies as liberationist, and he also calls it—presumably in a nod to Freire—"a problems approach" (*Getting* 1989, 35). Kincheloe decries "the typically required map work and state capital memorization" found so often in compulsory education, arguing that such assignments "contribute little to individual emancipation or critical social education" (*Getting* 2001, 678). Kincheloe's conclusions have been mirrored elsewhere, as in Sam Wineburg's comparisons of professional historians and high school students, a comparison that seems unfair on the surface. But Wineburg found that the high school students performed admirably well on factual exams: "two high school students answered more of the identification questions (e.g., 'What was

Fort Ticonderoga?' 'Who was George Grenville?' 'What were the Townshend Acts?') than one of the historians, and another historian got only one more answer than most students." The students were therefore—and this makes sense, given the fact-based emphasis of compulsory education—masters of the surface of the texts that they analyzed. But they routinely failed at historical exercises that required thinking that went beyond the activity of receiving, storing, and returning bits of information. The students had difficulty finding subtext, tended to reduce historical documents to representations of one "side" or another, and became "flustered in the face of contradictions" as they searched "for the right answer." Given the students' mastery of facts and inability to engage critically with historical documents, Wineburg concludes that for the study of history, there must be "something more than knowing names and dates," something more than the fact-based banking model used in compulsory education (*Historical Thinking,* 77).

It is this line of thinking that has led history teachers such as Kincheloe to argue that "social studies must get beyond the facts" (*Getting* 1989, 35): centering texts for young readers around their "authenticity" is not just questionable, it might even be actively harmful. For Freire, the banking model of education not only teaches students facts, it also teaches the students who quietly receive those facts habits of interacting with authority and information that will discourage the students from being part of a functional democracy. "The more students work at storing the deposits entrusted to them," he argues, "the less they develop the critical consciousness which would result from their intervention in the world as transformer of that world. The more completely they accept the passive role imposed on them, the more they tend simply to adapt to the world as it is and to the fragmented view of reality deposited in them" (*Pedagogy,* 60). While the mode of education that privileges "truth telling" rewards students for storing and displaying the bits of data for which objective tests search so well, it also helps them practice a kind of nonparticipation in their own social realities. Students who are congratulated for their mastery of facts, Freire fears, will grow comfortably into the habit of passing information along without questioning it. Kincheloe has noted exactly this phenomenon extensively:

> The notion that history could possibly constitute more than just political and military facts is generally rejected by students with a few social studies courses in their pasts. This is not at all surprising when history, as viewed by the students, is a course that exists only to test one's ability to memorize facts for the test. The "good" history student is the one who memorizes minutiae, not the one who makes connections between the materials in the course and those encountered in the lived world. To say that the concepts of interpretation, historical continuity, and historiography are alien ideas in the teaching of history to elementary and secondary students is, at best, understatement. (*Getting* 2001, 594)

Significant in Kincheloe's complaint is that it is not the student who has *yet* to experience social studies education who faces this problem but the student who has *already* learned about history through conventional, fact-centered social studies courses. The structure of such courses punishes students who might be inclined to think of history in terms of Wineburg's "something more" and rewards students who are what Kincheloe calls "literal-minded." "This puts many students in a bind," he explains. "Intuitively, they know there can be more than one right answer, but their school-trained literal minds deny this" (*Getting* 1989, 342). And this literal-mindedness feeds on itself, as the very students being harmed by fact-based education become some of its most vocal defenders:

> It is a challenge to teach a group of students who have rarely been exposed to non-literal thinking to value non-literalness. The teacher may encounter student resistance at unexpected points. Some of the strongest opposition, for example, may come from the above average student who has succeeded in a literal-based educational system. These students are comfortable with a literal-minded emphasis. When placed in a context where abstractions and interpretations are emphasized these students may experience great discomfort. They may call for the teacher to dispense factual data in class and objective tests which call for student regurgitation of the data. (*Getting* 1989, 336–37)[3]

In this way, the banking model of education, which is made possible by a valorization of facts as the proudest sign of education, invests students in the very system of education that discourages them from engaging critically with information. Kincheloe therefore concludes that "as important as the bogus historical data or civic attitudes that programs sometimes try to inculcate are the unintended patterns of thinking and the perspective toward learning with which students leave the history classroom" (*Getting* 2001, 596–97).

These concerns about the way that a fact-based education can be harmful to students parallel the threat that materials written for children pose to critical engagement, a threat especially obvious in textbooks. In her study of textbooks, Avon Crismore finds that social studies texts participate in the culture that Kincheloe has condemned. "American Social Studies educators assume, apparently, that the typical Social Studies textbook should be a body of facts without exposition," she explains. She continues,

> The role of the textbook writer, then, is to report the facts, not to explain them or their significance for the reader and certainly not to explain the writer's plan for reporting the facts or his point of view. The role of the student reader is to receive the facts passively from the truth-giving authority who wrote the text and memorize them, not to understand the facts or the writer's attitude towards them and not to use the facts to build a larger picture or to think critically about what the writer said or did in the textbook. ("Rhetoric," 281)

This understanding of the relationship between textbooks and students helps to explain how classrooms devoted to the banking model of education can make teachers, students, and administrators comfortable. Resting on the seamless authority of the textbook and its cornucopia of truth, classroom discussion—if it exists—can safely sidestep the controversial work of critical engagement.

The solution is not a book with more information. As Wineburg argues,

> it is doubtful that teaching these students more facts about the American Revolution would help them do better on this task when they remain ignorant of the basic heuristics used to

create historical interpretations, when they cannot distinguish among different types of historical evidence, and when they look to a textbook for the "answer" to historical questions. ("Historical Problem Solving," 84)

Those cognitive moves, the "basic heuristics" to which Wineburg points, are actually obscured by an emphasis on facts. Students Wineburg examined who were comfortable in the authoritative authenticity of the banking model of education "simply overlooked or did not know how to seek out features designed to shape their perceptions or make them view events in a particular way." Such students, he goes on to say in wording that is directly relevant to the study of critical engagement in children's nonfiction, "may have 'processed' texts, but they failed to engage with them" (*Historical Thinking*, 76).

Crismore proposes that fact-centered education is likely to discourage critical engagement, and Wineburg's research indicates that it has already done so; I would like to take these observations a step further: fact-centered education and, more to the point, fact-centered literature *will inevitably* discourage critical engagement. A nonfiction that defines itself as truth bearer is one that cannot tolerate cracks in its authority, one that cannot make itself vulnerable to the inquiry and thoughtful tests of its readers. An insistence on truthfulness is self-satisfied, and therefore anticritical, in the sense that it willfully ignores history's lesson that facts are *constantly* under revision, that the facts any people of any period know to be true are *repeatedly* revised, even rejected by people of subsequent generations. The majority opinion that nonfiction is and should be a literature of final answers is an opinion that refuses humility, that refuses historical consciousness, the realization that answers have always been followed by questions. Defining nonfiction in this way makes it a literature that is opposed to critical engagement, with all of the consequences for human dignity and a functioning democracy that Freire, Kincheloe, Wineburg, and so many other authors have articulated.

However, support for a new way of thinking about the genre is swelling. Danielle J. Ford, for example, has noted the tendency to link nonfiction to authoritative accuracy in the case of nonfiction about science. "According to most sources," she observes, "children's science books ought to be error-free in text and illustration." After all,

> science books are about science; science is full of facts about the natural world; and children shouldn't be misled by inaccuracies, right? To some extent I would agree; however, the complexity of the (human-defined) realm of scientific practice isn't easily captured in a fact-centered text. Distilling science to isolated facts leaves out other, equally important qualities of science. ("More than Just the Facts," 211)

Ford's construction of the intersection of science and books is very appealing to me. It doesn't dismiss facts or the value of accuracy, but it figures science as an endeavor that is misrepresented when it is portrayed as something that exists outside of the human process of the production of science. Facts can, we might even say *must*, exist in the genre, but they cannot form the center of the book, at least not if the book is going to be in a legitimate sense "about science." Steve Jenkins, himself a writer and illustrator of children's nonfiction, proposes that "understanding that science is a way of thinking rather than a set of data is at the crux of the issue" ("Importance," 67). Jenkins is writing about misperceptions of science, not literature, but if we conceive of children's nonfiction in the same way he argues that we ought to think about science, an important redefinition of the genre becomes possible. Rather than a genre characterized by its commitment to finished knowledge, nonfiction becomes a place where experiments happen. As Ford argues, replacing data with an attention to thinking at the center of nonfiction is more than possible; it results in books that more accurately reflect the field that generates knowledge:

> A focus on facts alone might reward inherent interest in the subject, but it can be only a partial view of how science actually functions. Science is a dynamic social activity, where a "fact" is more a product of popular consensus than a truth to be uncovered. How those facts become stable is an important component of understanding the context in which knowledge is produced and of understanding the people who

are dedicated to investigating scientific questions. ("More than Just the Facts," 212)

Defining nonfiction in this way makes it a genre that is not fundamentally opposed to critical engagement but, as Ford indicates, inclined toward that engagement: "In the long run," she writes, "this is what we want for children—to be informed, skeptical interpreters of the scientific information found in newspapers, on television, or on the Internet" (214).

Others have made observations that suggest a promising link between nonfiction that invites critical engagement and the work of professional researchers in multiple fields beyond science. Victoria L. Bill and Idorenyin Jamar, for example, champion "disciplinary literacy" in the math classroom. They argue that in a class that avoids rote learning, which is to say in a class that instead engages students in conversations that probe at the nature of problems and solutions, "students learn content by working like mathematicians" ("Disciplinary Literacy," 84). Ronald Woodbury, in arguing for a decentered mode of teaching history, uses a phrase very similar to Ford's phrase about science:

> History is interpretation of the meaning and significance of the past, not the past itself. It is inevitably about alternative interpretations and for that, fundamentally dialogical, best understood through an interactive process of testing and refining ideas. To teach history as a one-way process from professor/scholar/authority to ignorant student is to obfuscate, to pretend away, how historians actually work. ("From the Traditional Lecture," 85–86)

How scientists, mathematicians, and historians "actually work," writers such as these maintain, is a process characterized not by monologue but by making vulnerable ideas that must continually be tested and refined, a far cry from ideas that must be regarded as stable and ready for memorization.

The ways those professionals "actually work" are also fundamentally critical in the sense that my argument endorses. Freeman and Person illustrate that connection while championing "presenting science learning as an inquiry-based discipline," arguing that in such a pedagogy, "children will learn science the way scientists learn: through asking questions about their world, through making observations, through inquiring and investigating phenomena" (*Connecting,* 33). As Jenkins argues in an essay tellingly titled "The Importance of Being Wrong," one of the primary tasks of children's nonfiction is not to give answers but to "encourage asking questions." He goes on:

> Most importantly, [children's nonfiction] can show that the conclusions of science are *supposed* to be questioned. Understanding how science works means that we know how to think critically about things—that we can observe things as they really appear to be, rather than as we are told they are, formulate new ideas about those things, and test them against what we already know. (68)

Jenkins, a popular author of children's nonfiction about science, here illustrates the punctuated plurality that is at the heart of critical engagement. Nonfiction presents conclusions that have been drawn, one might even say have been *earned,* by intelligent people asking intelligent questions and anticipating intelligent opposition, but even after those conclusions have been published—for example, in children's nonfiction—they are still "*supposed* to be questioned." For Jenkins, this cyclical process of producing and testing useful knowledge is intimately tied up not simply with a better understanding of facts but with a better understanding of ideology: one tests information to "observe things as they really appear to be, rather than as we are told they are." Wineburg, in a study of professional historians' strategies of reading, identifies a pattern of attention to subtext that is more than a "reconstruction" of authorial intention:

> In fact, many subtexts include elements that work at cross-purposes with authors' intentions, bringing to the surface convictions authors may have been unaware of or may have wished to conceal. These aspects fall into the second sphere, the text as a human artifact that frames reality and discloses information about its authors' assumptions, world view, and beliefs. Such a reading leaps from the words authors use to the types of people authors are, a reading that sees texts not as

ways to describe the world but as ways to construct it. (*Historical Thinking*, 65–66)

Wineburg sees such reading as a disciplinary habit, but what he describes is very similar to how other professional researchers work. And it is a habit identical to critical engagement.

There is some reason to believe that nonfiction has a promising potential to inspire children to engage creatively and critically with knowledge. Earlier, I summarized Jetton's study of the failures of narrative nonfiction to lodge a set of objective facts in the minds of readers. I argued that such findings pose a problem for the standard definition of nonfiction. They are not, however, a problem for someone interested in viewing the field as a place for dialogue between readers and books that invite children to the process of inquiry. Thus Jetton argues for "a need to provide instruction which encourages deep processing of text beyond simply restating the story" ("Information-Driven," 128). It is beyond the scope of her essay to theorize what that instruction might look like, but, in the final line of her paper, Jetton explains that "one encouraging finding is that students were able to expand on the existing story framework of the original text and create unique stories of their own" (129). This final observation, all but a throwaway, points to the idea that at the exact same time as narrative nonfiction fails to communicate pure data to its readers, it succeeds in inviting them to the dialogue of intellectual work. Again, this unsought result is a problem if the goal of nonfiction is to lead readers to the end of an intellectual endeavor, but not if the goal is to involve them in the analysis and production of knowledge.

Children's nonfiction has long been considered a literature of answers. When contemporary writers, editors, and critics talk about children's nonfiction, they often express excitement over the inclusion of literary techniques in new nonfiction, but they take for granted that whatever literary ornamentations it may bear, nonfiction is primarily a literature of facts. But there is a growing sense that children's nonfiction ought to be instead a literature of questions, and it is out of this perception of the genre that its real potential for critical engagement grows. Indeed, in some theories of education, especially those made by Freire and his intellectual descendants, it is only when nonfiction leaves behind an obligation to be authoritative that it has any potential for critical engagement at all. A literature of facts cannot be a literature of critical engagement. A literature of facts can only strive to produce a reading relationship between book and reader in which the book ushers in truth and the reader meekly receives what the book says—without questioning.

We can ask more of our nonfiction than authority. We can ask for a literature of questions.

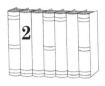

2

VOICE AND THE SEAMLESS NARRATIVE OF KNOWLEDGE

WHEN JOE L. KINCHELOE WRITES of the "seamless narrative" told by most history textbooks, he is not giving a compliment (*Getting* 2001, 592). For Kincheloe, a faithful story of the past requires a particular kind of telling, one in which conclusions are conditional, in which the voice with which the narrator speaks is characterized by what Sam Wineburg has called "humility" in the face of what we do not know and cannot understand about the past (*Historical Thinking,* 22). For Kincheloe, the effort that textbook writers spend to erase the "seams" of a narrative is problematic because doing so accrues to the narrator an authority that is unfair and to the story a confidence that is misleading. His complaint is that in presenting key dates in a linear tale of progress, attention to the slow, inconsistent drift of opinion, law, and ideology is ignored in favor of the moments in which the consequences of that drift become evident. History becomes a story of endings stitched together so tightly that the spaces between vanish. The firm, secure dates of change—when a president signs a law, when a general surrenders, when a ship sinks—remain, but the ideas and struggles that surround those dates, more difficult to explain, impossible to phrase in a multiple-choice question, these disappear.

In this chapter and those that follow, I want to begin to play with the idea behind Kincheloe's "seams." For Kincheloe, a textbook's seamless narrative erases the instances in which the work of history is more difficult, less knowable. As I turn to narrative nonfiction, I want to be alert to the places where the story attempts to draw attention toward the conclusions drawn at the expense of attention to the production of information. For Kincheloe, the spaces closed by seamless narratives were promising threats to a falsely authoritative version of history. For my study, the seamless narrative disguises where a book is most vulnerable to critical engagement.

I'll start by suggesting a different metaphor: think of the way that shoe polish works. If I see that my dress shoes need to be polished, what I am observing is that the surface of my shoes has begun to crack: minute fissures run across the face, reflecting the light in irregular ways and, more importantly for a skinflint such as myself, making the interior vulnerable to moisture and the sort of damage that could ruin the shoes entirely. When I polish my shoes, all I do is dye and fill in those tiny cracks. I do not, and this is an important distinction, actually repair the cracks; rather, I disguise them. I stuff them with a thick mixture of solids and liquids, and then I buff the excess polish off so that instead of a series of ridges, I have something like a black plane that runs evenly over the surface. I have not actually healed the shoe but disguised it so that the cracks are no longer visible to the eye or easily vulnerable to water.

The same is true of the process by which we make our arguments stronger. There are *always* things that we don't know about whatever subject we are explaining. There are *always* weaknesses in our arguments, places where even we know—though often we try to make ourselves forget—we might be wrong. To strengthen an argument, we tend to fill in, to conceal, those cracks in our argument. And although it is embarrassing to be caught doing so, I'm not sure that buffing our arguments to a shine is entirely unethical. In fact, I suspect that we would find it tedious to have to sit through every conceivable qualification, confession, and moment of self-doubt inherent in every argument that we ever hear. To a large extent, human communication relies on speakers to conceal the rough spots in our ideas.

But when a speaker—or, for my purposes, a book—*declines* to polish or indeed endeavors to draw attention to the cracks, what remains is an opening for critical engagement. Now, as my Conclusion will argue, readers—specifically children—frequently engage critically with texts whether those openings have been left plain or not. Nonetheless, the analogy still holds: when I polish my shoes, I prevent casual perception of their flaws, and I discourage easy saturation, but polish hardly fends off sharp sticks or deep puddles. Still, there is value to polishing our shoes as well as our ideas; if there weren't, we'd stop doing it. Similarly, there is a meaning to leaving the cracks visible. Wearing scuffed dress shoes communicates a certain lack of formality and authority. Expressing an idea and retaining in that expression the places where the idea cracks does the same thing. When a book declines to polish its presentation of information, the book communicates humility instead of authority; it leaves bare the gaps in understanding rather than presenting a unified front of finished information; it makes plain its vulnerabilities. These are what I am calling invitations to critical engagement.

In this chapter, I want to explore a few subtle rhetorical choices constellated around the concept of voice. When we think of voice as an aspect of literature, we tend to think of it in terms of tone, and to an extent tone is what I mean, but it's more accurate to say that for me, voice is the set of strategies through which a work of nonfiction cultivates an impression of confidence or doubt in the information that it presents. Certainly tone is relevant to such a concept, but the aspects of voice that I will consider, while indirect, are more objectively named than tone. For me, the most telling characteristics of voice in nonfiction are hesitancy, person, and multiplicity. In this chapter, I explore three terms introduced by previous scholars and directly relevant to those characteristics: *hedges, visible narrators,* and *necromancers*. I will be watching for how hedges signal hesitancy, visible narrators shift the voice to first person, and necromancers multiply the voices expressed, all in an effort to tease out how voice can contribute to encouraging readers to hear an opening for critical engagement.

Hedges

My way of thinking about voice is a bit counterintuitive, but it echoes concepts found in Bakhtin. When Tzvetan Todorov summarizes Bakhtin's understanding of the novel, he writes that "the novel starts out with a plurality of languages, discourses, and voices, and the inevitable awareness of language as such; in this sense, the novel is a basically self-reflexive genre" (*Mikhail Bakhtin,* 66). That self-reflexivity, that inherent complication of a single voice, is central to Bakhtin's idea of dialogism. The fracturing of a single ideology that Bakhtin reads in the novel is the product of what Todorov calls "voices," here indicating the means through which a text reveals rather than conceals the distance between ideas. When Bakhtin examines the comic novel, he argues that simply by placing multiple voices in the same narrative, an author of a comic novel

> utilizes now one language, now another, in order to avoid giving himself up wholly to either of them; he makes use of this verbal give-and-take, this dialogue of languages at every point in his work, in order that he himself might remain as it were neutral with regard to language, a third party in a quarrel between two people (although he might be a biased third party). ("Discourse," 314)

Bakhtin theorizes a space for debate—the sort of opening that I have been calling an invitation to critical engagement—framed by voice. Bakhtin champions the novel as a unique site for this sort of vocalization, but nonfiction, too, frequently uses techniques of voice to fracture the narrative of ideas.

The first of these techniques is what has come to be known among scholars as a hedge. Although research from the 1930s to the 1980s examined different forms of this technique,[1] Avon Crismore is today the scholar most closely associated with it and the scholar credited with coining the umbrella term. Crismore and her coauthor William J. Vande Kopple explain hedges as "linguistic elements such as *perhaps, might, to a certain extent,* and *it is possible that,*" elements that "writers use . . . to signal a tentative or cautious assessment of the truth of referential information" ("Readers' Learning,"

184–85). Crismore and Vande Kopple find that in certain situations, hedges can increase retention of the information contained in passages with hedges (199)—an important discovery for the study of children's nonfiction, considering how the genre is often used in classrooms—but more important to the study of critical engagement is how hedges can "signal" places that the information should be treated with significant skepticism. Myra Zarnowski has applied the concept of hedges to her use of nonfiction with elementary students, and she speaks highly of the potential for hedges to help children see how to engage with information critically. She writes about the tendency of older nonfiction for children to approach gaps in historical records creatively, feeling "free to fill in these gaps by creating dialogue and events that seemed plausible, even if they never actually occurred." But more contemporary nonfiction, she argues, uses hedges to "show how historians deal with gaps in information" (*History,* 53). She singles out *William Shakespeare and the Globe* (1999) by Aliki Liacouras Brandenberg (who publishes under her first name) and Diane Stanley and Peter Vennema's *Bard of Avon* (1992), praising them for using hedges to highlight the questions that remain in our study of Shakespeare as a biographical subject. "When Stanley and Vennema speculate about how Shakespeare's life might have been," for example, "they sprinkle words like *probably, some people think,* or *we assume* to highlight their uncertainty. Aliki, too, uses *perhaps, no one knows when,* and *some say.* All of this hedging makes it clear that there are gaps and uncertainties in the story of Shakespeare's life" (54). Zarnowski argues that hedges such as these show readers "that when huge gaps like this occur, the biographer has to look for other kinds of information" (53), and she finds that children are happily capable of following the inquisitive pattern laid out for them. In other words, hedges open gaps that invite critical engagement.

    One of the easiest places to find widespread, consistent uses of hedges is in Marc Aronson's *If Stones Could Speak: Unlocking the Secrets of Stonehenge* (2010). The book tells the story of how Aronson joined a crew of scientists as they explored Stonehenge and tested emerging theories about its origins. As such, one might expect a certain smugness about the scientists' conclusions, and there are

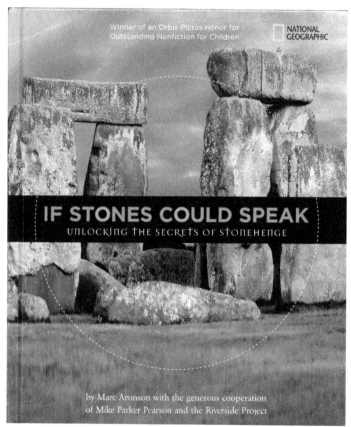

Marc Aronson, *If Stones Could Speak: Unlocking the Secrets of Stonehenge* (2010).

moments—such as when Aronson says that because of the unique viewpoint of one scientist, "suddenly we can look up, look around, and picture how people lived here thousands of years ago" (46)—when such is the case. But those moments are surprisingly rare; instead, Aronson peppers his book with hedges. As he explains a sixteenth-century sketch of Stonehenge, Aronson points to a depression drawn around the outside of the site and comments that "a bank like this with a ditch next to it is what archaeologists call a 'henge.' But the name Stonehenge probably has a different root: the Old English words for 'stone' and 'hanging'—possibly because the stones seem to 'hang in the air'" (7). This explanation does not shrink from providing information, but it suspends nearly all its conclusions, leaving them in the act of being considered rather than presenting them as finished thoughts. Aronson also uses hedges to communicate the stirring experience of being in the moment of discovery, as when he summarizes the "thrilling discovery" in 2009 of nearby Bluestonehenge. "This site may," he writes, "have been the original home of some of the taller bluestones now forming the inner circle at Stonehenge" (45). Indeed, one of the most interesting questions to emerge while scanning Aronson's book for hedges is on what subjects he does *not* use them, and for the most part, the pattern is easy to discern. The rare stretches in which Aronson declines hedges are moments in which he is expounding the book's central theme, which is that looking at subjects from a new perspective can provide important breakthroughs. The hedges indicate an eagerness on the book's part to invite readers to ask questions about the science, and when the narrator speaks with an uncharacteristic conviction, he insists that there is a need for new approaches to familiar materials. The hedges and their absence work together to make complementary points.

There is more range to hedges than one might suspect, even in books written well before contemporary styles in nonfiction. Priscilla Wakefield's *Perambulations in London, and Its Environs,* first published in 1809, consists mostly of detailed information about London, and the narrator frequently worries that the child reader will be bored by what it calls "the fruits of my research" (21). Nonetheless, Wakefield does at times break up the information with hedges. For example, she writes that following a disastrous agricultural season in 1315, "parents, rendered desperate by hunger, are said to have eaten their own children" (40). Elsewhere, she speculates that "it seems highly probable that the peculiar habits of the different companies, or guilds, originated" at about the time of Richard II's reign (51). These breaks in authority are rare, and there are no provisions from the narrative, the footnotes, or a bibliography to point to where a curious reader might follow up on the research, but Wakefield's text is just one example of how hedges have existed in children's nonfiction for more than two hundred years.

In more contemporary nonfiction, hedges continue to play a role, even sometimes multiple roles, as one word, *perhaps*, demonstrates. Pamela S. Turner's 2009 book *The Frog Scientist* uses the word in the context of an ongoing exploration about the effects of atrazine on amphibians. In one kind of frog, the presence of atrazine feminized the male of the species. "But perhaps the African clawed frogs were unusually sensitive," Turner muses. "Would atrazine have the same effect on a different kind of frog?" In this instance, "perhaps" highlights not exactly a crack in knowledge but a new way to approach knowledge, a new test to run, and indeed the titular scientist then proceeds to perform that test, this time on leopard frogs (26). In Susan Campbell Bartoletti's 1996 *Growing Up in Coal Country*, the word works differently. In a paragraph on the persistence of miners' superstitions, Bartoletti speculates that "perhaps, for them, it was better to let fate rest in the hands of the unknown" (63). In this case, "perhaps" points to a question that is *not* testable: without access to the thoughts of these miners, the great majority of whom are now deceased, our best knowledge is only a guess. Bartoletti's tone is sympathetic, and although her methodical research and careful documentation are at odds with the willingness of the miners to hold on to superstitions, "perhaps" hints at a sympathy for those miners, even a willingness to excuse behavior that, in retrospect, might seem naive. Julius Lester's 1968 *To Be a Slave* turns the word in yet another direction. "Perhaps," he offers, "the sound of other human beings marching to the fields for another day of forced labor was a 'pleasant' one. Perhaps" (75). Once more, the word indicates a guess into the minds of people who can no longer testify to the accuracy of the author's hunch, but here, the word also implies both that Lester is skeptical of the possible answer and that, unlike Bartoletti's hypothesis about the motivation of the miners, Lester is resentful of the people who would hold such an opinion. "Perhaps" encourages our skepticism and resentment, too. In each of these cases, the hedge chosen is the same word, and although each works slightly differently, in each case it flags a place where readers are invited to cultivate doubt.

Hedges are an aspect of voice in nonfiction that is not, however, common. Wakefield's narrator, for example, announces at one point that "it is time to fulfil my promise of enumerating the most striking events in the reign of Charles the Second," and "enumerate" is an excellent word for what follows, indeed, for what is characteristic of most of the book. Wakefield fills the next several pages with dates, events, numbers, names, and more numbers: 1665 (the year of a horrible plague), 63,596 (the number of people killed by the plague), Sir John Laurence (the lord mayor who tried to assist the needy), and 40,000 (the number of servants "turned into the streets to perish" [*Perambulations*, 89]). The secure knowledge offered in pages such as these allows Wakefield to proclaim lessons about spiritual truths: "Affliction is well adapted to draw forth and display extraordinary instances of virtue" (89), for one example; "Such benefactors are an honour not only to their own nation, but to human nature, and are the models we should endeavour to imitate" (90), for another. In more recent years, materials for children tend to be less overtly moralistic, but textbooks still avoid hedges, and for not-dissimilar reasons. Crismore speculates that writers of history textbooks "do not see themselves as needing to persuade young readers since they are the 'truth-givers'" ("Rhetoric," 292). What is at stake in hedges is authority, and when books avoid such qualifiers, they often do so with the effect of presenting themselves as dealers in a truth that is finished and in no need of further inquiry.

Visible Authors

In addition to her work on hedges, Crismore has made another important contribution to understanding the voices of informational texts. She notes that at times, the author becomes "present as the narrator," and she gives examples including "*It seems to me, We suggest, I think that*" ("Rhetoric," 293). To Crismore, such authorial presence is primarily a subset of hedging strategies, but other scholars have since isolated and developed that aspect of voice. Susan Bobbitt Nolen, for instance, builds on Crismore's research to demonstrate how "anonymous authors remain invisible to readers through the use of rhetorical devices, including passive construction, use of the third rather than the first person, and by not directly discussing their personal history, views, or personality" (47). In Nolen, "presence" drifts into "visibility," and today, that metaphor is the dominant word to explain the presence or absence of a personalized voice. Sam Wineburg adds that in most textbooks, "no visible author confronts the reader; instead, a corporate author speaks from a position of transcendence, a position of knowing from on high" (*Historical Thinking,* 13). Today, the term *visible author* is shorthand for what Crismore meant when she wrote about the sense of an author in the narration.

In the same way that the metaphor has drifted since Crismore's early work, the significance of such uses of voice has also changed. Although Crismore's work tends to be represented today as geared toward explaining how authors can open up opportunities for readers to question texts, the central point of her work was, according to Crismore, helping readers better understand what authors meant. "Metadiscourse," her term for hedges and other such rhetorical gestures, "is, simply, an author's discoursing about the discourse; it is the author's intrusion into the discourse, either explicitly or non-explicitly, to *direct* rather than inform the readers. Metadiscourse can be considered directives given to readers so they will understand what is said and meant in the primary discourse and so they will know how to 'take' the author" ("The Rhetoric," 280). But as scholars have continued to develop the concept of the visible author, its value has become more closely tied to encouraging inquiry. Richard Paxton, for example, has found that when a text used an anonymous narrator, students "were more likely to simply restate the text . . . rather than adding original thoughts, or pondering the meaning of the information presented" (239). When Paxton asked students to respond to anonymous texts, they often replied with "I don't know. I'm just reading. I'm not thinking anything." But texts with visible authors inspired students "to try to come to grips with the historical information presented" (241). In short, "when addressed by the visible author, students replied" (245). Furthermore, Zarnowski reports that her own students have replied with questions that show significant critical engagement: "Are my sources reliable? Are there gaps in my information? Is it possible to interpret the information another way?" (*History,* 52) Although research on visible authors began as a way to help readers correctly perceive authors' intentions, later research argues that visible authors can help readers engage critically with authors' ideas.

The visible author has a longer history in children's nonfiction than might be obvious. Some contemporary writers—Marc Aronson is probably the most obvious, and Zarnowski and Susan Turkel have examined the fruits of his efforts ("Nonfiction," 32)—make a point of showing themselves as active, opinionated stakeholders in the subjects that their books explore. But an earlier, clear example of the visible author comes from John Gregory, who, in 1761, wrote *A Father's Legacy to His Daughters*. The book was intended to be private, but after Gregory's death in 1773, his son published the book, which went on to enjoy many reprintings and international distribution. *A Father's Legacy* is a prototypical example of the visible author: the author speaks in the first person, narrating as himself, and the ideas are presented as endorsed by that narrator. For example, in one of his many comments on religion, Gregory explains, "I wish you to go no farther than the scriptures for your religious opinions" and continues, "I would advise you to read only such religious books as are addressed to the heart" (109). At the local as well as global level, this is a book that continually reminds its readers that there is a specific person espousing the opinions.

But the sentimentality of the book—which we have already seen in the advice to privilege books on religion "addressed to the heart"—gives Gregory a reason to invite to the voice of the narrative one other authority, and in doing so, he foregrounds his own fallibility. The book was written in the shadow of the death of his wife, the mother to the daughters to whom the book is directed. Gregory evokes her wisdom and casts his own as inferior:

> You will all remember your father's fondness, when perhaps every other circumstance relating to him is forgotten. This remembrance, I hope, will induce you to give a serious attention to the advices I am now going to leave with you.—I can request this attention with the greater confidence, as my sentiments on the most interesting points that regard life and manners, were entirely correspondent to your mother's, whose judgment and taste I trusted much more than my own. (101–2)

Although Gregory does not often refer to his dead wife, he does routinely remind his daughters that they "must expect, that the advices which I shall give you will be very imperfect" (102). The closing paragraph of the book ends with yet another iteration of his imperfection, with Gregory confessing that "I am conscious I undertook a task to which I was very unequal" (195). Gregory's book is therefore an example of how the visible author vastly predates our own period as well as an example of how a visible author can be a clear tool for complicating a text's authority.

I don't want to overstate the fractured authority that Gregory's selection of voice brings to his books. The text is, for instance, also overlaid with an awareness of Gregory's own impending death (early deaths ran in the family for Gregory, and he himself died unexpectedly before the age of fifty) that would make ignoring his sentimental pleas very challenging.[2] Too, it's difficult to regard much of Gregory's advice as especially empowering for his daughters. One of Mary Wollstonecraft's favorite themes in *A Vindication of the Rights of Woman* is how damaging Gregory's very popular book had been to women (at one point, she likens his advice to establishing "a system of slavery" [64]), and it's easy to see why: he discourages his daughters from applying "reasoning" to religion for fear it might shake their faith (108), grounds much of his advice in an effort to measure women by standards established by men (104), and warns his daughters to keep their intelligence "a profound secret, especially from the men, who generally look with a jealous and malignant eye on a woman of great parts, and a cultivated understanding" (122). Zarnowski, writing about contemporary books with visible authors, argues that "visible authors reach out to readers, inviting them into a dialogue about the past. They ask, What do you think?" (*History*, 50). Such is not the case in Gregory's book, even though its narrator is plainly a visible author.

Gregory rarely intends for his readers to argue with him, but the theory of the visible author does not quite call for intention. Rather, the theory is simply that by providing an embodied voice, a book attaches a person to an idea, and even if the book intends to present the idea as polished, the idea becomes humanized—which is to say that it becomes fallible—because of that attachment.

Zarnowski holds that, "unlike authors who give us the facts without revealing much about themselves or their thinking, visible authors bring us history with voice, attitude, and point of view. We begin to see the author as intertwined in the telling of the history—visible to us as a thinker, a person with opinions" (*History*, 50). In the case of Gregory's daughters, their hearts still raw from the loss of their mother, frightened by the thought of their father's mortality, this person with opinions would have been a very difficult one with whom to argue, but as the book has drifted further from its original audience, disagreement has become easier, and part of that shift is because Gregory makes himself a recognizable target. In texts with similar sensibilities from similar eras, we might have the same objections, but my guess is that we would be tempted to phrase our objections to those texts as objections to the way "people" during those time periods thought rather than pinning the ideas to a distinct proponent with whom we can argue specifically. Kincheloe, writing about the teaching of history, argues that it is not a search for an unbiased source that should be the goal of historical understanding but the recognition of sources themselves. "If a student is aware of the source of propaganda," Kincheloe explains, "he has made an important advance in protecting himself from it" (*Getting* 1989, 281). Wineburg agrees, arguing that when professional historians engage critically with a text, "the historian knows that there are no free-floating details, only details tied to witnesses, and if witnesses are suspect, so are their details" ("Historical Problem Solving," 84). Elsewhere, he finds that this kind of critical reading sees sources "as people, not objects" (*Historical Thinking*, 76). Visible authors make explicit the fact that their ideas come from human sources, which, in keeping with the authors' intentions or not, makes stronger the possibility of engaging with a book critically.

With the breadth of the visible author theory in mind, specifically the point that the author's intention is not crucial to the consequences of voice for critical engagement, I want to propose that we can broaden even further the idea of the visible author for an even wider examination of how children's nonfiction can invite critical engagement. Wakefield's *Perambulations,* whose mixed use of hedges I worked through above, provides an example of how this visible author might look. The book is written as a series of letters filled with information about the history, architecture, and culture of London, and as an epistolary book, it naturally gravitates toward the use of a first-person narrator, as, for example, when the narrator dryly mentions at the beginning of Letter IX that "I am glad to find that I have been able to render my historical detail tolerably amusing" (107). But, in a dialogical move that would delight Bakhtin, Wakefield writes *none* of these letters as though she were the narrator. Instead, each letter claims to come from characters of Wakefield's invention, including Catherine Middleton to her cousin Emma and a boy named Eugenius to Roland Spencer, a schoolmate. More than a quarter of the book is given, though, to one Charles de Vitry, around whom most of the other characters are constellated (Eugenius is a nephew). In one passage, de Vitry, an expatriate Swiss, proclaims the following:

> I believe there is no nation more attentive to domestic comfort than the English; nor more ingenious to contrive every accommodation to render the home-fireside the most agreeable spot in the universe, though it should happen to be in a narrow street, where the light of the sun can scarcely penetrate. This love of home may be attributed to the amiable character and excellent conduct of the females of middle rank, who are, in general, admirable patterns of conjugal and maternal virtue; devoting their time to the regulation of their families, with a cheerful perseverance, and well-directed attention, that endears them to their husbands, which would ill suit their modesty and diffidence, for which they are remarkable. (17)

This passage is typical of the adoring eye that the book casts on London, but because of this very strange case of a visible author, it takes on a delightful irony that shakes the authority of the book. Wakefield was herself exactly the kind of woman that "de Vitry" here praises: a female of middle rank who was not only admired and beloved by her husband and sons but reportedly saved her family from a house fire when her husband, in the words of a biographer, "fled to a corner in tears" (Shteir, "Wakefield"). Although her readers probably did not know her personal history, Wakefield was by the time of the publication of *Perambulations* an institution in children's nonfiction, with more than half a dozen books already published, including the very popular book *The Juvenile Travellers* (1801). Wakefield's name was widely associated with children's nonfiction, and at the time of *Perambulations,* published when *Juvenile Travellers* was a recent hit, her name itself was likely a marketing boon. Therefore, readers could easily have caught the irony of Wakefield writing de Vitry writing praise for women exactly like Wakefield. This situation does not fit the denotation of the term *visible author*—the "visible" speaker is not the author of the book—but it does provide a break in the book's seamless authority, as Wakefield/de Vitry brags about the "modesty and diffidence" of women such as Wakefield. If *Perambulations* were fiction rather than nonfiction, we might even call this scene metafictional, as it interrupts the immersion of the narrative to wink at the reader. So although this narrator is not in the strictest sense an example of the author herself speaking in first person as herself in the book, it is an example of a first-person narrator drawing attention to the author. It's strikingly similar, in fact, to what Nolen, in her study of visible authors, describes when she writes that "if an author's goal is to do more than impart knowledge, if instead he or she aims to help students become critical readers of research, then perhaps the author should emerge, like the Wizard of Oz, from behind the curtain" ("Effects," 59).

Kadir Nelson's 2008 *We Are the Ship: The Story of Negro League Baseball* shows a rare example of a contemporary work of nonfiction using a fictional narrator, and in doing so, it illustrates some of the significant political implications of knowledge that a visible author can help foreground. The narrator speaks in the first person from the opening page ("Seems like we've been playing baseball for a mighty long time. At least as long as we've been free" [1]) to the last ("We look at guys like Bob Gibson and Ken Griffey, Jr. and smile, because we made it possible for these guys to play in the majors" [78]). And if the fictionality of Nelson's narrator for a nonfiction book is uncommon, even more uncommon is that the narrator is both anonymous and plural. For Nelson, this choice has a specific, ideological impetus: "I chose to present the voice of the narrator as a collective voice," he explains, "the voice of every player, the voice of

Kadir Nelson, *We Are the Ship: The Story of Negro League Baseball* (2008).

we. Under the leadership of Rube Foster, who declared the leagues' independence from major league baseball by saying, 'We are the ship; all else the sea,' the owners and players formed and sustained a successful league, demonstrating the power of the collective" (80). As with Wakefield's first-person narrator, Nelson's plural narrator makes a virtue of the irony of the chosen voice. The narrator speaks of "those" black players of the 1860s, implying that the "we" of the narration did not play in those days, but when the history turns to the early twentieth century, the narrator relates "what we did" (3). The narrator implied by this voice also, however, has firsthand knowledge of players active at the time of the book's publication

(78). The voice created therefore requires a narrator who played in the Negro Leagues and is, by 2008, well over a century old. The irony in Wakefield's narrator offers a quasi-metafictional moment in which readers emerge from the narrative to get the joke, and Nelson's narrator, who cannot fit conventional models of nonfiction narrators both because of its plurality and because of its improbably long life, offers something similar, a prolonged metafictionality, as the identity of the narrator becomes ever more incompatible with the historical reality that the narrator describes. This narrator carries a sort of authority, but it is an authority that sits awkwardly enough to invite engagement and questions.

That unsettling authority is especially well suited to a book on the subject of how a disenfranchised group was pushed from the official version of history. As the book explains, black players were once part of professional baseball, but they were slowly and unofficially phased out of the game (1–2). When Rube Foster and other black men developed the Negro Leagues, they managed to carve professional and financial stability out of an athletic culture in which they were not valued, but much of the history of the Leagues cannot be told with confidence, and certainly not with the level of detail lavished on the history of the Major Leagues. The narrator addresses exactly this point:

> And stats? Well, some teams kept them. But it wasn't a consistent thing. Most guys kept their own stats, or if a player on the team was keeping them, a bit of the information was lost when he had to bat or play in the field. Occasionally, a local newspaper would send a reporter out to keep stats, but the papers wouldn't pay them to do it very often. Sometimes those guys would come late and have to ask around, "What happened in the first inning?" "Who did what?" or they'd just make up the stats. Even when the stats were recorded, they weren't always phoned in, or it was too much to try to stop and find a mailbox on the road while we were headed for the next town. Shoot, the white papers wouldn't run our scores anyway. Stats weren't kept consistently until later, after Jackie Robinson went up to the majors. (21)

One of the sad truths for a history on this subject is that the institutions for verifying and recording data are institutions bound up with the prejudices and inequities of their historical moments. Therefore, the decision to tell the story through a narrator who is present enough to be questioned is an aesthetic decision as well as one that more truthfully reflects the validity of the data. And the truth, of course, is that these data should be engaged with critically.

Necromancers

Sam Wineburg offers a general summary of what I think of as dialogical tools of voice, and he adds another tool with an especially pithy name. In general, Wineburg finds, "textbooks pivot on what Roland Barthes called the 'referential illusion,' the notion that the way things are told is simply the way things were" (*Historical Thinking*, 12). That illusion is synchronous with the attempt to close gaps in authority, to ward off critical engagement. Although Wineburg spends time on the effects of the visible author, he also explains that the voice of such informational texts can be much more fractured:

> Here reading moves beyond an author–reader dialogue to embrace a set of conversations—exchanges between actual and mock reader, between mock writer and mock audience, between mock reader and mock audience, and between any one of these characters and the "I" of the actual reader. Instead of a single "executive" directing a top-down process, mature readers of history may create inside their own heads an "executive board," where members clamor, shout, and wrangle over controversial points. Texts are not "processed" as much as they are resurrected, and the image of reader as information processor or computing device, which often dominates current discussions of reading, seems less apt than another metaphor: the reader as necromancer. (72–73)

Whereas the visible author humanizes information and provides a target with whom a reader can (and, if Paxton is right, does) argue, a text that puts its reader in the position of necromancer makes information too complicated to be absorbed simply. Necromantic nonfiction presents ideas in the act of being tested. It frequently attaches these ideas to people, thereby gaining the advantages of nonfiction narrated by a visible author, but it has the potential to go a step further, presenting ideas as things that are contested. When we are looking for places where nonfiction helps readers become necromancers, we are looking for where the text offers various legitimate positions in a debate rather than presenting only the conclusions drawn from a debate that has been long settled.

Katie R. Peel, in a study of newer children's nonfiction about Ethel and Julius Rosenberg, has made a point that gets to the heart of what I see as valuable in necromantic nonfiction. The texts that she studies cast the Rosenberg case as one that is itself unfinished, with new information coming to light decades after the federal government executed the Rosenbergs for espionage. Peel's arguments provide a clear link between Bakhtin's theories and Wineburg's "necromancy." The emergence of new evidence, she argues, presents nonfiction with the opportunity to allow "a multiplicity of voices," a sure echo of Bakhtin's search for where and how a text can be dialogical. A book written with such a multiplicity, Peel concludes, "requires critical thinking" of its readers ("Strange Fruit," 207). The relevance for a study of characters becomes more evident when Peel argues that "through the potential for critical thinking, [these] texts contain a sense of possibility and potentiality, even within narratives about lives already lost" (203). Peel is effectively demonstrating how even after the characters are dead, nonfiction can reanimate those characters and "invite active reader participation" (190) that insists on informed interpretation of historical information influenced by contesting theories. Information plays a key role; the readings of that information by previous authorities also play a key role. By animating the information and the people impacted by it, Peel argues, these texts create a reading situation in which they encourage their readers to engage critically.

Bartoletti, the author of *Growing Up in Coal Country* (1996), argues that writers of children's nonfiction frequently have just such a process in mind when crafting their work. She explains that she and writers like her approach material with suspicion, and she goes on to explain that her suspicion drives her to incorporate debate into her writing process. This involves, in part, recruiting someone inclined to argue with her:

> Despite the most diligent research, a mistake can slip by. To guard against this, many extreme researchers recruit a gaffe-protection force—an expert in the field willing to vet the manuscript. I prefer a "fault-hunting, mote-magnifying tyrant," as Mark Twain might say (and did say in *Life on the Mississippi*). When a curator publicly chastised a speaker for a slide that projected backwards, telling him that such a lack of attention to detail was inexcusable, I cringed for the speaker but later asked the curator to vet *Growing Up in Coal Country*, knowing full well that his fault-hunting, mote-magnifying nature might cause "dread at my heart" (Twain, again), but ultimately a grateful heart.
>
> As *Kirkus* editor and 2010 Sibert Medal committee chair Vicky Smith says, "Once you get over fuming, you'll probably have learned something. The recognition of opposition, even if it's unreasonable, can only make a piece of writing stronger and clearer." ("Extreme Sport," 28–29)

For Bartoletti, then, writing nonfiction should have a built-in component of opposition. This extends to a debate not only with a specific "mote-magnifying" audience member but also, as Bartoletti puts it, "with my sources—and myself" (30). Bartoletti is a widely read, widely praised, award-winning author of children's nonfiction, which I mention not to invest her with authority but to point out that if she is telling the truth about her writing process, then writing necromantic nonfiction is a safe professional decision.

Recent educational theorists of children's nonfiction have proposed a similar but importantly different way of resurrecting a heterogeneous group of voices on a given subject. Zarnowski has given the clearest theorization of this strategy. She proposes using "pairs, triplets, and quads," by which she means two, three, or four different books on the same subject, to "show students how to question what they read." Bringing these different texts into the classroom prompts "questions about how and why biographies of the same subject can be vastly different." This practice allows the class to "show that history involves *interpretation*" and undermines "the stubbornly persistent belief among students that one source—the RIGHT one—has the truth" (*History*, 28, 45). Zarnowski explains how she has used three biographies of Ben Franklin for this exercise. "By doing this," she writes, "the process of historical thinking [becomes] visible and open to discussion" (34). Patricia J. Cianciolo has proposed similar methods, offering multiple books about Tibet so that children can learn "to recognize the persuasive techniques" that authors use (*Informational Picture Books,* 13). Kincheloe even suggests putting textbooks into dialogue with one another in the classroom to reveal shifting understandings of history and the presentation of, for example, "the changing role of minorities and women in American social and political life" (*Getting* 2001, 182). These ideas are excellent strategies for provoking critical discussion in the classroom, but I am using Wineburg's metaphor to a slightly different end. For these theorists, the conversation occurs in a very real way between the texts, not within any one of them. But what Wineburg suggests is that inside a single text, there can be a variety of voices. Although these theorists have found a way to force a conversation, what I am searching for is where a book presents a conversation, where it shows a multiplicity of ideas rather than a monologue dedicated to one idea.

If we look closely, we can find many isolated examples of necromancy in children's nonfiction. *The Wonders of the Telescope,* an 1805 book probably written by Jeremiah Joyce, makes a point of animating the voices of debate in its section on sunspots, which it says "have been very differently explained." It continues,

> *By some it has been supposed,* that they are occasioned by the smoke and opaque matter thrown out by volcanoes, or burning mountains of immense magnitude; and that when the eruption is nearly ended, and the smoke dissipated, the fiery flames are exposed, and have the appearance of the faculae, or luminous spots. *Others have imagined* the Sun to be in a continual state of fusion, and that the spots we observe are the eminences of large masses of opaque matter, which, by the irregular agitations of the fluid, sometimes swim on the surface, and at other times sink and disappear. *Others have*

supposed them to be occasioned by a number of planets which circulate round the Sun, at a small distance from his surface. (20, emphasis added)

Much more recently, Sue Macy's 2001 biography of Annie Oakley uses a very similar structure when describing a 1901 train wreck involving Oakley and others who traveled with the Buffalo Bill show. "Annie was thrown from her bed and slammed into a trunk," Macy writes, "but sources differ on how badly she was hurt. Some say she received only slight injuries to her hand and back. Others say her back injury was quite serious, requiring several operations to repair" (*Bull's-Eye*, 46). These are straightforward examples of how a book can act as necromancer, giving voice to markedly different opinions on the information that the book explores.

At other times, necromancy is more a practice than an event. In these cases, individual moments of necromancy are instances of a widespread strategy throughout much of the book. Turner's *The*

Pamela S. Turner, *The Frog Scientist* (2009).

Frog Scientist, mentioned earlier, follows the research of Tyrone Hayes, who suspects that atrazine, a widely used pesticide, is provoking changes in the sexual makeup of amphibians. After Hayes has disseminated his results, others decide to pursue the question as well. "Some of the scientists found deformities," Turner writes, "and some didn't. The United States government decided more research is needed. The scientific and political debate over atrazine and other pesticides goes on" (48). In Turner's book, it is the questions that are important, and questions are validated by debate. Indeed, Turner's book defines science itself as a function of debate. "A scientific 'truth,'" she argues, "is usually decided after *a lot* of argument over data from *a lot* of experiments done *by a lot* of scientists. Each of Tyrone's experiments is a voice in the argument over the safety of atrazine and other pesticides" (42–44). Jim Murphy's *An American Plague: The True and Terrifying Story of the Yellow Fever Epidemic of 1793* (2003) is another book that tells its story as an unfinished conversation. Murphy features multiple debates, beginning with a heated argument between eighteenth-century medical doctors over what exactly the disease is that has hit eighteenth-century Philadelphia: some credit it to an imbalance of humors, but Benjamin Rush, one of the city's most respected physicians, makes the case for yellow fever (15). Even as Rush's diagnosis gains credibility, "most of the city's eighty physicians did not believe that the illness described by Rush was indeed yellow fever. They felt that the disorder must be one of the other common fevers that often struck during warm weather. Among the possibilities mentioned were jail fever, camp fever, eruptive military fever, and autumnal fever" (16). As the argument wears on, Murphy provides opposition for Rush in the character of William Currie, who believes that "whatever fever they might be facing had been imported from another area—probably from the West Indies by the recently arrived Santo Domingans" (26). Murphy also animates his story with debates over appropriate cures and preventatives, including breathing the fumes of vinegar (27), poisoning mosquitoes (28), scattering a two-inch layer of fresh dirt in every room of the house (29), "inhaling finely ground black pepper" (29), and imbibing any of a number of strange materials ("Peruvian bark, salt of vinegar, refined camphor," and a brand-name elixir with "so much pure alcohol that a glass of it could put a person into a drunken stupor" [31]). Even Rush, whose actions elsewhere in the narrative border on heroic, proposes (and administers on himself—twice) a combination of bleeding with a purge made of mercury and a poisonous root (61–62). Murphy puts these and other measures in pointed conflict with each other, tracing at length, for example, how "many doctors disputed Rush's cure rate and felt his 'Ten-and-Fifteen' purge and copious bleedings dangerous," leading some doctors to nickname him the "Prince of Bleeders" (62–63). The final chapter punctuates all of these debates with this chilling ellipsis: "despite years of research, *there is still no cure for yellow fever*" (138, emphasis original). Therefore, although this is a book about an event in the past, it makes a point of leaving open space for debate in the present. In these two books, the choice of subject itself is one that makes the necromancy routine.

Reading the Hallmarks Carefully

In this chapter, I have begun laying out the hallmarks that are central to my study. Here and in the next chapter, I offer rhetorical choices that often flag a text's willingness or reluctance to leave bare the seams of narrative, to invite or discourage critical engagement. Before closing, though, I need to provide two hedges of my own.

The first of these qualifications relates to a kind of moral relativism that critical engagement might seem to demand. It's tempting to think that nonfiction that privileges questions over answers forbids drawing a conclusion, but such is not the case. Bartoletti, whose thoughts on building debate into the writing of nonfiction I quoted earlier, is also the author of the celebrated *They Called Themselves the KKK: The Birth of an American Terrorist Group* (2010), and this book both sustains debate between different voices and offers stable conclusions. One example comes in a caption related to one of the most important early leaders of the Klan. Bartoletti describes how soldiers under the command of Nathan Bedford Forrest "slaughtered black Union troops and their white commander" in Tennessee. "In an official dispatch, Forrest said, 'It is hoped that these facts will demonstrate to the Northern people that negro soldiers cannot cope with Southerners.'" Bartoletti first makes a point of animating the debate that still surrounds the event: "Today," she writes, "historians don't agree on exactly what happened at Fort Pillow: some say the massacre took place after the Union commander surrendered; others say he never surrendered." But she immediately goes on to argue that "most historians agree, however, that, surrender or not, a massacre took place, in every sense of the word" (39). Necromantic nonfiction does not require intellectual paralysis; writers can and do still draw conclusions, and where evidence appears to be clear, necromancy does not insist that writers manufacture debate where none exists. Rather, in this and other works of nonfiction that animate the voices of different experts, the text can note debate and still show where dialogue has produced a measure of consensus.

My second qualification is one to which I will return again and again throughout my study. I have offered the first three of my hallmarks in this chapter, but none of the tools here or elsewhere in the book should be taken automatically to indicate an invitation to critical engagement; rather, they are hallmarks that I have found to indicate places where we ought to look closer for such an invitation. I realize that this is a fine distinction I'm making, but it's one very much in the spirit of the intellectual project that I'm proposing. In the first chapter, I tried to argue that what is important in children's nonfiction is not the facts that can be memorized but a humble approach to knowledge that eschews authority in favor of creative, critical engagement with information. A list of aspects of nonfiction that one ticks off to decide whether a book invites inquiry would run counter to that project. The current chapter and chapter 3 give a list of hallmarks of places in which books often invite or refuse critical engagement. That list, though, must be used as a tool to engage with the books in question, not as an excuse to end our own inquiry.

Sometimes, for example, nonfiction conjures a debate but casts it in a light that implies that one position is inevitably correct, making one of the positions in the debate untenable, effectively *discouraging* critical engagement. Kathryn Lasky's book on John Muir, for example, frequently shows debate, but sometimes that debate is disingenuous. Lasky recalls a horseback trip that Muir took with

Teddy Roosevelt, during which "he convinced the president to create a bureau of forestry to manage and protect the trees of forest reserves" (*John Muir*, 37). The book presents the scene as a debate—if Muir "convinced" the president, Roosevelt must have considered some objections—but that debate is incomplete in two key aspects. First, it dismisses any conversations that Roosevelt had before this meeting with Muir in regard to the formation of the bureau. The book doesn't say that no such debate took place, but it presents the voice of the hero of the book as the sole voice championing his position, far from the fracturing of authority that is supposed to come from necromancy. Second, it declines to articulate the reasons or even positions opposite Muir in that debate. Instead, Muir assumes an air of authority, hardly the kind of figure with whom one disagrees. Elsewhere, when the book does present debate, the contesting sides are barely comparable. Consider the side of the debate that the book endorses:

> As diligently as any hunter tracking an animal, John Muir began to track glaciers, for they left their marks. He began his studies in Yosemite by driving stakes into a glacier at intervals in a straight line. A month and a half later, he discovered that indeed the stakes had all moved downhill, one as much as forty-seven inches. Glaciers were alive and moving! (28)

In its description of Muir and his conclusions, the book uses punctuation to evoke delight. It also uses descriptions of his careful attention to detail that emphasize his reliability. The other voices in the debate take a very different tone. "But many important scientists disagreed," Lasky reports. "They felt that earthquakes were responsible for the sudden changes in the surface of the earth. These men of science had heard of Muir's ideas, but they called him a 'mere sheepherder' and even an 'ignoramus'" (28–29). Although there is debate present, one side is masterful, in tune with nature, and the other is anonymous and bigoted. The presence of debate suggests that questions can be asked, but the position the book offers from which to differ with Muir is vague and repugnant. In these places, presenting debate constitutes a disingenuous invitation to critical engagement: the conclusion to which the hero comes is the only conclusion to which a sensible, nonprejudicial person might come. The book does conjure different voices to disagree with one another, but in doing so, it argues *against* the need for critical engagement.

Similarly, although visible authors provide a person with whom to argue and therefore offer a possibility for critical engagement, nonfiction has also used a first-person perspective to nudge attention away from its underlying assumptions. *The Story Book of Houses* (1933), a volume in Maud and Miska Petersham's highly accomplished Story Book series (including, for example, *The Story Book of Iron and Steel* [1935] and *The Story Book of the Things We Wear* [1939]), is a case in point. The book uses a friendly tone that refers to the reader as "you" and, more importantly for the purposes of the visible author, a first-person plural perspective from which the authors offer a vision of houses around the world. Consider for example the final page, a section on skyscrapers, where the narrator observes that "our cities are full of tall buildings" (30). In this case, the pronoun does imply the existence of a person, but in contrast with the plural narrator in Nelson's *We Are the Ship*, this narrator joins with the reader, presenting not a separate entity with whom one might disagree or whose impossibility might border on the metafictional but a presence seamlessly aligned with the reader. Sometimes that alignment is dispensed with, as on the previous page, when the words alongside an image of a white girl and her pets in front of a modern house proclaim, "You have seen many houses like the one in this picture," but the close relationship of reader and narrator returns in the sentence immediately following: "There are thousands and thousands of [houses like this one] all over *our* country" (29, emphasis added). The consequences of that fused perspective become clear when contrasting this house in "our country" with an earlier description of "The Igloo." The house with the white girl is described as "a happy, comfortable place for the little girl and her parents and her brothers and sisters" (29). However, the narrator confides, "You would not find an igloo very comfortable," noting the lighting, temperature, and smoke (10). "The Eskimo's bed," it continues, "is not like ours" (11). In these examples, the narrator is visible but not as open to questions as the narrators imagined by the original theory. Rather, the narrator orients the reader with whom it is joined to note the strangeness of foreign ways, silently normalizing the culture of the narrator and supposed reader. Thus, when the narrator turns to "The Chinese Junk," it notes that "this is one of the queerest sorts of houses we have seen" (24). The voice employed in these examples marks houses in other cultures and times as strange, implying the normalcy of "our" own homes.

The Story Book of Houses is a reminder that although visible authors can—perhaps even should—encourage critical engagement, they can sometimes encourage the opposite. The Petershams' narrator in this book—who is not to be found in most of the other books in their series—is of a piece with the book's ethnocentricity, as becomes obvious in one sentence from the section "The Log House," which reads, "When people first came from Europe to the new land that Columbus had discovered, there were no houses for them to live in" (18). This sentence contains so many errors that one hardly knows where to begin correcting it. But as egregious as the factual errors may be, it is the narrator's cheerful way of naturalizing cultural norms, of discouraging critical engagement, that is my real focus. The perspective that underwrites that normalization of modern, Western, white, bourgeois culture is maintained in part through what certainly seems to meet the definition of "visible author," especially as I have broadened it in this chapter. Although previous research—and most of my own—has found the visible author to be a promising way to provoke argument with the author's assumptions and conclusions, there are also some cases in which that rhetorical structure can direct attention away from ideology.

Hedges, visible authors, and necromancy are not simple tools to use, from the perspective of either a writer or a reader trying to determine where a text is vulnerable to critical engagement, but they are signs of places where texts frequently choose to close or loosen their seams. Although textbooks have, as Kincheloe complains, traditionally been dedicated to presenting a "seamless narrative" of their subjects, children's nonfiction has more freedom to leave the seams visible. Wineburg finds that students who have excelled in the approach to knowledge offered by textbooks tend, when presented with primary texts, to work within "a knowledge system" in which they seek out authorities who can "serve as the arbiters of historical questions," a role that their textbooks have reliably offered to fill in the past ("Historical Problem Solving," 84). Nonfiction other than textbooks, however, can present knowledge as, to borrow a phrase, "contested discursive terrain" (Lankshear and Knobel, "Critical Literacy," 76). Nonfiction's use of voice—hesitant or certain, humanized or anonymous, heterogeneous or monological—is a marker for where to seek that terrain.

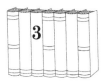

3 NONFICTION'S UNFINISHED CHARACTERS
The People Who Are Wrong, Flawed, and Incomplete

MY PREVIOUS CHAPTER explored a fairly subtle group of strategies in works of nonfiction. The techniques of voice that invite or resist critical engagement work mainly through implication: signaling confidence or doubt through hedges, narratorial person, or a dialogue about ideas is often an oblique task. However, those indirect techniques are fairly simple to mark: we watch for the presence or absence of certain words that imply hesitancy, of pronouns that suggest a real human being behind the words, or of debate. Now, I'd like to turn to techniques that are more direct but less simple to label, with more overlap between methods. In this chapter, I want to look not at how a text phrases its voice but at how it portrays the people it discusses. To use another term from the study of literature to illuminate nonfiction, I want to think about a book's characters.

By *characters*, I mean something quite broad. These can be the subjects about whom the authors write, certainly, such as the historical figures examined in a biography. They can also, however, be actors in the production of knowledge. These might be researchers working at the edges of their fields, students testing and extending the discoveries of their teachers, or even authorities of a former age who make mistakes as well as breakthroughs. Finally, and most abstractly, they can also be the community of researchers in which the study of the subject at hand is performed. The many ways in which a book portrays this community, its practices, the gaps in its knowledge, and the place it offers to young people are all part of how nonfiction populates its narratives with characters who invite or discourage critical engagement. If the voice of nonfiction can set the framework in which a book fosters or resists such reading, the characters of nonfiction can perform inquiry in ways that have similarly significant consequences.

Characters' Flaws

Take for example the complicated ways in which children's nonfiction about history has presented admired men and then attempted to draw readers' attention toward or away from the failings of those men. Examples of books that make a point of downplaying the faults of historical figures are too many to number, but I do want to pause over one eloquent example: *The Adventures of the Chevalier de La Salle and His Companions,* an 1875 history by John Stevens Cabot Abbott, one of the nineteenth century's major writers of children's nonfiction. This book is typical of Abbott's work and, indeed, children's historical nonfiction in general for its fawning attitude toward its subject. The first paragraph of Abbott's book on the seventeenth-century explorer opens with the words, "There is no one of the Pioneers of this continent whose achievements equal those of the Chevalier Robert de la Salle." The second paragraph intones that "fear was an emotion La Salle never experienced. His adventures were more wild and wondrous than almost any recorded in the tales of chivalry" (5). Elsewhere, Abbott remarks on La Salle's "characteristic sagacity" in dealing with indigenous Americans (98–99). Such unqualified esteem is typical for the book, and the consequences of such admiration for critical engagement are probably obvious: a character presented as so consistently admirable is hardly the kind of character whom one feels invited to question or criticize.

The contortions to which Abbott goes in an effort to maintain that admiration while explaining some of La Salle's more questionable choices is indicative of how nonfiction can attempt to conceal the ethical flaws in a historical figure whom the book wants to portray as above question. When Abbott writes of how La Salle's party suffered during an especially cold autumn in 1679, he explains that in their distress, they came upon a village where "two or three Indians were seen in the distance; but they did not venture to approach so formidable a looking band." A section of La Salle's party then came upon "a cluster of deserted wigwams, where the sagacity of their Indian guide showed them an abundance of corn, concealed from the ravages of wild beasts, in cells under ground." Near the end of their food stores, "these honest or politic men took all they wanted, and left behind them ample payment" (114). Although the presumable owners of the corn were too afraid to approach La Salle's party, and although La Salle seems not to have made any attempt to send a smaller (and less threatening) party to contact them, Abbott insists that we read the explorers' appropriation of the food in exchange for money as a fair contract. Paying for what they took, evidently, washes clean any other sins the party may have committed, despite the fact that they took food, food that had obviously been hidden during a difficult season in which the indigenous people might have needed it, leaving an amount of money that they decided upon without checking whether the owner of the corn was satisfied with the price. Abbott presents his protagonist, as it were, in an ethical framework (if you pay for something, you're not stealing) that conspires to draw tight the seams of the character's goodness.

In the following pages, the writer also takes great care to discourage his readers from questioning his characters' actions when La Salle behaves in the exact *opposite* manner. We find this challenge to Abbott's characterization when he describes how La Salle's stores began to dwindle again later that same year, and again he discovered food stored away by indigenous farmers:

> La Salle removed fifty bushels to his canoes, hoping to find the owners farther south and amply repay them. It would have been of no avail to have left payment, for it would be carried away by any band of Indians who chanced to be passing by.

> The hunger of his men, in his judgment, rendered the taking of the corn a necessity. (125–26)

The conscientious payment that earned La Salle and his men praise a few pages earlier is here brushed aside as foolish and unnecessary. The contradiction between the two acts means that one or the other must have been at least partially wrongheaded, but Abbott takes pains to distract from the cracks in La Salle's quality. He also neglects to mention whether La Salle ever found (let alone paid) the farmers whose food he had stolen. In these places, Abbott presents his character in ways that explicitly discourage critical engagement: where there is room to question La Salle, Abbott provides an interpretation of La Salle that implies that there is no need for debate.

This example of Abbott's burnished vision of La Salle is, unfortunately, typical for children's nonfiction up through today. Christina M. Desai makes a similar observation in her study of American picture books about Christopher Columbus published in the two decades immediately following the five hundredth anniversary of his encounter with the Americas. "Children's literature," she writes, "has its roots in didacticism and protectionism. Children's biographies of great men, including Columbus, have traditionally served to provide models of manly virtues such as courage and determination, and historic US values, such as scientific progress and westward expansion" ("Columbus Myth," 183). Desai notes how the books in her study carefully direct attention away from—or entirely fail to mention—flaws in Columbus and his behavior, instead paying "detailed attention . . . to his lowly origins, determined spirit, bold idea, and great discoveries" in order to convey upon him "great stature, whatever else he may have done" (186). Michelle Ann Abate sees the same pattern in Lynne Cheney's portrait of Thomas Jefferson in Cheney's 2002 "patriotic primer." Abate notes the "many achievements" of the third president Cheney spotlights as well as the many widely documented flaws and indiscretions that Cheney omits (*Raising*, 115). Abate's book focuses on right-wing literature for children, but, as Katharine Capshaw recalls, the pattern is hardly partisan. She explains that "children's historians use the generic expectation for truth in nonfiction as a means to convince the reader of a version of history influenced by ideology and social desire. Naturally, this is one reason for history's attractiveness to proponents on the right as well as on the left" (*Civil Rights,* 69). Kimberley Reynolds's work on British radical children's literature, for example, explores many examples of what she calls that literature's "complicated interaction between liberation and control," as leftist literature simultaneously "stirred readers up to challenge the status quo" and "tried to recruit and direct them" (*Left Out,* 9). "Stirring up" might signify a prodding to action that fits with Freire's ideas of critical engagement, but "recruiting and directing" sounds more similar to the propagandizing against which he specifically warns (*Pedagogy,* 107). The shaping of information performed by explicitly partisan books relies heavily on a style of characterization that plays down opportunities for critical engagement by remaining silent on a historical figure's flaws. Although partisan authors sometimes claim that their nonfiction is motivated by a deep love for children,[1] they often decline to encourage those children to nurture significant doubts about historical figures, especially figures who are key to a partisan narrative.

Children's nonfiction does, though, at times present characters, even admirable characters, as people to be read carefully and with discernment. An edition of Philip Stanhope's letters to his illegitimate son, which first saw publication in 1774, is an interesting example. As a whole, it's difficult to classify Stanhope's letters as children's literature: his son was an adult by the time the last letters were written, and Stanhope himself was a recently deceased fixture of contemporary British *adult* society at the time of their publication. But when John Trusler composed a new edition of the letters and published them in 1775, he packaged them under the subtitle "for the Improvement of Youth." Much of Trusler's edition focuses on Stanhope's recommendations for how exactly a young man might improve himself in social standing and character, and his presentation of accomplished persons shows a careful negotiation of how and when to engage with them critically. For example, Stanhope emphasizes the importance of using such people as a model: "Whenever, then, you go into good company, that is the company of people of fashion, observe carefully their behaviour, their address and their manner; imitate it as far as in your power" (qtd. in Trusler, *Principles,* 39). Such guidance calls for a studious absorption of the pattern of honored people, and it is obviously uncritical: their models are authoritative rather than open to question. However, Stanhope elsewhere insists that his son read these people critically and be judicious in imitation:

> Be it, then, your ambition to get into the best company; and, when there, imitate their virtues, but not their vices. You have no doubt, often heard of genteel and fashionable vices. These are whoring, drinking and gaming. It has happened that some men, even with these vices, have been admired and esteemed. Understand this matter rightly, it is not their vices for which they are admired; but for some accomplishments they at the same time possess; for their parts, their learning or their good-breeding. Be assured, were they free from their vices, they would be much more esteemed. In these mixed characters, the bad part is overlooked, for the sake of the good. (qtd. in *Principles*, 60–61)

In this passage, "the best company" is yet company that should be judged carefully and with attention to faults in order to avoid copying those faults. Stanhope continues in this vein, enjoining his son to

> imitate, then, only the perfections you meet with; copy the politeness, the address, the easy manners of well-bred people; and remember, let them shine ever so bright, if they have any vices, they are so many blemishes, which it would be as ridiculous to imitate, as it would, to make an artificial wart upon ones [sic] face, because some very handsome man had the misfortune to have a natural one upon his. (61–62)

In Abbott's history of La Salle, faults are downplayed when possible, and when they cannot be ignored, they are wrapped in an interpretation that strives to protect them from critical attention. For Stanhope, though, and for Trusler in his children's edition of Stanhope's letters, one is to look at great figures as texts to be read closely, as people who can be good in spite of flaws. These characters have flaws to which the reader must attend and then reject even as the reader admires and copies the strengths. Stanhope's approach to these great figures is fundamentally critical in the way that I have been defining it, and the technique he offers to his son for engaging with those figures is one that assures young people that they ought to question the actions of the admirable.

Characters' Vulnerability

Probably the best argument for giving children nonfiction about historical figures that presents them as above question is that such an image of historical figures allows children to have good role models to emulate. However, doing so is, as the contrast between Abbott and Stanhope demonstrates, anticritical, and I'm not even sure that it can help children in the way that I assume authors such as La Salle hope. Betty Carter, frequent reviewer of nonfiction for *Horn Book*, contends that children's "critical-thinking skills are often negated by our desire to use biographies to provide kids with positive role models" ("What Makes," 201). She argues that if we want nonfiction to be a part of the development of critical evaluation later in life, we need to be looking at biographies as places to point out rich, conflicted characters with flaws. Paulo Freire is even more pointed. He relates the story of a peasant revolt that faltered because the revolutionaries were too intimidated by the owner of the land, too awed by his status even to guard him. Freire is writing about oppressive regimes, and it's a stretch to compare those regimes with the characters of children's nonfiction, but what Freire is talking about is fundamentally authority, and it is authority that critical engagement troubles. Thus when Freire argues that "the oppressed must see examples of the vulnerability of the oppressor," he is naming a key strategy for fracturing authority enough that it can be engaged with critically (*Pedagogy*, 51). If we combine Freire's theoretical insight with Carter's notion of how nonfiction can play a role in the development of critical thinking, then highlighting the vulnerability of the characters of nonfiction becomes an important opportunity for critical engagement.

Nonfiction signals and even develops its characters' vulnerability in a variety of ways. Take for example Katheryn Russell-Brown's picture book about Melba Doretta Liston, the twentieth-century trombonist who rose to prominence through her legendary collaborations with Dizzy Gillespie, Count Basie, Billie Holiday, and later Quincy Jones and Randy Weston. One of the major points of focus in Russell-Brown's book is Liston's vulnerability, such as when Liston joined and quickly outpaced her high school's music club. "The other club members struggled to keep up with Melba," the narrator explains. "Jealous boys called her bad names. She tried not to care, but way down deep the names hurt" (*Little Melba*, 17). In this brief scene, the narrator draws attention to the character's emotional wounds, demonstrating her vulnerability. Elsewhere, Russell-Brown shows those wounds going so deep that they become not simply painful but a serious threat to the character's success. After an explanation of cruelties from fellow band members, racism from whites, and lukewarm or nonexistent audiences, the grown-up Liston "almost walked away from her trombone for good" (23). Pamela S. Turner uses the same technique in her book about Tyrone Hayes, a scientist investigating a mysterious epidemic affecting frogs. Despite trouble in his earlier life, Turner recounts, Hayes made his way to studies at Harvard. There, he discovered that "students could volunteer to help Harvard professors with research, [and] he knew he'd found what he wanted to do." But however satisfying volunteering might have been, Hayes did not have the financial wherewithal to give his time away, and the sole paying position that he could find in a lab "was washing test tubes, not doing research. Tyrone felt discouraged. His grades went down and he thought about dropping out of college. 'I was lost,' admits Tyrone" (*Frog Scientist*, 10–11).

These examples help demonstrate how encouraging critical engagement through characterization is often more difficult to flag than is encouraging critical engagement through voice. No specific words or perspectives are deployed; rather, the text focuses on a character's quality, on an ability to be wounded. Too, because both Liston and Hayes go on to become successful, one might interpret these moments not as cracks in the authority of the great figures but as examples of how their tenacity makes them even more admirable. After all, these scenes show the characters struggling and overcoming: like heroes on a quest, they encounter and overcome difficulty heroically. But my point in drawing attention to how these books emphasize vulnerability is that by emphasizing the internal struggles, the profound self-doubt and pain, the authors are asserting the capability of these great figures to be hurt. It is probably unrealistic to ask that nonfiction be written about people whose lives were failures, so our nonfiction will almost always be about people who struggled and overcame,[2] but nonfiction that shows great figures who can be wounded still offers something vital. Because these characters can be wounded, they are vulnerable, and because they are vulnerable, they are human, and because they are human, they can be engaged with critically.

Vulnerability does not, however, have to be quite so filled with pathos. At times, it can be documented by telling stories of characters on the brink not of tragedy but of comedy. Turner puts Hayes, the same scientist who felt "lost" at Harvard, in this position even while first establishing his character. As Hayes tries to capture a frog specimen in the wild, Turner recounts how "one frog gets sweet revenge. Tyrone lunges—the frog dives—and Tyrone quickly leaps back, snorting and laughing. 'Ugh! I just got a reed up my nose!'" (3). Sy Montgomery captures a similar scene in her story of a group of scientists chasing the so-called tree kangaroos of New Guinea. One of the teams manages to spot one of the extremely reclusive (and overhunted) creatures, but the scene does not end with its heroic capture. "As soon as it saw them," Montgomery writes, "the animal hopped away. Joshua took off after it. He might have caught it—if he hadn't tripped over a vine, then fell over a log, and then got a stick caught in his rubber boots" (*Quest*, 41). In these scenes, the characters seem more at home in a vaudeville routine than in a somber record of their fearless exploits. Each of these books gives extensive attention to the characters' successes, but the pratfalls that they experience while in the act of performing science humanizes them, their activities, and their inquiry.

When I argue that vulnerability makes the characters of nonfiction better suited for critical engagement, what I am effectively arguing is that vulnerability opens those characters up to dialogue. Rather than building for its characters a position in which their sins are explained away or faults are ignored, places where nonfiction invites critical engagement fracture the authority of the characters

86 ▪ *Nonfiction's Unfinished Characters*

by pointing to their humanity. When Freire explains the relationship between the leaders of a valid, democratic revolution—as opposed to a violent changing of one group of oppressors for another—he bases that contrast on the place that the leaders give to dialogue:

> Dialogue with the people is radically necessary to every authentic revolution. This is what makes it a revolution, as distinguished from a military coup. One does not expect dialogue from a coup—only deceit (in order to achieve "legitimacy") or force (in order to repress). Sooner or later, a true revolution must initiate a courageous dialogue with the people. Its very legitimacy lies in that dialogue. It cannot fear the people, their expression, their effective participation in power. It must be accountable to them, must speak frankly to them of its achievements, its mistakes, its miscalculations, and its difficulties. (*Pedagogy*, 122)

As I have already recognized, the comparison between oppressors and works of nonfiction is fraught with problems, but in this passage, Freire's point is the inverse of a point I made earlier: it is the maintenance of authority that threatens critical engagement. Freire sketches in this passage how an antidemocratic authority maintains its power through a refusal of dialogue, but an authentic relationship between those in power and those on its fringes will be characterized by, he hopes, "courageous dialogue." Notice, too, how dialogue in this model is enabled by naming one's vulnerability: to speak of one's mistakes, miscalculations, and difficulties is to draw attention to the *imperfections* in one's authority. Critical engagement is performed through dialogue, and dialogue is made possible when authority is vulnerable.

Characters' Mistakes

Freire calls for attention to the mistakes of figures in positions of authority, and some nonfiction devotes space to exactly this aspect of its characters. The biographical picture book that I mentioned earlier about Melba Doretta Liston, for example, gives special attention to her early difficulties with the trombone:

> Melba gave the horn a mighty blow.
> Hooooooonk!
> Haaaaaaahnnnnk!
> It sounded bad, like a howling dog.
> "I'm no good, Grandpa," Melba said, tearing up.
> (Russell-Brown, *Little Melba*, 11)

Rather than present only Liston's successes with her instrument, Russell-Brown establishes early in the narrative that her great figure made mistakes directly relevant to her later successes. The same is true of Jacqueline Briggs Martin's picture book biography of Wilson Bentley, an early photographer of snowflakes. Martin explains Bentley's successes, and she even details how Bentley was first able to photograph a snowflake, but much of the book is about Bentley's frustrated enthusiasm. She explains, for example, how Bentley tried for "three winters" to draw snowflakes, but "they always melted before he could finish" (*Snowflake*, 8). Later, when he switched to photography, "his first pictures were failures—no better than shadows." Martin tells how "mistake by mistake, snowflake by snowflake, Willie worked through every storm. Winter ended, the snow melted, and he had no good pictures" (14). Bentley does of course go on to succeed—again, a nonfiction that focuses exclusively on characters who fail seems unlikely to find a market—but Martin recounts his failures again and again. Even in nonfiction about historical figures who went on to become household names, some nonfiction will set aside space for those figures' mistakes. Shelley Tanaka's book about Amelia Earhart does so repeatedly, such as when it tells how the young aviator escaped a bank of terrible fog by putting "the plane into a tailspin until she emerged from the fog, and then landed." Rather than celebrate Earhart's daring, Tanaka immediately points out that Earhart's strategy was successful at least partly because of blind luck: "Suppose the fog had lasted all the way to the ground?" asks a more experienced aviator (*Amelia*, 13). Tanaka then records how Earhart "crashed, more than once," hurt herself in a cabbage patch, and, landing in a soft field, even "stopped the plane so suddenly that it flipped over, broke her seatbelt, and threw her out" (13). Freire calls for authority to make itself vulnerable by being frank about its mistakes, and these stories of important, successful characters do exactly that.

88 ◨ Nonfiction's Unfinished Characters

Thom Holmes's *Fossil Feud: The Rivalry of the First American Dinosaur Hunters* (1998) is, at first glance, a book about two scientists, but a more accurate summary of its topic might be their failures. Holmes's protagonists are Edward Drinker Cope and Othniel Charles Marsh, late-nineteenth-century paleontologists whose successes and profound mistakes still echo down through the study of dinosaurs. Specific, local mistakes are a frequent subject of the book, such as Cope's miscalculation of the length of a mosasaur specimen because he thought that a specimen on one side of a bank was the same specimen as another that came out of the other side of the bank (52–53) and his placement of the head of an Elasmosaurus at the wrong end

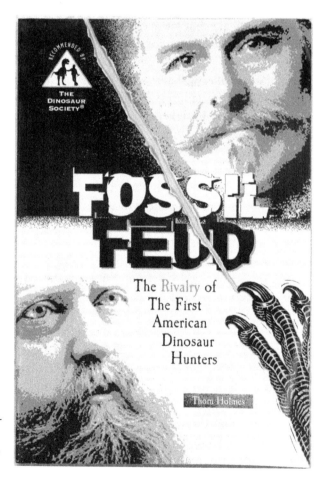

Thom Holmes, *Fossil Feud: The Rivalry of the First American Dinosaur Hunters* (1998).

of the creature's body (41). He also notes Marsh's mistakes, including his initial conclusion that the skeleton of a triceratops belonged to a buffalo (because "neither he nor anyone else had ever seen a horned dinosaur," 121–22) and a mistake that has proved especially persistent: declaring the existence of a kind of dinosaur he named the brontosaurus—when he had in fact already named the same creature something else (124–25). Cope and Marsh would, Holmes concludes, "sometimes name dinosaurs based on the thinnest of evidence. A jaw found here, a vertebra there, maybe only a solitary tooth. They believed they could identify an entirely new creature from tiny fragments. They were wrong, and many of the new species they named in this way have turned out to be incorrect" (122–23). *Fossil Feud* is a rare example in children's nonfiction: its subject is great scientific figures, and its main mode is recounting their mistakes.

Even more significantly, Holmes's book explains the base motivations that drove these scientists. Many of those mistakes, Holmes convincingly argues, "were made by Cope and Marsh because they were too eager to triumph in the fossil feud. They could have prevented many of them by taking more time to study the evidence and by looking for additional fossils to fill the gaps in their knowledge" (122). I began my analysis of this book by pointing to how we can find on its surface multiple examples of the scientists' mistakes, but what is especially impressive is that the book's central argument is that when we look at science, we should be alert to the prejudices that drove and limited the human beings who performed it, prejudices that have led to mistakes. Holmes explains how Cope and Marsh met early in their careers and started out as friends, "but greed and pride soon eroded their budding friendship" (34). The results, as we have already seen, were declarations of truth that were subsequently overturned, but some of the results are even more dire, with profound costs to scientific inquiry in the generations following Cope and Marsh. At an especially rich dig site in Wyoming, the competitors acted "as if they were at war," constantly watching for one another and documenting the other's movements. "The two teams didn't actually come to blows," Holmes explains,

> but, in one sense, they behaved even more childishly than that. Whenever Marsh's crew abandoned one of their many Como

Bluff sites, they used sledge hammers to destroy specimens still in the ground. They left nothing behind for Cope's crew to collect. Cope's men seemed to have done the same. Such destruction of future scientific resources was a shameful blot on both sides. (77–78)

Compare Holmes's handling of the Como Bluff scenes with Abbott's breezy explanations for La Salle's theft of resources he needed while exploring the mid-continent. Whereas Abbott reported but excused La Salle's unethical behavior, Holmes calls out "shameful," routine behavior by his characters. He uses an extended history of the petty feud between the two scientists to make a point about how science is done. He argues that Cope and Marsh were exceptionally awful, but he also concedes that "science is a *human* activity. Clashes of personality, jealousies, attacks on the work of rivals, and powerful urges to win fame by being the first to discover or explain something—all these are a normal, necessary part of real science." For Holmes, Cope and Marsh "went to extremes," but those are extremes embedded in the nature of the way that we do science (121). Holmes's explanation is not an excuse for science or for the scientists whom he repeatedly criticizes but a reminder that the disgraceful conduct of Cope and Marsh is not isolated. Myra Zarnowski praises nonfiction that shows "scientists hampered by assumptions that prove to be inaccurate" ("Reading," 16), but Holmes's book is more than a catalog of the errors of two specific scientists. *Fossil Feud* is a tour of how science as a method of inquiry is human, which is to say vulnerable. The scope of the book's implications goes beyond the specific scientists whose story it tells and on to the paradigm in which they—and we—produce knowledge.

"The Light of Becoming"

I have been documenting the many ways that children's nonfiction shows (or buries) the mistakes of its characters, but it is also possible to think of the time *between* failure and success as a space for critical engagement. Bakhtin offers a beautiful phrase for this period. As he praises how the novel focuses on the path of its characters as they journey toward success or failure, he writes of how "life and its events, bathed in the light of becoming, reveal themselves as the hero's experience" ("Discourse," 393). Bakhtin is writing about fiction, but his arguments about how narrative thrives in "the light of becoming" are exactly relevant to a study of how nonfiction can open room for critical engagement. Bakhtin admires the novel's attention to "the process of a man's becoming," by which he means "a certain duality, a lack of wholeness characteristic of living human beings, a mixture within the man of good and evil, strength and weakness." That mixture, when put into action in narrative, means that the novel avoids presenting "a ready-made character . . . an already preformed and predetermined hero" (392–93). The novel's presentation of its characters and the events that they suffer, "bathed in the light of becoming," insists on its subjects as incomplete, in transition, asking questions, making poor decisions, and succeeding (or failing) because they are caught up in a process rather than springing to success fully formed and unmarked by need, improvement, or testing. Freire makes a similar point about education. "Knowledge emerges only," he argues, "through invention and re-invention, through the restless, impatient, continuing, hopeful inquiry [people] pursue in the world, with the world, and with each other" (58). That ongoing inquiry is central to Freire's "problem-posing education," and Freire writes that such education declares human beings as "in the process of *becoming*" (72, emphasis original). The frankness that Freire calls for in the presentation of one's faults and mistakes is important, but that which comes after the realization of inadequacy is also key to education. Between Bakhtin's different, fundamentally aesthetic concerns and Freire's concerns about better education through fractured authority, we can develop a useful theory for children's nonfiction. When nonfiction focuses on its characters as in the process of becoming, it opens space for critical engagement.

One of the most obvious places to find characters in the light of becoming is on the heels of the mistakes about which I wrote earlier. Although I have pointed to the importance of how Russell-Brown focuses on her heroine's mistakes, the book also demonstrates that after her first, awful attempt at playing the trombone, Liston "stayed up real late and practiced" (*Little Melba*, 11). The book returns to this theme later, explaining that "even with her keen ear, teaching herself to play the trombone was no piece of cake. But Melba kept blowing her horn, getting better day by day" (14). Liston left behind an enormous, impressive body of accomplishments, but by attending to the period of her life during which she was in the process of becoming that great musician, Russell-Brown humanizes her. I also highlighted the comical section of Montgomery's book about the search for tree kangaroos, and Zarnowski and Susan Turkel have examined the same book, but their emphasis is different. For them, one of the most valuable elements of the story is Montgomery's consistent interest in the team's response to failure. "Even when they are challenged by surprising and unforeseen results, they persevere," write Zarnowski and Turkel. "When one solution doesn't work, they incorporate the new knowledge they have gained and try something else" ("Nonfiction," 33). What Montgomery demonstrates in such scenes is how the scientists *become,* and it is significant that this is the story of most of her book: the scientists are not presented in their polished completion but as they progress. Both texts present their characters in the light of becoming by following up on what happens to them after their missteps.

Characters in the Long Middle of Discovery

The process of becoming does not have to conclude, though, with the aftermath of mistakes. Elsewhere in *Quest for the Tree Kangaroo* (2006), Montgomery shows her characters in the act of inquiry. Specifically, Montgomery dedicates several scenes over the course of the book to showing the characters gathering information. Two of the scientists, for example, regularly track a pair of animals using signals from radio collars. That information is, Montgomery writes, "hugely important. From these telemetry recordings, the scientists will be able to see how much land each kangaroo calls home. They'll be able to learn the kangaroos' favorite kinds of trees." As one of the characters puts it, "This is how we'll know what habitat needs to be conserved" (52). Later, the team manages to capture a male and female tree kangaroo, and Montgomery carefully notes the extensive process of measuring each of the creatures, turning the event of data collection into a scene in its own right, even a scene with remarkable drama, as the scientists work feverishly around the sedated animals and Montgomery warns that "anesthesia can be dangerous" for the tree kangaroos, so one of the team members constantly monitors the creatures' breathing and heartbeats (58). The characters are not recovering from mistakes but performing the long middle section of research. They are "becoming" not in the sense of improving but of journeying toward a state of knowledge sufficient enough to allow them to draw reasonable conclusions.

Often, books that draw attention to how their characters gather information then go on to show those characters using data to perform experiments, and again the effect is one that can create space for critical engagement. In Turner's *The Frog Scientist,* Tyrone Hayes, the scientist who earlier suffered the indignity of a reed up his nose, travels to a pond in Massachusetts to gather "a few clutches of frog eggs to raise back in his laboratory" (4). Over the course of the book, Turner shows Hayes repeatedly testing the information he has gathered. He forms a hypothesis about frogs raised in water contaminated with a specific chemical and tests it, then forms a different research question—"how do mixes of pesticides affect frogs?"—and tests that question as well (31, 50). He tries an experiment first on one kind of frog, then on another (25–26). After considering the data generated by an experiment, Hayes questions his conclusions and returns to examine the information again. "That's the thing about experiments," Turner confides. "Even with careful planning, you can't always control everything. And sometimes you have to take a second look" (45). Another book, *The Snake Scientist* (1999), from the same series as *Quest for the Tree Kangaroo* and *The Frog Scientist,* portrays the researcher in the act of testing but then adds new instances for inquiry. This book, also by Sy Montgomery, follows Robert "Bob" Mason, a zoologist from Oregon State University, and his team. "They are always taking measurements," as the narrator says, and those measurements play directly into specific experiments (20). The book describes at length Mason's process for determining the chemical makeup of the scent emitted by female snakes, pausing over breakthroughs, frustrations, and setbacks as well as conclusions (28–30). But once Mason has "proved that red-sided garters use a pheromone to detect the presence of females," one of his students launches a new investigation: "Now Michael is trying to find out if snakes will follow these chemical signals over land. Can snakes use pheromones to determine which way another snake went?" (32). The following pages describe the student's multiple experiments, each with a different level of complexity (34–35). Interestingly, the book doesn't give all the results of these experiments. Rather, the emphasis is on the middle period of inquiry rather than the conclusion, an observation borne out by Montgomery's decision to follow Mason's finished experiment with another that finds a new question to ask. Zarnowski has argued that scenes such as these provide readers "with an up-close view of scientists who are engaged in problem solving" and demonstrate "how scientists learn" ("Reading," 16). To say that the characters are learning is to say that they are becoming, which is to say that they and their conclusions are portrayed as human endeavors that can be duplicated, questioned, and extended. As with Holmes's book about rival paleontologists, these books imply that critical engagement is necessary not only for the specific characters whom the story pursues but also to research itself.[3]

The Incompleteness of Inquiry

Zarnowski has also praised nonfiction that demonstrates how "scientific understandings are subject to change" ("Reading," 16), and the characters of nonfiction can have an important function in that demonstration, especially when they act out the process of corroboration. Nonfiction that shows its characters in the act of testing information and drawing conclusions from it frequently also offers examples of researchers corroborating the data that they have gathered. Take for example a scene from a 2010 book in which a paleontologist explores the remains of a mammoth and concludes that it was in excellent health at the time of death. Cheryl Bardoe, the author of the scene, then goes on to explain how the paleontologist verifies that conclusion by checking the original data against the layers in the mammoth's tusks (*Mammoths*, 16). Similarly, Marc Aronson's book on recent studies of Stonehenge explains how a contemporary team of researchers found exciting new evidence that argued for a new understanding of the ancient site, but those data did not match up with the findings of the great archeologist Richard Atkinson, so the new team went back to "carefully review" Atkinson's notes, discovering a mistake he had made and that had been taken as reliable ever since. Aronson then documents how the contemporary team put the new information next to their own discoveries as well as data from yet another dig to confirm their breakthrough (*If Stones*, 46–47). And Priscilla Wakefield's *Introduction to Botany* (1796) uses the strange first-person narrator I explicated in the previous chapter to encourage her fictional reader—and supposedly the actual child studying her book as well—to "compare my descriptions with the flowers themselves" so that, "by thus mutually pursuing the same object, we may reciprocally improve each other" (2). Zarnowski has complained about nonfiction that buries the work that its authors have done, specifically bemoaning the opportunities lost when authors fail to note evidence that they could not include "because it could not be corroborated" (*History*, 29). What we see in these scenes is that authors of children's nonfiction can, as Zarnowski argues, include their own struggles in their first-person narration, and they can also include scenes in which their *characters* struggle to corroborate their findings, similarly opening up opportunities for readers to see the incompleteness of inquiry and the human beings who perform it.

A major way that nonfiction can signal incompleteness is by pointing to that which we still do not know. Evelyn B. Freeman and Diane Goetz Person have complained about textbooks that "present science as a completed subject" (*Connecting*, 35), and Patricia J. Cianciolo, borrowing a pair of terms from Margery Fisher, concurs, arguing that good nonfiction should be "a starter rather than a stopper": "A 'starter' gives a clear and vivid outline or overview of a subject so that the reader wants to pursue it further. In contrast, a 'stopper' gives the reader the impression that the book is self-contained and there is no need to read further about the subject" (*Informational Picture Books*, 7). Freire would agree with these evaluations, because for Freire, "the very roots of education" as a human enterprise are in the recognition of the incompleteness of that which previous generations have understood about the world (*Pedagogy*, 72). In the model of education that Freire condemns, teachers assume a persona *devoid* of ignorance and press onto students an identity *characterized* by ignorance. It is through this—false—opposition of knowledgeable teachers and ignorant students that a teacher in this model "justifies his own existence." By maintaining such a dichotomy, a teacher "negates education and knowledge as processes of inquiry" (58–59). Freire is writing about real people who teach (or fail to teach) and their students, but the oppressive power dynamic he describes can easily be mapped onto the relationship between books—especially books explicitly dedicated to informing—and readers. When an informational book represents its knowledge of its subject as complete, when it is, as Cianciolo would have it, a "stopper," it constructs a reading position in which those who approach the book are empty of knowledge, with the consequence that it erases a truer portrayal of learning as a process of inquiry. To transfer Freire's observations about real-life teachers to books and how they construct their audiences is to provide, first, a theory to explain the frustration of Freeman, Person, Fisher, and Cianciolo and, second, a justification for seeking places where books divest themselves of their authority by being honest about what they do not know. These pointed confessions of ignorance can come in the books' representation of their characters and, as we shall see, their authors as well.

Zarnowski has identified the willingness of some books to be honest about what they do not know as part of the pleasure in reading them, and the characters of those books contribute to making that pleasure possible. She compares nonfiction to mysteries, pointing specifically to nonfiction that foregrounds unanswered questions. But in the nonfiction that Zarnowski prefers, the process of answering questions almost always prompts more questions. "The satisfaction that readers get from a science mystery is not in tying up all the loose ends," she argues. "Instead, the satisfaction comes from participating in the process of solving part of an even larger mystery" ("Reading," 15). Some of the books that I have studied in this chapter offer such pleasure, such as Aronson's book on Stonehenge, which follows a group of archeologists as they make mistakes, collect data, conduct experiments, and corroborate their findings. Aronson is also careful to point to those questions that remain, as when he explains that "usually, when visitors see the stones they ask how the builders moved 35-ton rocks over hill and dale." The head of the research team, Aronson confides, "is sure we will never be able to answer that" (*If Stones*, 15). Montgomery, too, points out how her protagonist in *The Snake Scientist* "has made some exciting discoveries," and yet "still hasn't found all the answers" (12). In fact, after he "became the first person ever to find a pheromone in a reptile," a new series of questions appeared. "That's what's fun about doing science," Montgomery quotes him as saying (30).

In the previous chapter, I noted how authors can forgo the invisibility of third-person narration to make a target with whom to argue, and similar strategies allow them to acknowledge the gaps in current understanding. Tonya Bolden, a contemporary writer, often makes use of this technique when she speaks in first person about knowledge that "we" lack. For instance, in her book about an early-twentieth-century black girl who found herself in almost accidental possession of an enormous amount of wealth from oil fields, Bolden traces an exchange between W. E. B. Du Bois and the judge who named a white man as the girl's guardian. Du Bois, rightfully suspicious, wrote to inquire about the choice, and the judge replied that "the parents himself selected him." Bolden writes, "We'll probably never know if Du Bois frowned, scratched his head, or fell out of his chair when he read that. *The parents themselves selected him?*" (*Searching*, 35). Bolden uses this brief, even humorous gesture toward what we don't and can't know (how a historical figure reacted in a private moment) to highlight the heavily racialized context in which the girl's wealth and its protection were read at the time, and she uses that context to prompt questions about the white guardian, the white judge, and their connection to the girl, her family, and other marginalized people of the early century. Bolden is hardly the only writer to use such a technique. Agnes Giberne's late-nineteenth-century book about astronomy, for example, which in general presents itself as taut with finished knowledge, points on occasion to its own ignorance. Giberne writes, for example,

> We do not in the least know how long the Stellar System has existed. Calculations have been attempted, with a view to discover how many millions or tens of millions of years our own sun may have been a sun; and the reckoning baffles

human powers. The answers arrived at amount to hardly more than guesses. How much more is the effort vain, if we speak of the entire Universe, and try to picture *its* probable duration. (*Radiant*, 318)

The last page of the book again conjures the limitations of human knowledge. Giberne writes of the discovery of a new star and confesses that it "lies beyond reach of parallax measurement. We can only conjecture its probable distance" (322). Unlike Bolden, Giberne's tone in most of her book is more suited to the oppressive teacher whom Freire imagines: she positions her book as full of the knowledge that readers will, by definition, not possess. Finding moments such as these in Giberne's book, then, suggests that even the most self-confident nonfiction can open moments in which readers can see knowledge as a process rather than a finished cache of information.

I have been arguing that pointing to where our knowledge is incomplete constitutes an implicit invitation to critical engagement, but at times such invitations run toward the explicit. Montgomery's *Snake Scientist,* for example, explains how school-age children witnessed a phenomenon that had escaped the notice of scientists and thereby launched a new set of scientific questions. "In 1995," she writes, "middle-school students on a field trip in Minnesota discovered hundreds of frogs with missing eyes or with extra legs. Is something in the water responsible? The same water the people drink? Researchers are trying to find out—thanks to the amphibians' tip-off and the observant students" (42). Bardoe, the writer who told of how a paleontologist corroborated evidence concerning the death of a young mammoth, returns to that same scientist shortly after he has made a breakthrough, but the emphasis is not on how her readers should assume that the questions have all been answered:

> Dr. Fisher says this success is just the start of how a technique that was developed by studying mammoths and mastodons can help elephants. Every year research methods grow and new discoveries are made. Dr. Fisher expects that in 20 years a new generation of scientists will exclaim "Aha!" while examining a tusk or the incredible specimen of Lyuba. With hard work and luck, we might unravel the secrets of these animals

from the past—and prevent elephants from following in their footsteps.

And so a new generation—maybe you!—will write the next chapter in the mammoth story. (*Mammoths*, 41)

And the invitations to perform the necessary work remaining become yet more explicit in, for example, Rebecca L. Johnson's *Journey into the Deep* (2011), a book written in second-person perspective, with constant references to the work "you" do as "you help the science team scoop" up samples or "help preserve dozens of animals in alcohol" (35). Near the end of the book, a sidebar asks, "Do you wish you could *really* explore the ocean firsthand?" (54). It then offers advice on subjects to study, resources to consult, and conversations to join. The back matter of Montgomery's *Quest for the Tree Kangaroo* includes a page titled "Tree Kangaroos Near You," on which Montgomery explains how to learn more about the animals and what children can do next (76). The book also gives a list of advice from the main scientist on how readers can become scientists doing similar research themselves (74). Such moments obviously fulfill Cianciolo's call for "starters" as opposed to "stoppers," and they also open the possibility of solving what Freire calls "the teacher–student contradiction." They reconcile "the poles of the contradiction so that both are simultaneously teachers *and* students" (*Pedagogy*, 59).

Phineas Gage

I want to close with an extended look at a book with which I have struggled for a long time, John Fleischman's *Phineas Gage: A Gruesome but True Story about Brain Science* (2002). Fleischman's book is rife with examples of invitations to critical engagement, as it examines Gage's life and the controversy surrounding him at length, using techniques of voice that I suggested in the previous chapter as well as the techniques of character that I have been developing in this chapter. The book opens with a pivotal scene about which there can be no solid answers: Phineas Gage, a nineteenth-century railroad construction foreman, suffered a terrible accident on whose details there is no clear record. Some witnesses "remember seeing Phineas standing over the blast hole, leaning lightly on the tamping iron."

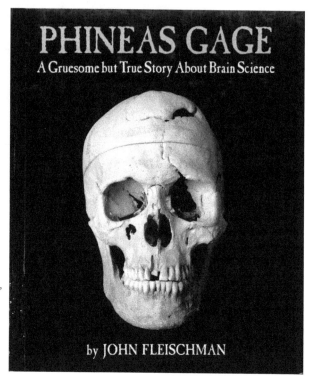

John Fleischman, *Phineas Gage: A Gruesome but True Story about Brain Science* (2002).

Other witnesses "say Phineas was sitting on a rock ledge above the hole, holding the iron loosely between his knees" (5). Fleischman's focus on the difference between the two begins the narrative by drawing attention to a gap in the knowledge on the subject and animates a debate between different positions. Following his accident, Gage becomes the central example in another debate, this one between two major contingents of medical doctors. Because Gage survived the destruction of a very specific part of his brain, he tests both the theories that Fleischman defines as championed by the "Whole Brainers" ("They think of the cortex as a chamber holding a formless cloud or jelly driven by a mysterious 'vital force.' Through this force, every part of the brain is connected to every other part") and the "Localizers" (they "believe that 'organs' inside the brain control specific functions") (34–35). This debate drives much of the book;

to a large extent, it is actually a book not about Gage but about the questions his case inspired and the disagreements people had about the possible answers. Too, Fleischman writes the book in present tense, an excellent choice for a book making lively a debate that took place in the past. This choice also allows the book to talk repeatedly about the scientific discoveries being made around Gage's historical moment, narrating the unfolding of knowledge rather than blending the thoughts and tools of different periods into one long-finished story. In animating the argument between these two contingents, Fleischman writes his book as an extended modeling of and invitation to inquiry.

There is, however, one way the book suggests that critical engagement is not necessary, and this suggestion lies at the intersection of voice and character. Consider this passage, in which Fleischman explains how the Localizers and the Whole Brainers were both wrong and right:

> In the long run, the Localizers will turn out to be somewhat right about localization but completely wrong about phrenological organs. The Whole Brainers will turn out to be right about the complex interconnections of the brain but wrong about the brain acting as a whole. The 10 billion neurons in your brain are not connected at random. They are organized into "local circuits" within the cortex; the local circuits form "subcortical nuclei," which together form "cortical regions," which form "systems," which form "systems of systems," which form you. (40)

In my previous chapter, I complained that Kathryn Lasky's book on John Muir presented debate but made one position so unattractive that the potential of the debate was badly weakened. Fleischman, however, gives neither the Whole Brainers nor the Localizers such a status.

Still, there is another position implied in this passage and others, a position so clearly superior that it, at least, does not require critical engagement. That position becomes important again later in the book, when it is more explicitly contrasted with the competing scientific models of Gage's era:

> In our time, we control most epileptic symptoms with powerful drugs called "anticonvulsants," because uncontrolled seizures can cause their own brain damage.
>
> In 1860, severe epileptic seizures are not controllable. All the doctors in San Francisco can offer Phineas are theories, useless drugs, and nursing instructions. (50–51)

The position that was masked in the previous example but that becomes visible here is the position of today's knowledge, from whose elevated position we "control" the disorder with drugs that are "powerful," and Fleischman contrasts that position with "theories" that have no hard data, "useless drugs," and inadequate advice. In the previous example, the contrast is not quite so mocking, but it is equally self-assured: the positions in the debates of the past "turn out to be" partly right and partly wrong, and, the book implies, we can tell the difference between the two because in the present, we have arrived at what is true and are now able to measure the thoughts of the past objectively. The same tones appear elsewhere in the book, as when the narrator mocks the Localizers' theories. Although they "haven't seen a single thought or brainwave ... that doesn't stop them from identifying thirty-seven 'organs' of the brain. How do they do it? Bumps. That's right. Bumps on the head" (37). In the book's final chapter, Fleischman shows contemporary neuroscientists at work with marvelous new technology to study patients with injuries similar to those of Gage's, and it recalls the deductions of John Harlow, who used "the best medical theories of his day" (17). As Fleischman explains the advances enabled by the equipment of the new millennium, he confides that Harlow's theory "was good enough for 1868. It isn't good enough today" (67). The book enthusiastically animates the voices of different opinions in the past, but it conjures the present as homogeneous and right. What is real and true is that which we know today.

The problem, from the perspective of critical engagement, is that this portrait of a past filled with debate and a present characterized by accuracy is teleological. The value of the past is measured in its similarity to the present, and whatever "becoming" was at work in the characters, their arguments, and the theories they tested is now at an end. In such a venue, critical engagement risks becoming a work of nostalgia, of looking back to a time when—unlike today—such engagement was necessary. Such a vision of the past as foolish in comparison with the present conflicts with Freire's claim that knowledge comes from "invention and re-invention, through the restless, impatient, continuing, hopeful inquiry [people] pursue in the world, with the world, and with each other" (*Pedagogy*, 58). Specifically, Freire warns against a way of looking at the world and its people that encourages "accommodation to this normalized 'today'" (80–81). Fleischman's winking condescension to science of the past in comparison with the orderly, correct understanding wielded by science today helps normalize the present. Our thinking is not becoming but finished.

I said, though, that I have been struggling with Fleischman's book, and I didn't mean that I was struggling with it because I was disappointed. Rather, I meant that the book also includes other elements, elements that we are now in a position to consider and that might rescue it from the complaint that I have been making. I ended the previous chapter by demonstrating that although I'm offering ways to recognize invitations to critical engagement when we see them, we have to take care not to apply the terms that I have developed unreflectively. I want to end this chapter by pointing out how these terms overlap, reinforce, and contradict one another. For the sake of clarity, I have been exploring these terms independently, but in practice, they frequently intersect with and complicate one another. *Phineas Gage* can help us see how that happens.

Again, my main frustration with *Phineas Gage* is how it portrays the past as foolish in comparison with what reads to me as a remarkably smug present. However, the authority granted to the present, which implies that inquiry is no longer necessary, is thwarted in a few places by mistakes in our current understanding and even gestures toward what we do not yet know. In an aside about changing notions of the brain from the distant past, Fleischman points out that "three hundred years ago, everybody 'knew' that anger was controlled by the spleen," and "the ancient Greeks 'knew' that the heart was the center of emotion and thought." Even Aristotle, Fleischman reports, "'knew' that the primary function of the brain was to cool the blood." Not until 1800, Fleischman writes, did an authoritative figure determine "that the brain is the seat of the intelligence, the emotions, and the will." So far, of course, this history is just another example of the foolishness of the past, but Fleischman then goes on to point out that we still retain many of the sensibilities of earlier understandings of the brain: "Even today," he correctly points out, "we don't talk about a lover who's been dumped as feeling 'broken-brained'" (26–27). The "even" here still carries a certain hint that what we think today should normally be assumed to be superior to thoughts of the past, but by drawing attention to a continuing mistake, Fleischman does break up some of the authority otherwise implicit in the present. Too, although most of the book measures the imperfect knowledge of the past against the knowledge of the present, there are places where Fleischman highlights that which we still don't know. "It's been 150 years since his accident," Fleischman writes of Gage, "yet we are still learning more about him. There's also a lot about Phineas we don't know and probably never will" (2). Indeed, there is a time in Gage's life that remains murky, and Fleischman points to a contemporary researcher, writing that until he "turns up solid proof, we can't say for sure" exactly what Gage did during that period. Even on the subject of brain science, Fleischman does sometimes—if rarely—explain that we have more to learn, as when he writes that "we know so much more about the brain today than the Phrenologists and the Whole Brainers did in 1850, yet we really understand only the rough outlines" (40).

As I continue to revisit *Phineas Gage,* it is moments such as these that strike me as an antidote to the paralysis of inquiry encouraged by the book's picture of the past in comparison with the present. By presenting the characters and ideas of the past as less than "good enough" in comparison with the characters and ideas of the present, the book implies a history of becoming that is finished. However, Fleischman also includes occasional reminders of the continuing mistakes of the present and of the knowledge that remains to be discovered, and they explicitly name the space left for growth. I'm not exactly sure that the latter cancels out the former, but in searching for invitations to critical engagement, all we have to find are cracks in the book's teleological authority, not a sweeping rejection. Putting the book's consistent conviction of the superiority of today's knowledge together with these moments in which Fleischman draws attention to the work left to do suggests that the book invites a skepticism of the past that is not exactly necessary in the present. It also suggests that there are breakthroughs yet to come. There is room in that imagined future for the work of gathering information, testing and corroborating it. There is a space for critical engagement.

Phineas Gage is a reminder of the complicated role of characters in a story of inquiry. Fleischman's portrait of some of the characters as foolish and others as confident indicates a faith in the progress of knowledge, one that takes for granted at least a vague linearity to the upward tick of human understanding. This portrait does imply a diminishing need for skepticism as we approach the contemporary moment, but it also implies a continuous future where more discoveries always remain to be made. The book's presentism, then, is not quite teleological, a distinction that becomes clear through the tug of these different modes of critical engagement against one another. In Fleischman's book, as in so much nonfiction for children, the characters—touched by vulnerability, prone to mistakes, unfinished—can open up or defer possibilities for critical engagement, frequently in ways that interfere with one another.

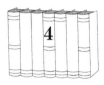

4 INQUIRY AT AND IN THE MARGINS
How Peritexts Encourage Critical Reading

I HAVE BEEN ARGUING that certain rhetorical choices in the narrative of children's nonfiction flag where books often invite or decline critical engagement. One way of reading nonfiction, however, relies heavily on elements that are *not* narrative. JoAnn Portalupi and Ralph Fletcher, for example, in articulating how exactly nonfiction is unique as compared to other children's literature, point out that "the format of the book offers support for the nonlinear way a student researcher might approach the book." The "format" of which they speak includes "the table of contents," "the introduction," and "subtitles, picture captions, glossaries, charts, and graphs" (*Nonfiction*, 10). While fiction, poetry, drama, and other literary modes use some or even all of these elements, nonfiction offers them as key to the reading experience, so much so that, Portalupi and Fletcher argue, it is the presence of such an apparatus that most immediately suggests that a specific work is in the genre of nonfiction. Similarly excited by the potential of such nonlinear reading, Myra Zarnowski claims that "sidebars and related graphics, captions, timelines, and author's notes provide readers with options. A reader can approach a book by examining the pictures first, by reading the sidebars, or by sampling a bit of

107

each—all of this before even beginning the main text" (*History*, 69). For these and other champions of children's nonfiction, nonnarrative elements of a book simultaneously signal a book's presence in its genre and invite a way of reading that is rare elsewhere but common in nonfiction.

This remarkable quality of nonfiction has potential to magnify invitations to critical engagement. Zarnowski reflects that when she reads a biography for children, she usually turns to the back matter first, "looking for the sources, and then I check for an author's note. Once I get a sense of who is writing the biography and the research that underlies it, I am ready to consider what the author has to say" (69–70). Zarnowski's way of reading children's biography, a way that she successfully shares with her own students, is a clear example of reading according to what Sam Wineburg has called "the sourcing heuristic," in which a historian first learns "a document's author and the place and date of its creation" in order to "develop hypotheses about what would be in the body of the document, the stance it might take, and its truthfulness or accuracy" ("Historical Problem Solving," 79). Wineburg's argument is that professional historians who habitually engage critically with evidence do so with specific contextual knowledge, and Zarnowski demonstrates how a reader of children's nonfiction can practice a similar approach using information given by the nonnarrative elements of a book. What this means is that the apparatus that characterizes nonfiction can—and, if Zarnowski is any example, *does*—play a key role in enabling critical engagement.

The narrative elements are frequently the most memorable aspects of a work of nonfiction, but previous scholarship reminds us that an analysis of the field must also attend to these *peritexts*, to borrow a word from Gérard Genette. Peritexts are bound up with the genre of nonfiction. They both signal that a book is nonfiction and facilitate a particular way of encountering it. Reading these nonnarrative elements of nonfiction closely can illuminate the genre and, because the specific way of reading that they encourage is fundamentally dialogic, tell us something exactly relevant to critical engagement. Peritexts offer an extraordinary opportunity for us to point to what is rare in other literature but common in nonfiction, to think about how that which is common to nonfiction has clear potential to invite or discourage critical engagement, and even to address questions about children's literature in general.

Defining Peritexts

Some of Genette's terminology can be confusing, but it is inevitable for a discussion about a book's nonnarrative apparatus. The peritexts are "such elements as the title or the preface and sometimes elements inserted into the interstices of the text, such as chapter titles or certain notes" (*Paratexts*, 4–5). In children's nonfiction, the list of items that qualify under this rubric is lengthy, including titles, prefaces, chapter titles, and notes as well as sidebars, captions, epilogues, bibliographies, and more. In addition to peritexts, Genette also explains *epitexts,* by which he means information that does not come packaged with the text itself but that attempts to shape our understanding of the text. At times, such information reaches readers through other texts: "messages that, at least originally, are located outside the book, generally with the help of the media (interviews, conversations) or under cover of private communications (letters, diaries, and others)" (5). But epitexts might include information that floats through public consciousness, impacting the perception of a text: Genette lists as examples an author's age, sex, "membership in an academy (or other exalted body)[,] or receipt of a literary prize" (7). Together, the peritext and the epitext compose the broader term for which Genette is more famous: *paratext.* For this chapter, it is not paratexts in general or epitexts at all that are my concern but the peritexts, those parallel texts that accompany the main text.

The Limitations of Peritexts for Critical Engagement

The history of peritexts in children's nonfiction is lengthy, and it shows a complicated relationship between texts and their anticipated audiences. Contemporary children's nonfiction published in the United States shows tendencies indebted *and* opposed to the uses of peritexts in children's nonfiction of earlier centuries, which leaves me with the task of untangling how to recognize peritexts that invite and decline critical engagement. Although Zarnowski and others have pointed out how the peritexts of children's nonfiction present important opportunities for readers actively involved in inquiry, it is more accurate to say that peritexts are places to look for invitations to and implied limitations upon critical engagement, often in tension or accordance with historical precedents. As contemporary nonfiction authors continue to experiment with the uses of peritexts, they find ways sometimes to sequester, sometimes to highlight paths for critical engagement in the sidebars, author's notes, captions, and other elements that accompany the main text.

Zarnowski has given us reason to be optimistic about how readers will use the peritexts of children's trade nonfiction, but Sam Wineburg has argued that peritexts conventionally represent, in children's textbooks, a way of pushing opportunities for doubt to the margins. He lists many ways in which contemporary history textbooks eliminate "traces of how the text came to be," including the primary evidence from which professionals have drawn conclusions about history. Such a process leaves students to accept those conclusions rather than engage with the evidence itself. Obviously, when the main text of a book encourages students to accept its conclusions without reflection or even a sense that the conclusions *are* conclusions with a history of debate and dissent, that text discourages critical engagement. On the rare occasions when textbooks do present a primary source, Wineburg claims, "it is typically set off in 'sidebars' so as not to interfere with the main text" (*Historical Thinking,* 12–13). In Wineburg's understanding, then, an invitation to critical engagement presented in a peritext is an invitation safely insulated from the main text, whose authority it never really threatens. This accusation is a serious threat to the project of critical engagement in the genre. If it is true, as others have argued and as I have agreed, that peritexts are a conventional part of nonfiction, and if it is also true that textbooks, the cousin of contemporary trade nonfiction, use peritexts to obscure the production of knowledge, then it is possible that peritexts should be regarded as a tool for resisting, rather than enabling, critical engagement.

The uncomfortable truth is that contemporary children's nonfiction does sometimes justify Wineburg's fears. Consider Larry Dane Brimner's *Birmingham Sunday* (2010), which tells the story of the 1963 bombing of the Sixteenth Street Baptist Church in Birmingham, Alabama, which resulted in the deaths of four black girls. In explaining the larger context of the attack, Brimner shares the story of a photograph that became famous almost overnight and that has remained in the public discourse about the civil rights movement ever since: Bill Hudson's May 3, 1963, photograph of Walter Gadsden. In the main text of his book, Brimner writes,

> Photographs of police dogs going after Ullman High School sophomore Walter Gadsden, a bystander who had gone downtown only to see Martin Luther King, were published in newspapers around the globe. The event helped to transform public opinion about the plight of Negroes in the South. (20–21)

This explanation includes no obvious invitations to critical engagement. It explains that there was a person in a specific situation with known motivations and that photographs of "police dogs going after" him received certain distribution, all of which contributed to a subsequent shift in public opinion. Contrast that description, though, with a nearby peritext, namely, the caption of the accompanying photograph:

> When Walter Gadsden was "attacked" by [Commissioner of Public Safety] Connor's dogs and the image was published in newspapers around the world, it helped transform public opinion in 1963, although today there is some controversy as to whether he was being attacked. (20)

In two places—the scare quotes around the first use of "attacked" and the final clause about conflicting interpretations—this caption opens up cracks in the authority of the photograph. But the disagreement between credible sources—something that I, inspired by Wineburg, labeled in chapter 2 as a kind of invitation to critical engagement—exists only in the sidebar. As such, this brief example looks very much like the sort of sequestering of critical engagement away from the main text that Wineburg protested.

A more sustained example comes from Suzanne Jurmain's

Forbidden Schoolhouse: The True and Dramatic Story of Prudence Crandall and Her Students (2005). This history of Crandall, a nineteenth-century Connecticut educator, explains how she integrated her school for girls and then, when the parents of white students withdrew their children, switched the focus of her program over to black girls. The school eventually closed amid raging controversy in Crandall's hometown of Canterbury, but fifty years later, the state legislature awarded Crandall a pension in honor of her efforts, and in 1995, ten years before the publication of Jurmain's book, Crandall was named Connecticut's official "state heroine." Well before Jurmain's book, then, Crandall's status as a heroine had been well established, and that status, taut with authority, makes her a difficult subject for critical engagement.

Not surprisingly, the narrative portion of *Forbidden Schoolhouse* rarely paints Crandall as anything other than reasonable and courageous. Multiple examples might serve, but two in particular stand out as especially resistant to questions. When townsfolk expressed their outrage, Crandall wrote a letter explaining her position. "She did it as politely as she could," the narrator reports. "In a calm, well-written letter to a local newspaper, Prudence laid out the facts." "It was a good, clear, sensible letter," Jurmain concludes, "but it didn't change a lot of minds in Canterbury" (54–55). In this scene, the book presents Crandall and directs readers to interpret her as being as polite as possible, evenhanded, honest, and a good writer. The narrator does not offer the words of the letter but a conclusion about them. Readers are not invited (or even enabled) to consider the letter and test conclusions about it; they are instead given conclusions. Later, as Crandall and her supporters considered how to widen support for the school, they bemoaned a lack of positive press and decided to found a new paper, "one that would print *all* articles about the school—both pro and con." "Two weeks later a new," and, the narrator insists, "unbiased paper called the *Unionist* was rolling off the presses" (70). Probably what Jurmain means here is that the paper, by including two sides of an issue, made some attempt at balance, but in dubbing the paper "unbiased"—again, without reproducing any of the essays from the paper, simply telling the reader how to interpret them—it presents the *Unionist* as beyond criticism. Avon Crismore argues that "young readers need to see author biases and evaluate them at an early age; textbooks and teachers need to teach them how to do this" ("Rhetoric," 296). Labeling one source as "unbiased" certainly does not advance that cause, and it probably discourages the evaluation for which Crismore argues. Together, examples such as these from the main text present Crandall, her cause, and the book's knowledge of them as above question.

The first appendix, though, breaks that pattern. In these lines the author speaks with a humility that is uncharacteristic of the main text. She writes,

> Although no complete school roster exists, evidence suggests that there were probably about twenty pupils. Very little is known about most of these young women. In some cases, even their exact names are in doubt, but researchers have uncovered a few facts about the pupils listed alphabetically below. (121)

This peritext does not abandon the possibility of reasonable knowledge: it explains what conclusions the evidence suggests, and it even refers to "a few facts" that earnest research has produced. But it repeatedly points to the *limitations* of knowledge, to a lack of evidence, and in doing so, it demonstrates where questions remain and are especially pertinent. Such rhetoric fits the patterns I have been arguing constitute invitations to critical engagement, but they appear mainly in the peritexts. The humility of these lines contrasts directly with the bulk of the narrative, which avoids mention of any lack of security in the narrative's information or interpretation of that information. Instead, the book produces a Crandall whose actions, discourse, and allies were above reproach. Doubt is set off in the peritext, where it is less likely to interfere with the main text.

The Potential of Peritexts for Children's Nonfiction

Wineburg's skepticism about peritexts is well founded, as these two examples demonstrate, but I want to introduce some nuance to his skepticism. These books by Brimner and Jurmain feature main texts that rarely invite doubt when considering the authority of either the narrator or the information offered. As a result, occasional peritexts that speak with humility stand out as aberrations at best, as means of closing off inquiry at worst. But peritexts do sometimes interact with their main texts in richer ways, so although Wineburg issues a useful reminder that peritexts can effectively work against a text's invitation to inquiry, I want to explore some important examples of peritexts that magnify such invitations.

Emily Arnold McCully's *Marvelous Mattie: How Margaret E. Knight Became an Inventor* (2006), a picture book, keeps critical reflection mainly to its peritexts, but it uses those peritexts in a way that enriches rather than departs from the main text. The text itself is trim, more evocative than descriptive. For example, early in the book, the narrator explains that

Emily Arnold McCully, *Marvelous Mattie: How Margaret E. Knight Became an Inventor* (2006).

when [Knight] thought of things that could be made with the tools, she drew them in a notebook labeled *My Inventions.* Her brothers called the sketches her brainstorms.

Mattie made a whirligig for Charlie and a jumping jack for Jim. For her mother, who sat up late on cold nights sewing to earn a living, she made a foot warmer. (4)

This section of the text largely skims over the process of invention, the struggles and mistakes that are part of Knight's own critical engagement. But the bottom quarter of the spread on which these words appear is given over to a series of sketches that illustrate designs for the projects that Knight here invents. The first sketch is of a boy labeled "Charlie" holding and preparing to blow into a whirligig, and the next two are of a jumping jack labeled "For Jim" (4). These cues indicate that these sketches come from Knight's notebook. As such, they demonstrate exactly the process of invention that the main text erases. The sketches annotate Charlie's whirligig with arrows and movement lines indicating how the air will move through the device, and drawings of Jim's jumping jack use a rotated view to imagine the working jack, then the connections that will allow that work to take place. Later, when her brothers ask her to build a kite, the main text says, "Mattie sketched a few kites with different shapes and struts. She picked the best one and set to work on it" (6). Again, the bottom of the page imagines Knight's notebook to tell the story of the girl's unfolding logic as she designs the kite. On the far left is a familiar diamond-shaped kite. The next two illustrations compare that kite with a box kite, and the next page shows a rough sketch of a bat-shaped kite next to a small sketch of bats; a careful, scaled, refined design for a bat–kite hybrid in a firmer hand then shows a design for a "bat kite." This final sketch comes complete with notes on wingspan, placement of dowels, and material. The sequence shows a standard design, then experimentation with another design, then rejection of the second and adaptation of the first: it's a narrative of reflection, experimentation, and even humility in the face of the realization that a previous idea was not perfect, and that narrative is told entirely in the peritext. McCully uses the same technique in sidebars throughout the book. These peritexts routinely illustrate the sequence of critical thought that is implied in the main text.

116 ◨ *Inquiry at and in the Margins*

Wineburg would be justified in saying here that the critical process is removed from the main text, but that removal has a richer effect than simply marginalizing inquiry. The book invites readers to the project of inquiry through the interplay of text and peritext, in which the sidebars expand on the steps of invention that might have been tedious in the main text. The information in those sidebars might fairly be said to have been placed so that it would not be "interfering" with the main text, but it does await the reader, prominent, even alluded to in the main text, and it fleshes out the story told by the main text in a way that is rewarding for readers who take the time to contemplate the sidebars.

Furthermore, McCully's sidebars make use of the picture book form in a way that Wineburg's complaint, which targets textbooks, cannot anticipate, and in doing so, they deepen the invitation to critical engagement. First, the sidebars rarely use a narratorial voice; indeed, they use it only once, in the last of the sidebars. As such, they leave to the reader the action of closing the gap of meaning between the main text and peritext, of linking these sketches with the journal mentioned early in the story and moments of invention that constitute the main beats of the plot. The dovetailing of narrative and illustration to produce meaning is frequently isolated as one of the defining traits of picture books,[1] so the fact that the illustrations of Knight's critical process are separated from the main text cannot represent the isolation of question from answer in Wineburg's theory: picture books *assume* that readers will connect the main text with the illustrations that surround them, not leave them isolated from one another. Second, because picture books tend to anticipate a reading situation in which a proficient, literate reader reads the words aloud while a preliterate reader listens to the words while looking at the illustrations, the fact that this book locates its representation of the critical process in the illustrations might be an indication that children are *more* likely to think through the process in the sketches than they would have been if that process were placed in the main text. It's possible, that is to say, to think of the illustrations as more efficiently directed at the child audience of the picture book than at the literate, presumably adult, audience. I think, then, that although Wineburg is on the whole right about how peritexts can represent places where books sequester critical engagement, and although I think that we should be alert for this disappointing potential, there is also good reason to think that peritexts that contain invitations to critical engagement can issue those invitations in unique, even compelling ways.

The Historical Roots of Peritexts in Children's Nonfiction

One technique for distinguishing between the problems that Wineburg finds in textbooks and the potential that I am seeking in trade nonfiction is to look back at examples of peritexts in textbooks and how that precedent has influenced contemporary nonfiction. Textbooks of previous eras often declined to include a significant apparatus at all, and the peritexts that they did include indicated strongly that those peritexts were to be used either by the teacher or under the teacher's direction, hardly the sort of self-directed critical engagement in which I am most interested. Frances L. Strong's late-nineteenth-century reader on nature, *All the Year Round, a Nature Reader, Part 1: Autumn,* contains a "Note to the Teacher" in the front matter, a five-page document followed by 102 pages of readings and drawings for the students, these with no apparatus at all. J. Hamilton Moore's *The Young Gentleman and Lady's Monitor, and English Teacher's Assistant,* first published in the late eighteenth century and reprinted throughout the opening decades of the nineteenth century, includes no index, table of contents, or footnotes. It does include a preface, but, in a decision that would remain typical for much of the history of children's publishing, the preface appears to be intended to give advice on how a teacher might use the selections found after the preface. The editor numbers each paragraph of those readings (but not the preface), perhaps better to aid in assigning specific sections to be studied or read. Such numbers do of course count as a kind of peritext, but their function is probably to facilitate instruction, perhaps even to direct rote memorization, not to invite a child's questioning of the material. I draw that interpretation of the text in part from works such as J. Madison Watson's nineteenth-century reader on elocution, whose preliminary section "To Teachers" instructs educators to use peritexts such as the included "dictionary and cyclopedia" to practice and repeat the readings without reflection. Watson even directs instructors to use the peritexts to help students practice reading the assignments *backward* so that the children will absorb the manner of delivery, to memorize rather than reflect (*Independent,* iv). When these textbooks used peritexts—something not to be taken for granted—that use was even more resistant to critical engagement than in the contemporary textbooks about which Wineburg has complained. They not only pushed the production of knowledge to the margins, they actually indicated that the ideas in the peritexts were intended to serve either one-sided instruction or the noncontemplative memorization of the information on the page.

Trade nonfiction often followed the pattern established by textbooks, but not always. For example, Ann Taylor's *City Scenes, or a Peep into London for Good Children,* published in 1828, follows the lead of textbooks in limiting peritexts, with neither an index nor a table of contents in place. It does on rare occasions include footnotes, but they generally serve to reinforce the main text, as in the case of one footnote that adds information about the grisly fates met in the Tower of London (14–15). Taylor's book also numbers the paragraphs of the main text. If I am right to read such labels as a guide for assignments, repetition, and perhaps even rote memorization, then here, too, the implication of the peritexts is that the content of the main text is to be absorbed rather than questioned. The work of Priscilla Wakefield, the prolific early-nineteenth-century author, presents a telling contrast. In the previous chapter, I made the point that Wakefield uses her nonfiction to demonstrate characters in the action of learning. My conclusion was that dramatizing the process of testing information constitutes an invitation to critical engagement with the text: rather than simply asking readers to absorb, memorize, or recite assigned sections of dense information, when a book tells the story of discovery, it is presenting *that* activity, not the activity of passively receiving discoveries made by others, as attractive. I argued specifically that Wakefield's *Introduction to Botany* invites critical engagement through its scenes of characters reading and applying Linnaeus's methods of classification, and here

I want to argue that its peritexts facilitate such engagement. The back matter includes one hundred illustrations of named plants, followed by a twenty-four-page "Catalogue of the Most Approved English Names" and their classifications (class and order), which is then followed by a nine-page "Vocabulary of Botanical Terms," which is itself followed by a two-page "Tabular View of the Classes and Orders." All of these are arranged clearly, with layouts that make skipping from one group of information to the next easy and intuitive. Within the main pages of the text, the book also includes a foldout giving twenty-four classes of plants, important hallmarks, examples, and a list of the numbered illustrations that follow each of the examples. Wakefield fills the final letter from Felicia to Constance with footnotes that tag different plants according to Linnaeus's method. The peritexts throughout *Introduction to Botany* encourage readers to join the process of considering the features of real and illustrated plants and deciding which names are indicated by the evidence at hand. Although early textbooks for children either ignored peritexts or put them in service of transferring unexamined information into the minds of young readers, and although much trade nonfiction followed that model, some very popular nonfiction demonstrated how to use peritexts in a way that made readers part of the project of inquiry rather than just its beneficiary.

The Real Audience of Peritexts

Wakefield's use of these parallel materials alongside a main text that models their use indicates that her peritexts are aimed at her young readers, but as we have seen, other authors labeled their peritexts in such a way as to announce that they were not for children but adults. Because today's nonfiction descends from that tradition, we are justified in suspecting that, at least traditionally, peritexts that invite critical engagement might actually be inviting the adults looking over the shoulders of the children rather than the children themselves. Even today, an assumption remains in educational theory that children will not read the peritexts unless adults direct them to do so. Rebecca L. Perini argues that teachers ought to use author's notes, forewords, and afterwords better to understand an author's intentions. In arguing that adults need to share these things with children, she is underscoring a conception that these parts of the book are not already read by or intended for children. When she advises that "the author's note may help guide teachers to select related resources and better prepare themselves to address unfamiliar themes and topics," she highlights how such peritexts can encourage readers to continue the process of inquiry past the end of the book, but the readers whom she imagines following that prompt are adults ("Pearl," 431). Given that, for most of the history of the genre, peritexts have served the caretakers of children more directly than they have served the children themselves, Perini is probably on solid ground. If so, whatever invitations to critical engagement we find in the peritexts of children's literature cannot count for very much.

Monica Edinger, however, a grade-school teacher and frequent writer about children's literature, offers some hope that if peritexts are present, children will read them regardless of how their authors intended them. In an essay on historical fiction, she confesses that she cannot remember paying attention to extra materials included in books she loved as a child, but she also suspects that whatever her memory now might say, her passion for these books would have driven her to "read any and all back matter, had there been any" ("After 'The End,'" 80). She points to recent works and observes that "whether young people read the notes (and I can only hope they will), the back matter for these two books seems absolutely necessary." After summarizing Katherine Sturtevant's author's note in *A True and Faithful Narrative* (2006), Edinger says, "I suspect that quite a few young readers will be as eager as I was to know more and will be equally appreciative of this extra material" (82). Again, she is writing about historical fiction rather than nonfiction, but for Edinger, the deciding factor in whether a child will seek out peritexts is not genre, or even age, but passion. In my Introduction, I noted that Patricia J. Cianciolo has pointed to interest as the defining criterion for a child's willingness to read nonfiction, including nonfiction out of the child's supposed reading level. Therefore, if Edinger is right that children will be "eager" and therefore read the peritexts of historical fiction, it is reasonable to expect that children who are passionate about the subject of a work of nonfiction will look at its peritexts, too.

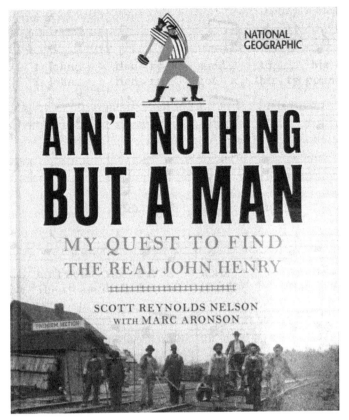

Scott Reynolds Nelson, *Ain't Nothing but a Man: My Quest to Find the Real John Henry* (2008).

If children today find themselves motivated to consider the peritexts, contemporary nonfiction, despite its precedents, shows signs that authors are making room in their peritexts for child readers. Scott Reynolds Nelson's *Ain't Nothing but a Man: My Quest to Find the Real John Henry* (2008), written with Marc Aronson, offers many encouraging examples. Aronson's six-step "How to Be a Historian" appendix explains the difference between primary and secondary sources, then urges the reader to "gather as many . . . as you can and compare them." Because this invitation to critical engagement comes couched within a larger explanation of something that one might assume that adult readers of nonfiction already know (namely, the difference between the two kinds of sources), I think it's fair to consider this as an example of a peritext anticipating a young reader. On the same page, Aronson advises researchers who have hit a dead end to "ask a librarian for other ways to frame your search" (61). Finally, the opening appendix, this one written by Nelson, explains how "a group of teenagers" is continuing the search for historical evidence: "Maybe the teenagers will find out more about John Henry," he suggests, "or maybe you will" (58). The "you" of these peritexts seems to imagine a reader who needs words explained that adults probably would not, requires advice more obviously relevant to a student than a teacher, and exists in a category comparable to teenagers doing similar research. None of these explicitly names young readers as its audience, but each creates space within the readerly position for young people. And each of these peritextual examples encourages readers to be part of the continuing work of history.

I opened by saying that peritexts present an opportunity not only to understand nonfiction better but also to think through some of the difficult questions of children's literature, and it is on the question of the true audience of the peritexts of children's nonfiction that I find myself inevitably stumbling over one such question. One of the most contentious points in the study of children's literature has been whether a child's book can really be said to be *for* children. The most famous attempt to answer this question is Jacqueline Rose's 1984 *The Case of Peter Pan, or, the Impossibility of Children's Fiction*. Rose concludes that children's literature is really always by, about, and for adults, and considering the ubiquity of adults and adult concerns in the production, editing, reviewing, awarding, purchasing, shelving, gifting, and teaching of children's literature, it's hard to argue with her. Nonetheless, nearly everyone *has* argued with her. Major books in the field frequently contain sections spanning several pages in a row dedicated to explaining why she is wrong (Reynolds, *Radical Children's Literature*, 4–9; Gubar, *Artful Dodgers*, 39–33; and Nodelman, *Hidden Adult*, in which a revision of Rose is one of the central themes). In 2010, the *Children's Literature Association Quarterly* dedicated not simply a few pages but an *entire issue* to continuing the argument with Rose's book.

The next year, *PMLA*'s first issue featured three essays on children's literature using different theoretical models to disprove Rose's contention as well as one essay using a different theoretical model to argue that we haven't paid *enough* attention to Rose.[2] What I draw from this continuing, one might even say compulsive, argument is not so much the impossibility of children's literature but the impossibility of stating a categorical answer to the question of whether children's literature is really for children. All of which makes it, of course, foolish of me to try to answer that question myself.

In trying to answer that question myself, I want to narrow my focus from children's literature in general to books, indeed to parts of books. I think, as I have argued elsewhere,[3] that we can use formal cues to infer whether at least part of a book is anticipating a child audience, an adult audience, or some mixture of the two. I want to attempt that same strategy here. I am especially interested in the difference in a book's font size and line spacing, by which I mean the amount of vertical blank space between typed lines of the printed words. Specifically, I want to trace these variables from one part of the book to another. Conventionally, in adult literature as well as children's literature, font and spacing in the main text are generous, but the font and spacing in prefaces, bibliographies, appendices, and other peritexts are traditionally much smaller. No doubt that shift in size is in part the result of publishing efficiencies: printers, looking to minimize costs, condense the parts of the book over which readers spend less time. But in children's literature, font and spacing are aspects of the book that have been carefully theorized, especially those aspects that signal the intended audience. Kathleen T. Horning's handbook to children's literature gives a concise explanation of this phenomenon. Although larger font and spacing increase a publisher's costs, for Horning, those aspects of print are concessions to the developing physical capabilities of children. Specifically, because children have not yet developed the fine control of ocular musculature necessary for reading lines of language of the size conventional in print for adults, publishers who anticipate child readers who are new to reading will routinely print their pages with more generous font and spacing (*Cover to Cover*, 127–28). Thus "most books for adults are set in typefaces of 10 to 12 points," but "the standard size typeface for beginning readers is 18 points" (135). Such an increased font size gives children a larger target as they force their eyes to move along the horizontal line of type, a task that they have little reason to practice before learning to read. Similarly, the spacing between lines is increased "so that a child can easily keep his or her place in a line without wandering down into the next line" (136). There are multiple reasons that a publisher might increase font or spacing—including, at the most conniving, trying to *appear* child-friendly to adult reviewers and buyers—but given the increased costs of publishing a book with such traits, the font and line spacing are uncommonly solid indications of whether a child or adult is anticipated as the audience of that specific line.

Any of a number of examples could illustrate this point, but I'll choose two books a little more than a hundred years apart to demonstrate how reduced font size and spacing indicate that adults are the intended audience. I mentioned earlier Strong's 1896 *All the Year Round*, the book that opens with a five-page "Note to the Teacher" and then contains 102 pages of readings for children. That opening peritext serves well as an example because it declares that its audience is an adult reader. The note also indicates that the main text is intended for children (vi). We can compare the number of printed lines in each of these sections and, informed by the announced audiences, draw some contrasts between font and spacing in a section for adults as opposed to a section for children. The fourth page of the note, the text for adults, contains thirty lines of vertical type, but the fourth page of the readings for children contains merely twenty-six. As Horning's contemporary analysis of font and spacing leads us to expect, the section for adults makes miserly use of vertical space in this older informational text, whereas the section for children makes more generous use. That principle continues to guide very recent nonfiction. Take for example Marc Aronson and Marina Budhos's *Sugar Changed the World: A Story of Magic, Spice, Slavery, Freedom, and Science,* published in 2010. The back matter includes the three-and-a-half-page "How We Researched and Wrote This Book: A Short Essay on a (Very) Long Process, for Teachers, Librarians, and Other Interested Parties." As the (archaically verbose) title indicates, this section is for adults. The opening sentence confirms that interpretation, stating, "This essay is not aimed at young readers, but rather at those who challenge, instruct, and assist them" (127). The essay goes on to make a case for the ability of young readers to thrive in the sort of narrative provided in the main text, further indicating, if there were any doubt, that the *main* text is for children. The first full page of the peritextual essay (page 128) has thirty-five lines of vertical type, but a typical full page of main text (take, for example, page 87) has only twenty-eight. Again, the font size and space are expanded on pages for children, but pages primarily for adults use denser text.

I think that the safest inference to draw from this comparison is that when a peritext uses a font and line spacing that are especially generous, that peritext is signaling that it anticipates child readers. This conclusion does not really answer the broader question of whether a work of children's literature is for children—Kathleen T. Isaacs, for example, suggests that nonfiction authors craft their peritexts in part to draw favorable responses from (adult) reviewers and award committees (14)—but it does give some stability with which to analyze how contemporary children's nonfiction wants to distance its use of peritexts from the traditional habit of talking to adults in the margins and children in the main text. It's also important not to put too much trust in the inverse of the inference I'm drawing. Although I do think it is reasonable to conclude that a larger font and greater space between lines signal an anticipated child readership, I do not think that more cramped font and spacing preclude a child readership, especially today. Aronson's back matter in Nelson's *Ain't Nothing but a Man*, to take one of many examples, anticipates a young readership, but those lines are in a smaller font than the main text. In fact, it's my perception that contemporary children's publishers increasingly use comparable font sizes in their main texts and peritexts. The significance of tighter fonts, then, seems to be disappearing, but if we are concerned that a line of text might be for adults rather than children, then larger fonts—which are counterincentivized by the increased cost of printing—can help us determine what parts of a book anticipate a child audience.

Peritexts for Children in the Work of Tonya Bolden

Two books by Tonya Bolden, a prolific writer of black American children's history, use broader font and spacing in the main text as well as the peritexts, and in both cases, these books place invitations to critical engagement in those child-friendly peritexts. Take for example Bolden's 2005 *Maritcha: A Nineteenth-Century American Girl*. *Maritcha* is a biography of Maritcha Rémond Lyons, who became, as a child, a pivotal figure in the desegregation of New England schools and, as an adult, a school administrator. The font and spacing send a clear message about audience. The maximum number

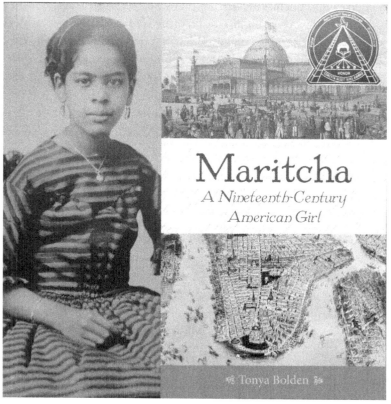

Tonya Bolden, *Maritcha: A Nineteenth-Century American Girl* (2005).

of vertical lines on a page of regular text, while not perfectly consistent throughout the book, tends to fall within a range of twenty-eight to thirty lines per page.[4] Not all of the peritexts have such generous spacing, but the preface and author's note both do. In fact, the two full pages at the middle of the author's note have twenty-nine lines per page, exactly in the middle of the normal range of the main text, and although the preface is less than one page long and therefore offers no perfect comparison, it appears to have the same font and line spacing. If we accept that the main text is designed with child readers in mind, the font and spacing indicate that the peritexts are, too. Again, I don't want to imply that narrower spacing indicates a resistance to the readers of the main text as readers of the peritexts.[5] I do, however, see the increased font and spacing in these pages as a signal that Bolden anticipates younger readers.

And *Maritcha* provides abundant rewards for children who consider the peritexts. Bolden makes powerful use of a first-person narrator, what Crismore calls (and as I discuss in chapter 2) a visible author, in the preface as well as the author's note. The preface opens with a dramatization of Bolden at work in the early stages of discovery: as she looks over the scant primary documents on Lyons's life, "Xs blot out some words. Information gaps and blanks bewilder," she writes, but she is "too intrigued to stop reading" (3). Here the visible author makes the pursuit of knowledge itself a component of the narrative, and part of that pursuit is the realization that the information on her subject is incomplete. Bolden does not keep such epistemological uncertainty to the peritexts, either, but incorporates it early in the main text, as when she points to the lack of a diary with descriptions of a daily life, meaning that we now must infer such details from parallel evidence (7–8). From the very beginning, the preface establishes the theme of working through an incomplete but rewarding body of knowledge, as Bolden confides that although she "dreamed of telling [Lyons's] story," such a job "would require a fair amount of detective work—dots to connect, facts to ferret out—because the memoir [that Lyons] never lived to revise and complete is the main source of information about her" (3). The author's note after the main text returns to this theme, explaining where Bolden first encountered the memoir, how she researched Lyons's life at the

Schomburg Center for Research in Black Culture, and the way that Lyons's story wove through Bolden's career. The author's note also shares a behind-the-scenes moment with important implications for critical engagement:

> My editor and I decided against presenting the story with illustrations by a contemporary artist because the Schomburg had photographs and other keepsakes from Maritcha's life. Not to draw on these holdings would be a missed opportunity to bring historical artifacts into wider view. To further add texture to Maritcha's story, I sought out images from other sources. In some cases, given the scarcity of nonderogatory images of blacks in pre–Civil War America, I settled on images that match Maritcha's era and experiences, but are not precisely of her life and environs. (41–42)

Bolden's explanation of her process demonstrates that the book in the reader's hands is a construction, that it is a result of choices and selection, including ideologically informed decisions about how the past should be represented. In this author's note, Bolden draws attention not to the conclusions of her research, not to the finished product of knowledge, but to choices she made in stitching that product together. In the peritexts that appear at the beginning and end of her main narrative, Bolden emphasizes that the information in the main text is a product of research that is constituted of work done by filling in gaps and choosing what texts will represent the truth.

If her 2005 book uses its peritexts to present information as the result of a process, the peritexts of Bolden's 2014 *Searching for Sarah Rector, the Richest Black Girl in America* present that process as frequently characterized by imperfect information and mistakes—when the information is available at all. Again, the peritexts are designed in such a way as to make them easier for children to read, with the prologue, author's note, and even acknowledgments printed with a font and spacing comparable to the main text.[6] *Sarah Rector* is an ideal book for the theme of filling in incomplete information, as its subject matter is a black girl whose luck in oil rights made her one of the wealthiest black people in early-twentieth-century America—or, more accurately, its subject matter

Inquiry at and in the Margins   129

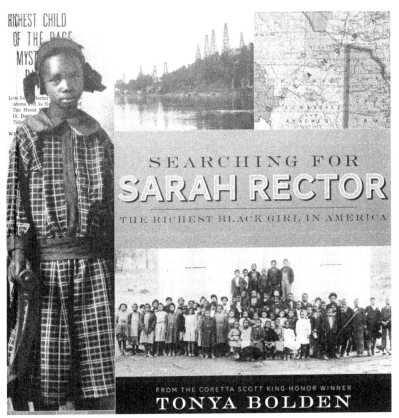

Tonya Bolden, *Searching for Sarah Rector, the Richest Black Girl in America* (2014).

is her *disappearance*. Searching is therefore a central theme at the narrative level. The author's note sustains that theme at a metatextual level, as when Bolden points to a continuing lack of information about the relationship between Rector's father and the white man who became her guardian and the evidence that almost but not quite confirms that a set of surviving photographs is connected to that guardian, T. J. Porter (52). The author's note also makes a point of explaining Bolden's research strategies, including how she investigated Porter by tracking down a man whose name appeared on a legal document alongside Porter's: "Among the court documents I acquired was the guardianship bond Porter had provided the court, a document I initially gave only a glance. When I finally gave it a hard look, I saw that one of the guarantors was an E. T. Werhan. As Werhan is a less common name than Porter, I went in search of E. T. Werhan" (52). This short paragraph again points to knowledge as a process, explaining the method rather than just the conclusion, and as such it constitutes what I have labeled as an invitation to critical engagement. But notice, too, that it points to the author making a mistake in her research: Bolden first dismissed the evidence without looking at it closely, and only in rectifying that mistake did she find her next lead. Elsewhere in the author's note, she similarly highlights a misconception she had when she began her research, again in connection with her investigation of Porter:

> At the outset I expected to find evidence that he was a fiend, because for decades the word was that during Oklahoma's oil boom days *all* white guardians of people with valuable land were grafters. There was also the claim that no blacks were allowed to be guardians of wealthy children. Finding neither to be true—well, there's another lesson: Better to rest on research and reason than on scuttlebutt. (51–52)

These points are beats in the narrative of the main text, too: W. E. B. Du Bois made a public call for a black guardian for Rector and her staggering wealth, assuming that Porter had been forced on the family and that he would of course take advantage of her, but Bolden keeps for her last chapter a lengthy examination of evidence that Du Bois was wrong, and she follows that with an author's note in which we learn that Bolden was wrong, too. In this way, the questions of the main text—what happened to Sarah Rector, and did her white guardian profit from her disappearance?—dovetail with the peritext. The book becomes a better story of searching for Sarah Rector because it dwells not on the answer—she was at home in Oklahoma the whole time, being seen after by parents, a white guardian, and a fair-minded judge who carefully protected her—but on gaps in knowledge, well-intentioned mistakes, and errors in the interpretation of evidence. It also does a better job, for all these same reasons, of inviting critical engagement.

Bolden's books serve as a good example of how, despite Wineburg's concerns about historical uses of peritexts and despite the tricky process of deciding whether a line of text is for children or adults, the peritexts of children's nonfiction can play a crucial role inviting children to the project of inquiry. Her books also demonstrate that in issuing invitations to critical engagement, peritexts can help nonfiction authors attain their aesthetic goals for a book. The implicit argument of this chapter has been that evaluation and analysis of children's nonfiction can profit from attention to the peritexts, but I want to close by pointing out that attention to peritexts can also profit the producers of children's nonfiction. Indeed, there is abundant evidence that contemporary children's nonfiction is increasingly invested in developing robust peritexts. Many children's literature professionals, such as Roger Sutton, list peritexts as crucial aspects of the genre. Sutton is the editor in chief of *The Horn Book,* a periodical that has served for generations as a professional magazine for authors, illustrators, editors, librarians, and teachers. In his editorial introduction to a special issue of the magazine focusing on children's nonfiction, Sutton writes, "Perhaps most important to librarians and teachers is the fact that nonfiction books don't only provide information about a subject, they also teach kids how to use a book, how to navigate an index, how to scan chapters, headings, and sidebars" ("It Won't Be on the Test," 7), and of course, these activities mirror Zarnowski's practice of reading nonfiction, a practice I described in the opening of this chapter as deeply connected to critical engagement. Karen Patricia Smith has argued that the Orbis Pictus, an award for nonfiction sponsored by the National Council of Teachers of English, places high value on a book's documentation—through "sidebars, correspondence, a glossary, and a selective bibliography"—and credits it with improving a child's delight in reading and researching ("Acknowledging," 40). When the Young Adult Library Services Association, a division of the American Library Association, explored the establishment of its own award for nonfiction, the appendix on "Expanded Criteria for Excellence in Nonfiction" paid special attention to the excellent use of peritexts, including "subheadings, sidebars, captions, and appendices" as well as a "table of contents, glossary, timeline, and index" (11).[7] I have been arguing that the peritexts are key to nonfiction's identity and to the potential for critical engagement that I prefer in children's nonfiction. What this swell of interest in a book's apparatus by the teachers, librarians, and reviewers of children's literature indicates is that peritexts are also key to how the field in general defines good nonfiction.

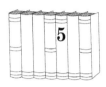

5 SEEING PHOTOGRAPHS
Breaking the Authority of Nonfiction's Favorite Medium

"PHOTOGRAPHS," writes Susan Sontag, "which cannot themselves explain anything, are inexhaustible invitations to deduction, speculation, and fantasy" (*On Photography*, 23). From this perspective, photography holds enormous potential for critical engagement. Rather than voicing an interpretation, Sontag here seems to say, photographs present evidence that is to be interpreted. Although the data of the photograph await readings that will transform them into meaning, they do not wait passively: Sontag posits that a photograph "confers on each moment the character of a mystery" (23), thus providing the atmosphere—one might even say extending an invitation—for investigation. Although other aspects of nonfiction that I have examined elsewhere in this book have existed to one extent or another in children's nonfiction for well over a century, widespread use of photography is simultaneously a relatively recent feature of children's nonfiction and, if these comments are right, a dramatically rich venue for invitations to critical engagement.

That potential for inquiry, however, becomes more complicated as we look closer. In praise of photography, Sontag also writes that "in teaching us a new visual code, photographs alter and enlarge our notions of what is worth looking at and what we have a right to observe" (3), which I take as a fair representation of photography's ability to extend our range of perception and to give us time and authority to examine the information in a photograph. Such luxuries enhance our ability to perform the work of analysis, which certainly strikes me as enabling critical engagement. But Sontag's friend and colleague Roland Barthes takes a more cynical stance on our "enlarged" and enabled perception. When he writes that photography "photographs the notable," he is perhaps agreeing with Sontag in that a photograph makes the infinite aspects of reality into a discrete object of study. But the same sentence argues that photography also "decrees notable whatever it photographs" (*Camera Lucida*, 34). In doing so, a photograph not only isolates aspects of reality but bestows authority on that which it shows. By virtue of having been photographed, an object, person, or moment becomes more important than the objects, people, and events that surrounded it when the shutter snapped. The augmented value given to the subject of the photograph is arbitrary at best (an accidental photograph snaps an image with little intent to persuade viewers of a specific meaning), misleading or even coercive at worst (a skillfully composed shot disingenuously neglects the subject's context). In decreeing its subject notable, the camera does not invite endless speculation but frames data in a way that predetermines their bloated importance. In this way, photography closes down the possible meanings of the subjects it captures, imbuing them with authority. And since authority tends to deflect rather than foster critical engagement, Barthes's pessimism threatens the faith we might have in Sontag's observation of the "inexhaustible" interpretations inherent in the medium.

If it is true that photographs are coercive, that they allow us to see while telling us what is worth seeing, their coercive power may be driven primarily by their rare ability to present information while disavowing their interpretation of that information. Kate Sampsell-Willmann writes that "photography allows the viewer to see the subject supposedly 'transparently.'" Such is not the case with most other visual media. "Painting," for example, "is clearly subjective, 'reality' processed through the mind and hand of a painter; photography is mechanical and therefore apparently more objective. This 'objectivity' misleads and does so convincingly" (*Lewis Hine,* 12). It is this misleading quality of photography that Barthes references when he argues that "a photograph is always invisible: it is not it that we see" (*Camera Lucida,* 6). A photograph presents itself as a window to truth, encouraging what Anne Higonnet calls an "absolute belief in photography's objective neutrality" (*Pictures,* 10), asking viewers to attend not to the artifice of photography but to the purportedly ingenuous representation that it offers. This skepticism of photography's claim to untouched truth is a common refrain in theory about photography, so much so that even though Sontag praises the medium's ability to spark speculation, much more of her work is dedicated to reminding readers not to trust what a photograph tells them:

> Whatever the limitations (through amateurism) or pretensions (through artistry) of the individual photographer, a photograph—any photograph—seems to have a more innocent, and therefore more accurate, relation to visible reality than do other mimetic objects. (*On Photography,* 5–6)

Vicki Goldberg echoes these sentiments when she argues that photography "is at once the most faithful and the most seductive of witnesses" (*Power,* 19). A photograph's transparency (Sampsell-Willmann), invisibility (Barthes), innocent accuracy (Sontag), and seductive witness (Goldberg) are direct threats to critical engagement, for they pretend that although viewers are welcome to interpret the data presented in a photograph, those data come to the viewer free of bias (which cannot be seen) and full of authoritative truth (which should not be questioned). From the beginning, Goldberg writes, photography "seemed to promise truth that no mere representation had ever given." Neither has a contemporary familiarity with the medium utterly shaken the lure of that promise, Goldberg continues, for "even today, when a large audience supposedly 'knows' that photographs lie, the most sophisticated observers instinctively believe the camera's report, at least for the brief pulse of time before the mind falls back on its education" (19). Unlike the other visual media that preceded it, photography offers authority in its image, and it does so quietly. The medium has a tendency to disappear, leaving behind only information whose provenance cannot be located and is therefore beyond question.

To be sure, not every photograph fits this description. There are photographs that call attention to themselves as photographs, that make a point of calling into question their authenticity, or that make a point of highlighting their artistry. But the kinds of photographs that tend to be featured in texts bent on conveying information are rarely such photographs. Barthes describes what he calls "unary" photographs, which he dubs "the most widespread in the world" (*Camera Lucida,* 40). "The Photograph is unary," he explains, "when it emphatically transforms 'reality' without doubling it, without making it vacillate (emphasis is a power of cohesion): no duality, no indirection, no disturbance" (41). To Barthes, unary photographs are artistically disappointing because they try to throttle any opportunity for alternative interpretations: they attempt to speak univocally, to communicate one piece of information from a specific (and anonymous) perspective. He finds that the unary photograph is especially common in news reports, and considering the similar impulse of reportage and nonfiction to disguise bias and speak with authority, it is reasonable to think that unary photographs will be similarly common in nonfiction. Such photography quietly insists on its own authority to speak about the information it contains and to limit the understanding of that information. And an insistence on authority is the surest sign of a resistance to critical engagement.[1]

Katharine Capshaw's extraordinary book *Civil Rights Childhood* provides some hope, though, that we may look to photography in children's literature for opportunities for critical engagement, and this chapter will follow her lead. She examines how children's photobooks have participated in social justice movements, especially those invested in securing the civil rights of black Americans in the second half of the twentieth century. Capshaw theorizes that the photobook as a form routinely "spurs consideration of [its] own constructed nature," meaning that the photobook is, in fact, an "it" that we see. In a turn of phrase with direct relevance to my own study, Capshaw writes that "the stitches and seams of a photographic book become apparent" because of the photobook's constructed nature (xiii). Capshaw's entire analysis is dedicated to children's books—some of them nonfiction, some of them fiction—that use photographs, and as such, she has to struggle with exactly the same insistence on authority that threatens the use of photography in nonfiction. Her point is not that photographs themselves reveal their "stitches and seams" but that something about the aesthetics of the photobook, something about that form itself, transforms the authoritative photographs into an argument with which readers can grapple. Following Capshaw, I do not contend that nonfiction as a genre works to undercut the authority of the photographs it deploys but that there are specific aesthetic choices that can pull those seams tighter.

This chapter asks how a work of nonfiction wants its readers to interact with the photography in its pages. Are we asked to take the photographs as transparent truths? Are we guided to focus on certain information within the photograph? Are we urged to ask questions about the content of the photograph or how the photograph was made? Are we supposed to doubt either the photograph's content or its origins? In short, are we supposed to see the photographs, or are we supposed to see through them? Photographs pose an obstacle to critical engagement, at least as dominant theories of photographs would have us believe. How and when do works of children's nonfiction present photographs in ways that treat them as venues for testable information produced by fallible human beings? This chapter explores how books use captions, prose, layout, and other elements to indicate that a photograph is something to be interpreted. In some cases, the photograph remains more or less transparent, but even in cases such as these, when the photograph is not the "it" that we see, the picture still offers as its subject matter evidence that readers are invited or even directed to analyze. More interestingly, a book can point us to a photograph in a way that makes the photograph opaque, thereby asking us to think about it as a photograph, as something taken and shaped and therefore shot through with perspective, intention, imperfection, and bias. Photography has a long history of authority, and this chapter examines how moments within children's nonfiction sustain and complicate that history.

The Voices and Characters of Critical Engagement in Photography

My previous chapter dealt with peritexts and began an analysis of captions, and much of the point of that chapter extends to this one, often in fairly simple and straightforward examples. Tonya Bolden's *Maritcha*, whose author's note explains the provenance of the images in the book, uses captions with hedges that explain, for example, what toys Maritcha "may" have played with (8). Here the caption accompanies a photograph of an image from the same period as Maritcha's childhood, and the caption encourages a reading that keeps in mind that the photograph should not be taken with utter confidence: Bolden has a good reason to believe that the toys in the photograph match those of Maritcha's experiences, but her hedge (as defined in chapter 2) places a filter of doubt over the information in the image. Susan Campbell Bartoletti's book on the Ku Klux Klan provides a photograph of a scene of devastation and accompanies it with a caption that reads, "This 1865 photograph of ruined houses shows the total destruction that some planters suffered in Savannah, Georgia, possibly as a result of the Union bombardment or General Sherman's campaign, known as the 'march to the sea'" (*They*, 8). This caption retains the sense of desolation implicit in the photograph but confesses that this photograph—much like those Bolden uses—is only *likely* to be exactly relevant to the historical event under consideration. A caption in Marc Aronson's *If Stones Could Speak* accompanies a wide-shot photograph of an archaeological dig and explains that "natural ridges" such as the ones in the photograph "may have looked like parallel lines running to Stonehenge and were marked by ditches and banks" (50). This caption directs attention to specific parts of the photograph (the ridges) and explains both what the archaeologists still question—whether the ridges had a specific relationship to the path to Stonehenge—and that which the archaeologists no longer debate: how ridges are marked in the geological evidence. In each case, these captions protect a space for legitimate skepticism and make a visible point of explaining how the evidence in the photograph probably validates a specific conclusion. In doing so, they imply that photographs should be read as sources of information that can be evaluated, not as evidence that appears before the reader already tested and approved.

In my second chapter, I borrowed Sam Wineburg's idea of the "necromancer" to explain how a text can help readers reanimate the voices of a debate, and this strategy, too, presents a fairly straightforward opportunity for captions to frame a photograph as a target of inquiry rather than a transparent window to truth. Sue Macy's biography of Annie Oakley uses this technique in its captions on more than one occasion. A caption accompanying one early photograph says, "Some people believe this picture shows Susan Moses, Annie's mother. Others, however, believe it is Matilda Shaw, the first wife of Annie's stepfather Joseph Shaw" (*Bull's-Eye*, 10). Later, alongside a reproduction of a greeting card, Macy's caption explains, "According to some sources, Annie's 1891 Christmas card, mailed to her friends and family from England, was one of the first personalized greeting cards ever sent out at the Christmas season" (39). In these cases, the captions present photographs as contested knowledge, enriching Macy's presentation of Oakley's life as a story in which legend and truth mingle endlessly. Captions such as these present their photographs as evidence about which sensible people disagree, which discourages an automatic submission to the photographs as truths to accept unreflectively.

At times, captions will point to what the current state of research does *not* know, a technique that I argued (in chapter 3) often signals an invitation to critical engagement. This, too, is a fairly simple technique for a book to use or a reader to spot, but its presence is especially significant in the context of the theory of photography that I have sketched out. In Bolden's *Searching for Sarah Rector,* one caption gives a few specifics of which it is confident but then identifies other details about which it is unsure:

> Cushing-Crumright Field, c. 1912–15. In the car on the left is Bernard Bryan "B.B." Jones, riding shotgun with his brother Robert E. Lee Jones. The white man in the second car is another brother: Montfort. Precisely who the Indians are in both cars is a mystery. Like Sarah, they could be the owners of land Jones leased for oil drilling. (22)

Scott Reynolds Nelson's story of his search for the man behind the story of steel-driving John Henry contains a similar caption. Alongside a photograph of a black man, Nelson writes, "John Henry, a worker in the headquarters of the 3rd Army Corps, in 1863 (opposite). I would like to think that this was the John Henry later arrested in Prince George County, but we may never know" (*Ain't Nothing but a Man,* 43). Both captions contain a note of poignancy, Nelson's perhaps especially so, as their comments provide a tension with the security that photographs generally offer. The photographs give evidence that someone existed, someone whose name and fate was known at the time of the picture, someone whose meaning was significant, but the captions draw attention to the void where that meaning is for contemporary viewers. Bolden and Nelson are writing books about the process of looking for someone, about the mystery of research, and these captions skillfully turn photographs—which generally represent answers and the end of a mystery—into reminders of the knowledge that we have not finished discovering.

Before I move into more complicated techniques for inviting critical engagement with photographs, I want to highlight one more straightforward strategy, one that gets right to the heart of the problem of photography's authenticity. An easy example comes from Macy's biography of Annie Oakley, where a caption for a portrait of Oakley reads, "With a brown wig covering her white hair, Annie looked a lot younger than her 51 years when she posed for this photograph in 1911" (*Bull's-Eye,* 48). This caption does something remarkable: despite the consensus opinion that photographs tend to be read as reliable windows to truth, this caption tells readers not to trust the photograph. And I am delighted to say that such counterintuitive moments are surprisingly common in the field. Another book notes that although the date of a historical event is inscribed on a piece of metal featured in an accompanying photograph, "someone . . . got the date wrong" (Fleischman, *Phineas,* 73). Bolden's *Maritcha* provides a photograph of documentation that the girl's father submitted following a riot and notes that this date, too, is incorrect (30). A caption in Aronson's *If Stones Could Speak* directs skepticism toward not just a detail of a photograph but the entire professional ethos symbolized (and apparently testified to) in that photograph:

> [Richard] Atkinson was a brilliant man and a skilled archaeologist who directed work at Stonehenge between 1950 and 1978. But while in this photo he takes precise measurements with measuring tape, he chose not to write up and share his research with fellow scholars. That is one reason archaeologists today are carefully reviewing his work to understand what he did and where he was right or wrong. (32)

These examples directly contradict the reliability that is part and parcel of so much photography. Such handling effectively turns photographs into evidence that should be read skeptically rather than being accepted as testaments to truth.

Even more dramatically, Bartoletti frames a photograph of Civil War veterans in a way that specifically resists its evidentiary qualities. The context she offers drenches the photograph in irony:

> Former Yankee and Rebel soldiers shake hands in reconciliation at the 1913 Peace Jubilee, marking the fiftieth anniversary of the battle of Gettysburg. That year also marked the fiftieth anniversary of the Emancipation Proclamation. By 1913, most of the nation had embraced white supremacy and had sanctioned Jim Crow laws. That year alone, white mobs lynched fifty-one black Americans. (*They*, 144)

The irony of the photograph encourages a reading that directly opposes the photograph's unary intention. Accompanied by this caption, the photograph becomes a biting condemnation of the official (which is to say, white and wealthy) story of the Civil War and postwar reconciliation. The caption pierces the narrative that the photograph wants to tell instead of taking the photograph as a complete, true story. As such, Bartoletti's handling of the photograph, and the handling of all of these photographs, makes these images into, as Sontag would have it, mysteries, packed full of intrigue, disingenuity, and outright lies.

Directing Inquiry That Ends

These examples show fairly simple ways that captions can complicate the authority of photographs, widening opportunities for critical engagement, but the prose and photographs of nonfiction can also interact in more nuanced ways, often with more complicated consequences. Take for example Bolden's book about a black girl at the beginning of the twentieth century who owned a piece of land under which was discovered a very lucrative oil deposit. Bolden follows a photograph of a legal document with this caption:

> Above: An important piece of paperwork in the 1905 application for Sarah's allotment. This affidavit (statement of facts under oath) says that Sarah's parents were members of the Creek Nation. Therefore, so was she. The midwife, Amy Jackson, who attested to Sarah's birth on March 3, 1902, was most likely Sarah's maternal grandmother. (*Searching*, 19)

This caption meets many of the standards for an invitation to critical engagement that I have outlined earlier in my study. It treats the photograph not as a lifeless testament but as a piece of evidence to be scrutinized in sections. It draws attention to the information provided in the photograph about Sarah's parents, and it walks its reader through the process of drawing a conclusion. It also highlights information about the woman identified as the midwife and speculates—with a hedge that gives it an air of humility—about her relationship to the girl. Such modeling of critical engagement is clearly in the spirit of the sort of invitation for which I have been searching throughout my study.

Myra Zarnowski praises this sort of caption, but I have some—perhaps unfair—qualms all the same. Zarnowski considers books by two important authors and produces a list of six ways that these authors "ma[k]e their captions meaningful." Authors using these techniques might, she explains, "point out details we might not have noticed." They can also "give additional information beyond what is in either the text or the illustration," "give opinions," "speculate," or make use of "relational terms to direct the reader's attention" to one part or another of the photograph (*History*, 79). One of the authors whom Zarnowski examines is John Fleischman, author of *Phineas Gage: A Gruesome but True Story about Brain Science*, which I discussed in chapter 3. When I look at this book, I see many examples of the sorts of captions that Zarnowski notes, such as the following description facing a photograph of nineteenth-century surgeons at work:

> Notice two things about Hawes's picture. First, it's all men. There are no female hospital nurses, let alone female doctors. The second thing you should notice is what the doctors are wearing—nothing special. They are in street clothes—black frockcoats, shiny satin vests, and linen shirts. No one is wearing surgical scrubs. No one is wearing surgical gloves, masks, or booties. These doctors may not wash their hands until *after* the operation. These men know nothing about bacteria—but they think they know all about the brain. (24)

Fleischman guides the reader to notice specific elements and provides interpretations of them. He also provides an opinion of the photograph, one that pokes holes in the authority of the somber, impressive men populating the photograph. Indeed, in this one passage, he does nearly all the things that Zarnowski notes in her list. And Zarnowski's claim that such language makes the photograph more meaningful can hardly be contested: these words foreground the sexism, arrogance, and frankly deadly ignorance of the men pictured. It's an evocative frame of reference in a powerful book with important implications for critical engagement.

But in this example and Bolden's caption following the photograph of some of Sarah Rector's paperwork, I worry that the language bears the trappings of an invitation to critical engagement without exactly inviting such engagement. Photographs in children's nonfiction have a strong potential to offer what Freire calls "codifications." As I observed in my Introduction, Freire even mentions photographs as the kind of isolated observation that can be presented to students to represent "an existential problem" in the ubiquitous ideology of their oppressive societies (*Pedagogy*, 106n). The consciousness raising that is enabled by critical engagement begins, in the words of Janet L. Freedman's book on feminist vision, with an "aha" moment in which "women become aware of how sexism affects their lives" (*Reclaiming*, 11), and the technique of severing one moment from those around it, a technique that all but defines photography, can serve that purpose very well. Bolden's caption only alludes to the structures of power and dispossession encoded in paperwork documenting the ownership of property, but Fleischman's caption is an admirable, even prototypical example of how to use a snapshot moment to unveil the ideologies implicit in it.

Still, there is something in these captions that narrows rather than opens room for critical engagement. Recall the line from Sontag with which I opened: "Photographs, which cannot themselves explain anything, are inexhaustible invitations to deduction, speculation, and fantasy" (*On Photography*, 23). I offered that observation as evidence that photography has great potential for invitations to critical engagement, and in this quotation, Sontag's point links directly with Freire's definition of codifications, which Freire explains will "offer various decoding possibilities in order to avoid the brain-washing tendencies of propaganda" (*Pedagogy*, 107). Although these captions do model the process of interrogating information, they lack the *multiple* possibilities for interpretation on which Sontag and Freire insist. Both captions model a process of critical engagement, but the captions do not so much invite readers to the process of that engagement as they do lead readers into one *solitary* conclusion. They provide the meat of interpretation and then narrow the possibilities down to one. Zarnowski's argument in her discussion of captions and throughout her work on nonfiction is that such modeling is sufficient for a child to learn to imitate the process, especially when that child is guided by a good teacher, and I can hardly argue with her, considering her remarkable career as a teacher and scholar. Still, from my probably uncharitable perspective, there is something about these sorts of captions that *almost* succeeds. Modeling critical engagement in a way that leads to preordained conclusions feels to me like a step toward enabling critical engagement, but not precisely an instance of inviting a reader into the immediate act of engaging critically. Rather, I read it more as a record of the author's critical engagement than as an opening for a reader to perform original critical engagement, and as such, it retains the authority of photographs, this time routed into the authority of the final conclusions that the captions draw.

Studying Photographs

What, then, are methods for a more profound invitation to critical engagement in the presentation of photographs? Zarnowski mentions briefly one technique that I think does much more to present information in a way that invites original analysis than does the previous technique. In praising Fleischman's book, she pays specific attention to "how several captions suggested comparing one illustration with another" (*History,* 78). This insight is very useful in opening up how books label and position photographs. At times, the photographs, their layout, and their accompanying text offer little to no guidance in how to interpret the pictures, but the scope for comparison is significant. Patricia Lauber's *Volcano: The Eruption and Healing of Mount St. Helens* (1986) uses this technique repeatedly, as on one page where a caption above two large photographs says simply, "Boot Lake before and after the eruption" (19). The photographs, evidently taken from almost exactly the same vantage point, provide multiple opportunities for thoughtful contrast, from the shape of the hill hidden by evergreens in one photograph and laid starkly bare in the next to the multihued pond in the first picture and the dull slate water in the second. And of course the list goes on and on: there is no way to anticipate all of the points of comparison between the two photographs, and every single one is another opportunity for original critical engagement. In each such pairing, Lauber sets the evidence up to encourage a certain conclusion (in this case, the stunning lifelessness of the forest after the mountain's eruption), but I have said all along that inviting a reader to critical engagement at no point requires authors to pretend that they have no interpretations themselves. The idea that authors should write without bias is absurd, so I don't object to an author having a position. Lauber presents her photographs in such a way as to encourage comparison between them, and that comparison requires treating the photographs as pieces of evidence to pit against one another, which complicates the tone of authority in photographs that makes them a threat to critical engagement.

I am especially fond of Lauber's photographs because they model how to offer evidence through which readers can find their

Two images presented next to each other allow unstructured comparison without sacrificing an implied conclusion. Patricia Lauber, *Volcano: The Eruption and Healing of Mount St. Helens* (1986), page 19.

own paths, but nonfiction's handling of photography does not have to be quite so lenient to invite critical engagement. Millicent E. Selsam's *Hidden Animals* (1947), a rare example of experimental nonfiction in an early reader, frequently uses photography and layout to allow a more directed but still reader-centered exploration of data. As an early reader, *Hidden Animals* works within very tight genre constrictions. Such books must use language and illustration in ways that support the struggling efforts of children transitioning from the reading position encouraged by picture books—in which an older person reads the book aloud to the listening child—to the reading position required by novels, in which a child must be enough of a master of the written language to understand more complicated syntax and vocabulary. With such limitations, early readers often ignore more artistic, metaphorical uses of language and image, preferring to offer simple words with illustrations that directly mirror the explicit meaning of those words. Selsam's book, however, often asks readers to pause in their reading to consult an illustration and search it carefully. For example, one page facing a photograph asks,

> This animal lives on the floor of the sea.
> It is called a stonefish.
> Do you see it? (17)

A black-and-white photograph opposite the words displays a stonefish on a sandy floor, underwater, with other, similarly colored rocks surrounding it. Picking out the stonefish certainly is a challenge at first, at least until one notices the open eye on one of the supposed rocks. On the next spread, the book presents the same image, this time with everything in the image except the stonefish grayed out, delaying the revelation of the stonefish until after readers have had an opportunity to search for it on their own. Selsam uses this technique twice more—once with a snake concealed in leaves (25), again with birds (30)—and each time, she offers a photograph for exploration before a page turn that reveals the conclusion that she wants her readers to draw. The careful use of layout allows for a reader-directed search for evidence, and although the conclusion—the fish/snake/bird is *here*—is foreordained, the photographs support a period of examination of and, perhaps, comparison between images that is the essence of critical engagement.[2]

One recent book demonstrates the fine distinction that I am attempting to draw between the sort of modeling that Zarnowski praises and the openness to interpretation for which I am searching. Nelson's *Ain't Nothing but a Man: My Quest to Find the Real John Henry* tells the story of how the author developed a powerful theory about the origins of the John Henry mentioned in so many folk songs, and that story centers around a photograph. Nelson mentions

The postcard image referenced in Scott Reynolds Nelson, *Ain't Nothing but a Man: My Quest to Find the Real John Henry* (2008). The back of the card identifies it as a "view from Gambles Hill Park" of the state penitentiary in Richmond, Virginia. Nelson introduces the importance of the image as key evidence and provides information to help readers search the evidence for relevant information, but he refrains from giving his own interpretation until after the page turn. Image courtesy of Cardcow.com.

the photograph early in the narrative, where he portrays himself frustrated by a lack of direction in his research. He recalls, "I had a book open on my lap. I had scanned an old postcard from the period I was studying to be the background of my computer monitor. I was surrounded with research, and I did not know what to write" (7). Two pages later, Nelson returns to the mention of that photograph, and this time he flags it as a key breakthrough in his research. "I was sitting at my computer," he remembers, "cruising, trawling for anything that might come my way. And then as I stared at the scanned postcard I had seen a thousand times before, I suddenly saw it, the clue that changed everything" (9). In these and other hints throughout the book, Nelson points to the photograph—or more accurately, something in the photograph—as key to explaining the mystery of the book. Most of the middle of the book explains other aspects of the historical context for the photograph, but throughout, Nelson skillfully builds a mystery, narrating in first person (thus qualifying as a visible author) the mistakes and frustrations of all his failed attempts to solve the mystery. The photograph itself doesn't appear until page 34, and the order of presentation of information both models a process of reading a photograph for a certain interpretation and delays explaining that interpretation long enough to open a space for readers to try to solve the mystery first on their own. Here on the left-hand (verso) page, a simple caption accompanies a large photograph. The caption reads, "The postcard from 1910 that I used as my desktop wallpaper" (34). Readers have been directed to consider this image carefully, and its delayed appearance as well as the caption's identification of this picture as the photograph to which Nelson has been alluding throughout work together to dramatize the importance of the evidence without quite saying what is important about it. On the facing (recto) page, Nelson's prose again prompts the reader to consider the photograph and even drops the hint on which Nelson himself finally seized. Nelson reproduces a verse of a song that "kept coming into my mind":

> *They took John Henry to the white house,*
> *And buried him in the san'*
> *And every locomotive come roarin' by,*
> *Says there lays that steel drivin' man,*
> *Says there lays that steel drivin' man.* (35)

Nelson then writes that he "looked up at my screen, where I had saved the postcard shown on page 34. The image had become a background blur to me; I hardly paid attention to it. And then I saw it, and I finally understood the picture that unlocked the secret of John Henry" (35). Just after the page turn—and that placement is significant—Nelson reveals the connection that he made between the song and the photograph: "Most of the buildings were tinted red, suggesting the color of brick. One, though, blazed white. And running by the prison were train tracks" (35–36).

This sequence—foreshadowing the importance of the photograph, presenting the photograph, offering the linking song, and then finally explaining exactly what connection Nelson made—answers Zarnowski's call for modeling critical inquiry, and despite my qualms about such modeling in other examples, even I have to admit that the repeated delay of giving the answer to the book's persistent mystery allows space for readers to run through the "various decoding possibilities" that Freire said must be possible in a codification. When Zarnowski and I agree on the value of encouraging comparison, a technique we can find in Lauber's book, what we are really agreeing on is creating a venue on the page in which readers can process evidence themselves. Nelson's thoughtful—and, let's not forget, compelling—mystery narrative, with its early planting of evidence and late solution to the question, is a more eager invitation to critical engagement. These books by Lauber, Selsam, and Nelson use photographs to provide evidence, and even if the authors draw a certain conclusion from the illustrations, they provide room for the exercise of study and interpretation.

Photography in Russell Freedman's *Lincoln*

For the rest of the chapter, I want to turn to one author whose influence and major works have been closely tied to photography: Russell Freedman. Two writers, Seymour Simon and Patricia Lauber, significantly contributed to the popularization of photography in children's nonfiction at about the same time that Freedman was rising to prominence. In fact, Lauber's book about Mount St. Helens, which I examined in the previous section, won a Newbery Honor in 1987, the same year that Freedman's most famous book was published, and the heavy reliance of Lauber's book on photography signals that the field was beginning to skew toward that medium before Freedman made his mark. Nonetheless, Freedman's *Lincoln: A Photobiography* (1987) represents a turning point for the market. Kathleen T. Isaacs argues that "although Freedman was not the first to use photographs to add interest and information to children's books, his use of photos from the times [about which he wrote], combined with in-depth research and eloquent writing, became both a trademark and a model for authors who followed" ("Facts," 11). Leonard S. Marcus credits Freedman with inventing the name "photobiography," and he points out that when the Lincoln biography won the Newbery Medal, "it had been more than forty years since a work of nonfiction last won the big prize" (*Minders,* 307). Photography had appeared in earlier children's nonfiction: an 1893 book for children about the World's Fair published by Century, for example, is bursting with photographs (Jenks, *Century*), and Katharine Capshaw's recent work on photobooks documents their wide distribution and political use from the 1940s to today (Capshaw, *Civil Rights*). But when Freedman's book won the most prestigious (and potentially lucrative) award for American children's literature, the first time a work of nonfiction had won the award in generations, that win provided evidence that nonfiction heavily illustrated with photographs could be a financial success in the contemporary market. The year of its publication fell during an explosion of growth in children's literature, a market that doubled between 1986 and 1990 (Schwebel, *Child-Size,* 2). Its influence on photography in children's nonfiction, then, is hard to overstate.

Many of the strengths of photography in contemporary children's nonfiction are evident already in the Lincoln book. For example, Freedman places photographs next to each other to encourage comparison between them. Often, such comparisons foster a grim tone, as when four photograph portraits of Lincoln taken in 1861, 1862, 1863, and 1864 appear across a page break from a full-page portrait of Lincoln taken on April 10, 1865 (116–17). A caption reads, "The strain of war. A sampling of photographs taken during Lincoln's four years in office shows how the pressures and anxieties of the war became etched in his face" (116). As with Lauber's photographs of Mount St. Helens, in these images Freedman encourages drawing a particular conclusion from the photographs, but again, inviting the reader to perform the act of comparison is an invitation to handle evidence, which fits the sort of invitation to critical engagement I am seeking. Earlier in the book, Freedman uses the same technique to foster a lighter tone, as he places four photographs next to each other, and the captions highlight Lincoln's decision to grow the beard that is so familiar today. The first picture bears a caption reading, "Lincoln's last beardless portrait, August 13, 1860," and the caption for the next picture reads, "The president-elect sprouts whiskers, November 25, 1860" (64). On the facing page, Lincoln continues to grow his beard, first in a photograph with the caption

"Lincoln with a full beard, January 13, 1861. 'Old Abe is... puttin' on (h)airs!' a newspaper joked." The final photograph in the sequence shows the completion of the beard he would wear throughout his presidency, this one labeled "February 9, 1861. Two days later, Lincoln left for Washington to become the first bearded president of the United States" (65). The series highlighting Lincoln's beard is of course more trivial, but it operates in much the same way as the "strain of war" series in the penultimate chapter. Although the captions clearly encourage a particular conclusion, they also offer the opportunity and invitation to practice the comparison of evidence. Too, by animating Lincoln's life and pointing out how he changed, these photographs humanize Lincoln, a technique that I argued in chapter 3 often works to make historical figures more welcoming to critical engagement. In fact, the levity in the beard sequence might even make Lincoln more vulnerable to such engagement than the other, more serious sorts of humanizing I have explored. Freedman's presentation of photographs alongside one another and indication of points for comparison is hardly original to his work, but his skill with it creates opportunities for critical engagement from a variety of approaches.

One of my points in this chapter is the challenge that photography poses to critical engagement through its transparency, its ability to hide the fact that it interprets the data that it shares even as it is in the act of sharing, and the photobiography's treatment of the medium offers a powerful response to that concern. One of the major themes of the book is photography itself, by which I mean photography as a newly emergent technology and, more importantly, an unreliable technology. In Freedman's section on the Gettysburg Address, for example, he writes that "a photographer in the crowd fiddled with his camera, preparing to take a picture of the president as he spoke. But before he could get the camera ready, the speech was finished" (101). In this brief scene, photography fails. The photographer and the camera were not ready and could not capture the truth, and I don't think it unfair to hear in this statement the implication that if photography was not fast enough for this moment, there are infinite other moments for which it has been equally inadequate. Freedman also notes that

> Lincoln was the most photographed man of his time, but his friends insisted that no photo ever did him justice. It's no wonder. Back then, cameras required long exposures. The person being photographed had to "freeze" as the seconds ticked by. If he blinked an eye, the picture would be blurred. That's why Lincoln looks so stiff and formal in his photos. We never see him laughing or joking. (2)

Freedman applies the same skepticism even to the photographs he furnishes in the book. He provides a photograph labeled "Thomas Lincoln" and then immediately questions its reliability (10). He records an instance in which Lincoln looked at a portrait of himself and compared its truthfulness to the others he had seen (facing page 1), and he later records Lincoln's observation that although he found one portrait "very true," Mary Todd Lincoln "and many others" did not (40). In a caption to the last portrait Lincoln would live to have taken, a photograph with a plainly visible flaw in it, Freedman writes, "As [Alexander] Gardner was taking the photograph, the glass-plate negative cracked across the top" (117). By drawing attention to the flaw in the photograph and connecting it with the process of making a photograph, Freedman ensures that the medium itself is visible. Over and over again, photographs in the photobiography are exactly the "it" that we see, a medium that fails or produces information whose meaning is contested from virtually the moment that the shutter snaps.

I have an enormous amount of admiration for this book. It represents a watershed moment in the history of children's nonfiction: its critical and financial successes helped move nonfiction back into the mainstream for children's trade publishing, and its heavy reliance on photography did a great deal to set the style of the genre in the decades that followed. My most profound admiration for the photobiography, though, springs from the fact that in this book that dedicates so much space to photography, Freedman makes one of his major themes the reminder that photography should not be trusted. In the very book that made photography a nigh-inevitable element of children's nonfiction, there is a resistance to the authority of photography that is taken for granted in so many other venues.

The photobiography does, though, allow some photographs to

remain transparent, and the distinction between which photographs are made into objects of study and which are not is revealing. From time to time, the captions present the photographs as opaque, as when one caption nudges readers to pick out a specific detail, such as the "fashionable stovepipe hats" in the accompanying photograph (66). Perhaps the best example of opaque images is of a photograph from a rare genre. The caption Freedman provides explains, "Because cameras required long exposures, Civil War photographers could not take clear action shots. This photograph, taken at Antietam in September 1862, is believed to be the only actual battle picture of the entire war" (87).[3] This caption, of course, demonstrates a great deal of what I have been arguing in this chapter and the

Originally titled "View of Battle-field of Antietam, on day of battle, Sept. 17, 1862," this photograph was attributed to Mathew B. Brady but was probably shot by Alexander Gardner and his photography crew. Russell Freedman uses this image in his photobiography *Lincoln* (1987). My student called it a "terrible" photograph, meaning that its poor aesthetic qualities constantly remind us that it *is* a photograph. Image courtesy of the McMahan Photo Art Gallery and Archive.

last: the peritext invites critical engagement with the photograph, its provenance, and the adequacy of the medium. Furthermore, the photograph itself is one that all but refutes its own authority. When I taught the photobiography in a recent university course, one of my students, Rachel Smith, said, with no sense of disdain, "This is a terrible photograph." When I pressed her to explain, she provided a powerful insight: this photograph—with its unimportant, unnamed character in the foreground, its wasted space running up the middle, its barely distinguishable horses idling in boring contradiction with the supposed drama of the moment, its wispy smoke failing to highlight or tantalizingly obscure anything, its complete lack of a single clear human actor on the battlefield—is an aesthetic mess, missing all of the univocality of a good photograph. Echoing Sontag and Barthes, Smith went on to point out that this photograph constantly reminds us of the fact that it is a photograph, that its shutter was too slow, that its position was too far removed, that its composition failed to tell a story. It *is* a terrible photograph. A good photograph erases itself, but this one is more a testament to the fact that it is a photograph than to any content that it might document.

Brady's Antietam photograph appears on the recto, and turning to the following verso reveals a photograph that could hardly be more different. Here Freedman writes simply, "Dead soldiers lie where they fell on the battlefield at Antietam" (88). The caption focuses on the content of the photograph, not the medium itself, and the image above the caption is, to invert my student's observation, an excellent photograph. Every detail—the stones, the ruined grass, the pale fingernails in a corpse's grimy hand—comes through with sharp clarity. A wooden rail fence stretches diagonally from the right side, and the lack of a similar line on the left leaves the image eloquently unbalanced. The bodies splay in positions that suggest the action, violence, chaos, and surprise of the moment in which, as the caption puts it, "they fell."[4] This photograph, an exquisite photograph, speaks with one voice and erases its status as artificial. The caption similarly ignores the medium to consider only the content. Although a major theme of the book is photography itself, in this photograph, the medium is forgotten, and any opportunity to engage with it critically is buried.

156 ◼ *Seeing Photographs*

Originally captioned "View in the Field, on the west side of Hagerstown road, after the Battle of Antietam," this photograph was likely taken by Alexander Gardner and his photography crew on September 19, 1862. Russell Freedman uses this image in his photobiography *Lincoln* (1987). Freedman's caption, "Dead soldiers lie where they fell on the battlefield at Antietam" (88) and the photograph itself ask us to forget that it is a photograph and think about its content. Image courtesy of Wikimedia Commons.

As I have puzzled over the difference between these two photographs, I have come to think that there is a default position in this book and a position from which Freedman sometimes departs to make a different point. The default position of the Lincoln book—by which I mean the default position in the images as well as in the peritexts and prose—is one that encourages critical engagement with his subject. Specifically, the default position *about Lincoln* is one that encourages such engagement. Freedman opens the book with a mixture of praise and criticism of Lincoln: indeed, right after he first introduces the theme of untrustworthy photography, he gives eight paragraphs in a row of contradictions in Lincoln's personality. He seemed common, but he was actually ambitious. He was called sloppy, but he bought expensive clothes. He was abysmally educated, but he had all the hallmarks of someone well educated. He was funny but "melancholy," logical but superstitious, "an American folk hero" today but massively unpopular for much of his presidency (4–5). Later, Freedman describes Lincoln's troubled marriage, and although he concedes that life was difficult with Mary Todd, he also explains that it was difficult with Abraham:

> His untidiness followed him home from the office. He cared little for the social niceties that were so important to his wife. He was absent-minded, perpetually late for meals. He was away from home for weeks at a time, leaving Mary alone with a big house to run and children to care for. And he was moody, lapsing into long brooding silences. (41)

Freedman routinely lingers over Lincoln's failures, further complicating any narrative of a great man invulnerable to questions. He calls Lincoln's two-year congressional term "a disappointment" (36) and highlights Lincoln's Senate race loss to Stephen Douglas (60). Freedman even quotes Lincoln comparing himself to Douglas: "With *me*, the race of ambition has been a failure—a flat failure. . . . With *him* [Douglas] it has been one of splendid success" (55). Freedman's prose is filled with observations of Lincoln's flaws, and in writing Lincoln this way, Freedman offers Lincoln as a character so deserving of doubt that he doubted himself.

Elsewhere in the prose, Freedman also portrays a Lincoln vulnerable in his political positions. Freedman repeatedly highlights how Lincoln wavered in difficult decisions, including decisions that we now regard as his most incontrovertible. The decision to defend and supply Fort Sumter, for example, was made not by a Lincoln with a firm hand and clear conscience but by one who was profoundly unsure of what to do. "He consulted with his military staff and members of his cabinet," Freedman recounts, "but they could not agree on what should be done. Lincoln himself was uncertain. All the troubles and anxieties of his life, he later said, were nothing compared to the weeks that followed" (72). Such fluctuation is a routine part of Freedman's portrayal of Lincoln, even when he describes Lincoln's position on the single issue that most defines his legacy today: slavery. Although Freedman sometimes uses Douglas as a foil for Lincoln's string of public failures and gangly physical appearance, he pointedly refuses to turn Douglas into a caricature of Democrats friendly to slavery, instead recording the central points of the Lincoln–Douglas debates in a way that makes clear the rhetorical strategies and ideas of both men (59–60). As a result, Douglas never looks purely stupid and wrong or Lincoln purely sharp and heroic, which means that the two positions can be tested rather than immediately rejected or absorbed. And although during his early Washington career Lincoln did, as Freedman reports, claim a position against slavery, "for the most part, he sat silently in the background as Congress rang with angry debates over slavery's future" (46). Freedman even notes how, during the war, Lincoln hesitated over the issue of slavery, acting upon self-reflection and self-criticism rather than with righteous conviction. Freedman calls this Lincoln's "toughest decision," explaining that "early in the war, he was still willing to leave slavery alone in the South, if only he could restore the Union." "We didn't," Freedman records Lincoln as saying, "go into the war to put down slavery, but to put the flag back. . . . To act differently at this moment would, I have no doubt, not only weaken our cause, but smack of bad faith" (82, 84). Although Frederick Douglass, for example, excoriated the president for it, "Lincoln hesitated" (84). The book also confides that Lincoln wasn't even sure that he had the presidential authority to outlaw slavery in states where the institution was legal (85). James W. Loewen's 1994 survey of American history textbooks levels a scathing criticism of books that present Lincoln as a clear-sighted, virtuous leader who knew slavery was wrong and would let nothing stand in his way as he uprooted it from American soil (*Lies,* 154). In Freedman's 1987 photobiography of the president, we get exactly the complicated, hesitant, and ultimately human Lincoln for whom Loewen would later scour textbooks in vain.

The default position of Freedman's biography in the prose as well as the photographs is one that makes the evidence and historical figure under consideration available to interpretation, and the times when the book allows its photographs to remain transparent are much less common, but there is a pattern to those exceptions, too. Early in the narrative, for example, Freedman gives likenesses of Abraham and Mary Todd Lincoln. The first caption identifies the uppermost image as "Lincoln as a thirty-seven-year-old prairie lawyer in 1846" and explains that "this daguerreotype is the earliest known camera portrait of Lincoln." The caption for the second image reads, "Mary Lincoln as a twenty-eight-year-old wife and mother in 1846. The Lincolns had been married for four years and had two sons when they sat for these companion portraits. 'They are very precious to me,' Mary said later, 'taken when we were young and so desperately in love'" (26). Giving the dates of the portraits, naming them as "daguerreotypes," and providing the context for their shooting does something to remind us of the fact that the images are products, but on the whole, the tone of the captions encourages reading those images as transparent windows to truth, to the youth and early love of the Lincolns. The captions encourage not skeptical reading but trust in the testament to youth and romance implicit in the images. Later, during a chapter on the war, Freedman gives a photograph on the recto with this caption: "Many recruits on both sides of the Civil War were scarcely more than boys. This is a portrait of Edwin Jennison, a Georgia private, killed in action at Malvern Hill on July 1, 1862" (75). The caption makes the photograph a piece of evidence, but not one to be tangled with and questioned. Instead, the photograph mirrors a claim made on the facing page: "By early summer, both sides were training large armies of volunteers, many of them inexperienced boys who could barely handle a rifle" (74). Shortly thereafter, Freedman again pairs language on the verso with images on the recto, again in a way that suggests that the photographs are trustworthy evidence rather than information to be interpreted. On page 80, Freedman writes about Lincoln's agony following the death of his son Willie: "Lincoln plunged into the deepest gloom he had ever known. He had felt a special bond of understanding with Willie, and now he grieved as never before. Again and again, he shut himself in his room to weep alone." The facing page offers photographs of his two sons, accompanied by captions. The first reads, "Thomas ('Tad') Lincoln, the youngest son, in his colonel's uniform. Tad and Willie were the first presidential children to live in the White House." The second reads, "William Wallace ('Willie') Lincoln. His death in the White House in 1862 plunged the Lincolns into profound sorrow. 'He was too good for this earth,' the president was heard to say. 'It is hard, hard to have him die'" (81). Although most of the book takes as its default position that Lincoln and his photographs should be open to questions, these photographs—similar to the "good" Antietam photograph—act as transparent windows to truth, and the words with which Freedman accompanies them routinely support that approach.

Part of my argument throughout this study of children's nonfiction is that paying attention to those instances in which texts invite or discourage critical engagement can enable a better understanding of the texts themselves and the arguments that they are making. The striking contrast between these two ways in which Freedman treats photographs—most as opaque, some as transparent—similarly illuminates the project of his photobiography. In the examples of photographs in which Freedman deviates from his standard technique, what is at stake is grief. In other words, a grieving engagement is the sort of engagement for which Freedman appears willing, despite his broader pattern in the photobiography, to sacrifice critical engagement.

The examples that I have given adhere to the theme of grief in ways that are at times obvious, at times subtle. The "good" Antietam photograph, of course, takes grief as an obvious theme, so much so that it inevitably fits what Barthes calls a unary photograph: the details, the background, the composition, the candid positions of the corpses, all of these argue that the image should be regarded as heartbreaking. The portraits of the young soldier killed and of the Lincoln boys are more subtle. By themselves, these photographs do not explicitly speak of grief: the fact that they are so far removed from our current historical position threatens to dispel their emotional impact. Sontag tries to explain this phenomenon when she writes, "A photograph of 1900 that was affecting then because of its subject would, today, be more likely to move us because it is a photograph taken in 1900" (*On Photography*, 21). These portraits of the Lincoln boys—black-and-white images of faces we don't recognize attached to bodies wearing clothes rendered exotic by their unfashionability—are, at a glance, more eloquent on the point of their age than they are on tragedy. Freedman's language, though, restores the pain of the photographs. Similarly, his description of soldiers from both the North and the South as "scarcely more than boys" beneath Edwin Jennison's portrait directs readers to find the boy's youth in the picture (*Lincoln,* 75). His caption for the portrait of Tad Lincoln emphasizes his and his brother's youth during the White House years, and the next caption asserts that Willie's death "plunged the Lincolns into profound sorrow" (81). In these ways, Freedman encourages the photographs to be read not simply as old but as draped in heartbreak. Even the early daguerreotype of Abraham and Mary is cast in a way to suggest mourning for what has been lost: the caption alongside Mary's image explains that she loved these pictures because, as Freedman quotes her recalling, they were "taken when we were young and so desperately in love" (26). Sontag writes that "most subjects photographed are, just by virtue of being photographed, touched with pathos" (*On Photography,* 15), and Freedman's handling of these images makes sure to give them exactly that touch.

What does it mean that Freedman breaks from critical engagement in images that speak to grief? In part, he is doing nothing more than allowing photographs to carry the melancholy that is always implicit therein. In *Camera Lucida,* Barthes argues for the presence of "that rather terrible thing which is there in every photograph: the return of the dead" (9). *Camera Lucida* is simultaneously a meditation on the nature of photography and an exploration of Barthes's lingering grief over the loss of his mother, so the thoughts of the book might be too personal, even anecdotal, to extend exactly to other photography. But Sontag makes a similar point when she argues that "precisely by slicing out this moment and freezing it, all photographs testify to time's relentless melt" (*On Photography,* 15). If Sontag is right, then even if Barthes's argument is too specific to his situation, there is still a "return of the dead" implicit in photography, which at the very least reminds us simultaneously of that which existed and the fact that it can no longer exist in exactly this form anymore. Photographs tend toward grief, so perhaps Freedman's anticritical handling of these photographs is simply generic.

But the grief in these images is not inert on the page; rather, it is bound up with an argument. The sense of loss implicit in photography connects also to the polemical potential of the medium. Although Sontag believes that "photographs cannot create a moral position," she goes on to write that "they can reinforce one—and can help build a nascent one" (17). When Freedman suspends his invitations to critical engagement to allow—indeed, to foster—the grief inherent in his photographs, that grief itself becomes a moral position. It is a position that the story of Lincoln should be read as one of grief, which is a moral position in that it allows us to sidestep other, competing readings of Lincoln, positions that insist on Lincoln as the head of an invading force, or as someone who gambled with the life of the Union for a political position he did not always hold, or as a president who overextended his executive authority. I am hardly arguing that one of those positions—positions held by Confederates and McClellan-era Democrats and implicit in Giorgio Agamben's *State of Exception*—is better than Freedman's. Rather, I am pointing out that Freedman's willingness to suspend invitations to critical engagement in favor of invitations to read Lincoln primarily through grief allows for an understanding of Lincoln that extracts him from other, more complicated moral systems. That Freedman presents Lincoln this way is hardly a surprise: the dominant understanding of Lincoln in the late 1980s—and the dominant understanding today—is that he was a martyr. This position is safer for trade nonfiction than would be a position that allows for regional or ideological criticism of Lincoln.[5] When, in these less common cases in which the biography treats its photographs as transparent rather than opaque, Freedman emphasizes the grief inherent in the images, he invokes a tendency in photographs that is every bit as native to the medium as an implicit claim to authority, and that grief has, as Sontag would put it, a moral function.

Photography in Russell Freedman's *Kids at Work*

Freedman's photobiography of Lincoln represents a turning point in the history of children's nonfiction in the United States, but one of his later books deals even more extensively with photography, and again, paying careful attention to where and how the book invites critical engagement reveals a moral position that the book reinforces. After the Lincoln book, which won the Newbery Medal in 1988, Freedman's book about the Wright brothers won a Newbery Honor in 1992, and his book about Eleanor Roosevelt won another Newbery Honor in 1994. Also in 1994, he published *Kids at Work*, a biography of Lewis Hine, the early-twentieth-century photographer who all but defined the genre of documentary photography for later artists and activists. Freedman was a major, to my mind *the* major, American writer of children's nonfiction at this time, and he had received repeated approval from his field for the model of nonfiction, with its emphasis on photography, that earned him such renown in the Lincoln book.

The emphasis on critical engagement that characterizes so much of the earlier biography, though, is usually absent in Freedman's book on Hine, especially where the book discusses Hine's photography. Rather, Freedman often repeats claims to the utter trustworthiness of Hine's photographs. To that end, Freedman writes of Hine's use of unique strategies for accumulating as much data as possible about his subject. Hine was, Freedman explains,

> careful to document every photograph with precise facts and figures. Hine knew the height of each button on his vest from the floor, so he could measure a child standing alongside him with no one being the wiser. Hidden in his pocket was a small notebook. He used it to record the name, age, hours of work, daily earnings, schooling, and other facts about each child he photographed.
>
> "All along I had to be double-sure that my photo data was 100% pure—no retouching or fakery of any kind," [Hine] wrote. (*Kids*, 29)

Hine becomes in moments such as these a sort of visible author, but rather than therefore transforming into a photographer with whom one can argue, he is a photographer characterized by reliability. That reliability allows, for both Freedman and the National Child Labor Committee (NCLC) for whom he took the photographs, permission to read Hine's pictures as evidence whose truth is inevitable. "The photos publicized what many had refused to believe," Freedman explains. "They stood as graphic evidence that industrial America was exploiting its children. 'These pictures speak for themselves,' the NCLC declared, 'and prove that the law is being violated'" (71). Although Freedman sometimes points to Hine in the act of creating the images—as when he recalls how Hine would pose immigrants rather than leave them in their natural positions (12)—he much more often argues that the perception of Hine's subjects through his photographs is ingenuous. For example, shortly after his brief mention of how Hine posed the immigrants in his photographs, Freedman writes, "The respect that [Hine] felt for his subjects, his direct and courteous manner when he approached them, allowed the immigrants to relax and be themselves when they faced his camera" (15). Much later, he argues that Hine "had a way with children. With a smile and a few kind words, a touch of his hand, he let them know that he was their friend and ally. He saw the beauty that resided in every child, and kids responded by trusting themselves to his camera" (86–89). In emphasizing the purity of Hine's images, their trustworthiness as evidence, and lack of pretense in his subjects, Freedman presents Hine's photography as a source that is in no need of critical engagement.

As with the Lincoln book, Freedman's book on Lewis Hine reinforces a moral position, and again that position is one that is very much in keeping with a mainstream Western sensibility. The language of the book routinely interacts with the images to emphasize the fragility of children, as with the book's motif of children's damaged hands. "It wasn't unusual to see children with badly chapped hands pulling and topping beets in the middle of November," Freedman recalls, "as cold winds blew across the fields and ice formed in the furrows" (67). Elsewhere, Freedman opens a chapter by observing that "Lewis Hine took some of his most haunting photos in the dark tunnels and grimy breaker rooms of the nation's coal mines" (47). These comments explain that the photographs should be read a specific way, one that attends to the danger of the settings photographed rather than other elements captured by the camera. Similarly, the captions throughout the book routinely emphasize the age of the children, especially in contrast with the difficult and dangerous work they are performing. One caption explains that the children pictured are "cotton-pickers ranging in age from five to nine" (66).

Another clarifies that the child pictured is "Salvin," who is "five years old" and "carries two pecks of cranberries to the bushel man" (64). Elsewhere, a caption reads, "Four-year-old Mary shucks two pots of oysters a day." The photograph, though, features more than a dozen people in addition to Mary, and although the caption privileges the diminutive child, the person opposite Mary in the photograph is smiling. In each of these images, the possible interpretations are many, but the interpretations encouraged by Freedman's language are those that emphasize the preciousness of childhood and the monstrosity of anything that threatens that preciousness.

Paying attention to this book's extensive efforts to discourage critical engagement with Hine's photographs reveals how the book reinforces, as Sontag puts it, a moral position, namely, that children are defined by their fragility, a fragility that must be safeguarded.

Russell Freedman uses this photograph by Lewis Hine in his book *Kids at Work* (1994). Freedman's caption, "Four-year-old Mary shucks two pots of oysters a day," directs attention toward one aspect of the photograph and away from others, such as the smiling face nearby. Image courtesy of the Library of Congress, Prints and Photographs Division, National Child Labor Committee Collection, LC-DIG-nclc-00918.

But this revelation is not so much a revelation about Freedman's moral position as it is another example of a moral position ubiquitous throughout contemporary Western culture. James R. Kincaid has explored this topic extensively, writing about how British and American cultures have, "at least for the past two hundred years," defined children according to their blankness, and when that blankness disappears, the child ceases to be a child altogether (*Child-Loving*, 6). Kincaid's main focus is on the cultural imperative to define children as absent of sexuality, but his arguments transfer easily to texts—such as Hine's photographs—that take for granted that children are similarly creatures who do not know labor. For example, when Kincaid complains about how the Victorians and their descendants insisted on using "a kind of purity, an absence and an incapacity, an inability to do" to define children (70), he is opening up space for the consideration of how insisting on the monstrosity of requiring children to work is of a piece with insisting on the monstrosity of children as sexual beings. Elsewhere, he makes the overlap between the two points more explicit: "To allow [children] to avoid work," he argues, adults "force them not to work. We must have them playing" (79). To the observation that Anglo-American cultures tend to insist on the blankness of childhood, Kincaid adds the observation that children rarely benefit from such an insistence. "Unencumbered by any necessary traits," he writes, "this emptiness called a child can be construed in about any way we like" (71). And it is in the pleasure given to adults—for example, the pleasure in the ability to construe blank children as we desire—that Kincaid suggests we can find the real motivation for defining children through absence: "these stories are doing something for us," he argues; "we wouldn't be telling this tale of the exploitation of the child's body if we didn't wish to have it told" (*Erotic Innocence*, 5). Kincaid claims, and I find his claim very convincing, that in the repeated act of arguing that children are blank, adults please and empower themselves. However, as Kincaid puts it, "we do children no favor, in the long or short run, by insisting that their world and motivations are impossibly simple" (*Erotic Innocence*, 81).[6]

It frustrates me to see Freedman, whose Lincoln book so remarkably worked both with and against the generic tendencies of photography, reiterate a moral position about childhood that, like Kincaid, I find so odious. But in all fairness to Freedman, Hine's photographs of child labor might well be the one subject *most* impervious to critical engagement. Hine's body of work is so enormous as to defy comprehensive analysis, and although he took important photographs before and after his child labor series, the child pictures alone are so numerous as to stagger careful analysis. Hine worked for the NCLC for about a decade starting in 1908 (Gutman, *Lewis W. Hine,* 16; Kemp, *Lewis Hine,* 7; Sampsell-Willmann, *Lewis Hine,* 57) and then again briefly later (Mallach, "Introduction," 9). A year after he began at the NCLC, he had already taken "more than eight hundred photographs" (Kemp, *Lewis Hine,* 10), and Hine later estimated that by 1915, he had taken "approximately 5,000 child labor photographs" (Doherty, *Lewis Wickes Hine,* 20). Too, Hine approached the production of this enormous catalog in such a way as to discourage even the most skeptical viewers from questioning the argument made in his photographs. Goldberg explains that in the early century, "the yellow press's highly inventive approach to photographic documentation had inspired widespread distrust of the camera." Hine developed a set of deceptions that he would practice on the adults profiting from child labor in order to gain access to the places where children worked, so he knew, Goldberg reminds us, that his opponents would seize on any inaccuracies in the photographs themselves to discredit his argument. "That was one reason he was so careful with his written data," she explains, "noting time of day, place, height, age, and any other statistics he could obtain about the children he photographed. He was determined that his documents would be trustworthy" (174). Verna Posever Curtis quotes a letter from Hine in which he insisted that he must be "extra careful about getting data 100% pure when possible" ("Lewis Hine," 36). Hine's child labor photographs anticipated a hostile audience, and Hine went to great lengths to make sure that his images met such hostility with an authority that shut down questions. Between the scope and confidence of the child labor series, there is very little room to argue with the vision of truth on which these pictures insist.

Hine strove to make his child labor pictures impervious to

questions, and the generations that have regarded them have largely taken those pictures at their word. In the first monograph to study Hine exclusively, Kate Sampsell-Willmann writes that especially during the time of the child labor series, "photography provided a seemingly direct, unmediated, or unprocessed experience to all those who chose to look. Thus, while photographs were highly composed expressions of one individual, they *appeared* to the viewer to be *spontaneous* glimpses into a world different from his or her own. By directly affecting the viewer emotionally and intellectually, they communicated authenticity" (*Lewis Hine*, 13, emphasis original). Sampsell-Willmann makes a convincing argument for understanding Hine as someone who produced and shaped the philosophy of his day rather than as someone who merely consumed or reiterated it, but in this way, at least with his child labor pictures, Hine seems to have kept close to the pattern of the Progressive Era. Goldberg identifies "Hine's straightforward, undramatic, just-plain-facts style, with pictures generally taken from a middle distance and subjects often posing frontally for the camera," as key to his personal style as well as the "tone of documentary photography for decades" to come (*Power,* 173). John R. Kemp argues that the case made by the NCLC against child labor was all the more convincing because the "realism" of Hine's photographs "provided powerful, irrefutable evidence" despite the many voices who spoke out against the committee's efforts (*Lewis Hine,* 7). Alan Trachtenberg's praise of "certain photographs" that are "true facts as much as they are works of art" builds to the example of Lewis Hine, who, Trachtenberg argues, "belongs among these true masters of the camera's power. His pictures make a history for us" ("Ever," 118). For Trachtenberg, writing in the late 1970s,

> Hine's pictures have etched themselves in the minds of three generations of Americans. We have seen them in history books and taken them as facts. . . . Much remains to be seen: these pictures are not illustrations but visions of a man for whom the camera was an instrument of truth. (119)

For Trachtenberg, of course, these words are praise. However, combined with the observations of these other scholars, Trachtenberg's comments about the camera as "an instrument of truth" bode very ill for any hope of critical engagement with Hine's child labor pictures. Hine's attempts to compose his child labor pictures in such a way as to render them impervious to critical engagement were successful at the time of their publication, and, if these observations of Hine's place in contemporary culture are right, they have remained so ever since.

These powerful photographs came not from a cynical attempt to manipulate the public but, according to studies of Hine, from beliefs that the artist held deeply and genuinely. Stanley Mallach repeats a common observation when he writes that "Hine fervently believed that child labor should be eradicated" ("Introduction," 10). Sampsell-Willmann extends this point, arguing that Hine believed in the value of labor and that even much child labor, "such as work on a family farm or [in an] apprenticeship," was good for children. However, Sampsell-Willmann argues, "exploitative" work was bad for children *and* the society that thereby failed to prepare "the next generation to be productive members" (*Lewis Hine*, 75–76). According to her, Hine felt that such labor allowed wealthy industrialists to "profit financially from the misery of children" and then "pass the costs of that profit on to society in general" (82). The moral position enforced in Hine's photographs was a moral position to which Hine was intensely dedicated. It was also a moral position to which he saw his photographs as having an important duty.

For all that, though, scholarship on Hine has frequently pointed to a technique in his photography that *fractured* the message of his photographs, opening a dialogical space rather than the monological space more typical of photographs bent on enforcing a moral position. Immediately before he worked on the child labor series for the NCLC, Hine worked with the Pittsburgh Survey, a study of Pittsburgh as an industrial city and the people of Pittsburgh as the laborers who made that industry possible. When Trachtenberg reads these photos, he sees a photographer hard at work to make *and* undermine an obvious argument. Hine's volume on the steelworkers, Trachtenberg observes, "opens with a description of the 'glamour' of the industry, of the 'majestic and illimitable' power of steelmaking," but it then juxtaposes that positive view of the industry with "an antagonistic one: the insufferable 'working life' of the men who labor in the mills." As a result, Trachtenberg argues, the overlapping contraries framed the glamorous photographs as "not so much false as incomplete." He finds that the effect of the series is "to persuade the viewer that the full picture, the complete scene, includes contradictory evidence." If Trachtenberg is right, then in the Pittsburgh pictures, at least, Hine seeded his photographic series with evidence that would prevent the construction of stable arguments, that would indeed complicate any obvious argument about the value of industry. "The challenge for the viewer," writes Trachtenberg, "is to reconcile the opposing images: industrial power and human waste" ("Ever," 127). What Trachtenberg imagines is a text that invites critical engagement. Because Hine's pictures made an argument, then rejected it, then complicated and revised it, and finally left space in which viewers might "reconcile" the contradictions, these were photographs that anticipated and rewarded an audience that would engage critically.

This same technique appears in Hine's child labor photos, but the technique has a very different effect. When Trachtenberg praises the Pittsburgh photos, he places on one hand the negative effects of industry that Hine photographed—"crippled workers, crowded one-room dwellings, dirty streets"—and on the other "the strength and worthiness radiant in the faces of workers" (127). When Sampsell-Willmann praises the *child labor* photos, she notes "the objectively ragged" conditions in which the children lived as well as their "coal dust and fatigue," but she also singles out, in words highly reminiscent of Trachtenberg's, "the light that shines in their eyes." But whereas Trachtenberg found the contradiction an opportunity for viewers to puzzle through the complexity of the issue, Sampsell-Willmann argues that "it is that innocence that also indicts the viewer, the one who would have, in 1906 or 1911, *not* agitated for the end of child labor" (*Lewis Hine,* 92). Sampsell-Willmann then likens this strategy to a "jeremiad exhortation" (93). Even a photograph of children happily learning in an educational environment becomes part of this exhortation, she argues, "if shown in juxtaposition with a group of oyster pickers," as it narrates a tale in which children are unjustly removed from their rightful environment and forced into exploitative labor. The contradiction of evidence "becomes agitprop for a specific political outcome: passage of legislation" (84). For her, then, the contradictions in the images do *not* open a space for critical engagement but foster a specific reaction that condemns those who disagree with the photographer's conclusion. Interestingly, Jonathan L. Doherty shares a quotation from Hine that indicates that Hine may himself have been frustrated with the narrow ideological spectrum in which his child labor photographs could signify: "So many times have social workers told me," Hine wrote, "that the photographs of happy, healthy children do not make effective appeals in our child labor work, that I am sometimes inclined to think that we must mutilate these infants in industry before the shame of it can be driven home" (*Lewis Wickes Hine*, 21). Hine seems to resent the restrictions on his work, but even when he finds a way to sneak in the humanity and resilience of child laborers, the contradictions do not diffuse the photographs' exhortation. The technique of providing contradictory evidence to open room for critical engagement was one of Hine's hallmarks throughout his career. However, when he encoded (or simply found) contradictions in the subject matter of his child labor photographs, those contradictions served to reinforce a monological moral position, closing down exactly the sort of opportunities for engagement that his photographs about adult labor provoked.

There are, then, few texts more resistant to critical engagement than Hine's child labor photographs. As my last few paragraphs have demonstrated, there is a host of reasons for that effective resistance. Hine's body of work is enormous. Hine prepared for, shot, and labeled his photos in such a way as to defeat skepticism before it had even been uttered. Any critical engagement with these photos has to overcome nearly a century's worth of widespread acceptance of their argument at face value. Hine was legitimately, ingenuously, and deeply dedicated to the argument that these pictures made. Finally, Hine adapted the dialogical technique that marked his photographs of adults so that any contradictions would work together to make a monological argument in his child labor series. Although I am frustrated that Freedman's book on Hine abandons the critical engagement that the same author fostered so well elsewhere, his choice of subject here makes similar engagement difficult at best.

Too, there is a hint in Freedman's book that he made some attempt to dampen the shrillness of Hine's original argument. The first chapter of Freedman's book begins with a photograph of a boy holding two pots, standing barefoot in front of a heap of broken shells. Freedman's caption for the picture is "Manuel, a five-year-old Mississippi shrimp-picker." This caption highlights his age, location, and occupation, and certainly these three things together make a point synchronized with contemporary sensibilities about child labor. But Hine's caption, available through the database of Hine's photographs in the online Library of Congress catalog, makes Freedman's caption look subtle by comparison. Hine describes the picture as of "Manuel the young shrimp picker, age 5, and a mountain of child labor oyster shells behind him. He worked last year. Understands not a word of English. Biloxi, Mississippi." Although Freedman's caption focuses on information that offends Western sensibilities of childhood, his caption actually strips out some of the more explicit bits of Hine's caption that explained the argument Hine was making: gone are the references to last year's exploitation, the failure of the American infrastructure to educate him in the local language, and of course Hine's "mountain of child labor oyster shells." Later, Freedman gives one photo the caption "Climbing up on the machinery to replace bobbins" (37) in place of Hine's original caption: "The mill: Some boys and girls were so small they had to climb up on to the spinning frame to mend broken threads and to put back the empty bobbins. Bibb Mill No. 1. Macon, Georgia." The camera's focus in this photograph directs attention to the child's bare feet on the metal contraption, and Hine's caption similarly focuses on the photograph as evidence of the child's diminutive size and frailty. Freedman's caption, on the other hand, is understated. Finally, Freedman's caption to a much more complicated photograph of more than a dozen people of different ages explains that "Four-year-old Mary shucks two pots of oysters a day, Dunbar, Louisiana, 1911" (42). Although little Mary is in the foreground, another child barely older leans over a bin with a large smile on her face, something that, as I noted earlier, Freedman neglects to mention in the caption. In this way, of course, Freedman's caption slants the weight of the photograph toward the narrative of children's frailty that dominates the book. But as manipulative as I find Freedman's caption, the original is even more heavy-handed:

> Four-year-old Mary, who shucks two pots of oysters a day at Dunbar. Tends the baby when not working. The boss said that next year Mary will work steady as the rest of them. The mother is the fastest shucker in the place. Earns $1.50 a day. Works part of the time with her sick baby in her arms. Father works on the dock.

Freedman's caption attempts to narrow the meaning of the photograph by directing attention away from the girl smiling as she works, but Hine's caption not only ignores the smiling girl in the photograph, it also extends the narrative of children endangered by exploitative labor beyond the photograph to the labor Mary provides outside the work space, the imagined future of further exploitation, and the inadequate parenting prompted by the oyster industry.

I do, then, think that it is fair to criticize Freedman's closing down of room for critical engagement in the Hine book, especially in comparison with the expansion of such opportunities in the Lincoln book, but it is significant that, at times, Freedman actually appears to be taking pains to mute Hine's exhortations. It is possible, and in fact this is the reading I prefer, to read Freedman's rewriting of the captions as a sign that he was himself reluctant to provide a narrative as unary (as Barthes would have it) or monological (as Bakhtin would have it) as Hine intended. If this is the correct explanation for Freedman's tinkering with the captions, the conclusion I draw is that Freedman—who provided so many excellent spaces for critical engagement with photography in the Lincoln book—was less than enthusiastic about the expressly manipulative nature of Hine's photography. Therefore, when he had the chance to loosen Hine's hold on the meaning of his photographs in the captions, he took it.

But that said, these revisions to Hine's captions are rare exceptions to the general pattern of presenting Hine, his photographs, and the arguments they make as above question. Indeed, if I am right to read these exceptions as signs that Freedman resisted Hine's authoritative stance, then Freedman's larger pattern in the Hine book of reinforcing that stance is all the stranger. As I puzzle over this paradox in Freedman, I'm reminded of the paradox in Hine that photography scholars have faced when considering his child labor pictures. In general, Hine's work is marked by profound contradictions within the arguments those photographs make, and these contradictions complicate and enrich those arguments, leaving room for viewers "to reconcile the opposing images," as Trachtenberg puts it ("Ever," 127). That argumentative space is very similar to the spaces for resistance and questioning that I have, in previous chapters, been locating in various places where children's nonfiction invites critical engagement. But Hine's child labor photography uses the technique that elsewhere expands critical engagement to ward off resistance. Similarly, although Freedman's best-known book treats the subject of photography as a place for critical engagement, in his book on Hine, his treatment of the same subject discourages critical engagement.

The parallel between the two suggests that it is the topic of child labor itself that explains the difference in these two books that deal so extensively with photography. In this way, the insight opened up by attending to invitations to and deflections of critical engagement is an insight not so much about Freedman as it is about twentieth-century U.S. culture. When Hine was paid to shoot photographs about adult labor, he provided complicated, self-contradictory narratives that were well received; when he was paid to shoot photographs of child labor, he provided unary, monological narratives that reinforced and were rewarded by his culture. For Freedman, writing more than eighty years after Hine began his work for the NCLC, the story is the same. His study of the complicated, unstable intersection of Lincoln and photography received wide praise. Later, as one author put it in a starred review, Freedman's argument that photographs of child labor must be viewed with trust resulted in a book that was "thoroughly absorbing, and even those who normally shy away from nonfiction will find themselves caught up in this seamless account" (*Publishers Weekly,* "Unsigned Review"). The seams certainly are hidden in this book, as they must be to protect the moral position about children's labor that is so jealously guarded in contemporary Western culture.

Finally, the trust in photography that Freedman fosters in

the Hine book also protects a moral sensibility that is specific to children's literature. From the perspective of children's literature as a commodity, as an art form inevitably bound up with the reading situation of the children of its era and financial investments in the maintenance of that reading situation, it is perhaps inevitable that the presentation of Hine's argument is "seamless." To open up critical engagement with photography in this book is anathema to children's literature because to do so is to question the validity of Hine's social project, and that project is one that underwrites the idea that children should be in school or at home, quietly consuming knowledge rather than laboring in fields, factories, or mines. A children's book that is to be sold through the regular channels of adult approval for child consumption cannot question whether children ought to be reading rather than earning money. The Lincoln book could heap all the skepticism on photography it wanted to, especially when that skepticism was tied to a grief that helped it sidestep the more controversial (which, especially for classroom and library markets, translates to reduced sales) aspects of Lincoln's life. The Hine book—whatever Freedman's discomfort with Hine's captions—accepts the grief implicit in the child labor photos and thereby passes along without question the photos' argument that we should mourn children who work rather than consume. In both cases, the level of skepticism matches the market interests of the book.

Photography in children's trade nonfiction neither begins nor ends with Russell Freedman. However, his critical and financial success with nonfiction heavily illustrated by photographs points directly to the medium's deeply conflicted potential for critical engagement.

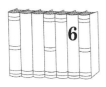

6. THE PURSUIT OF RELIABILITY IN *ALMOST ASTRONAUTS*

MY THEORY, the theory that nonfiction should be read for where it invites and discourages critical engagement, steps into a passionate debate already raging between authors, editors, reviewers, educators, and other adults who care deeply about children's nonfiction. In 2011, Marc Aronson, whose book on Stonehenge figures repeatedly in my earlier chapters, published an essay that touched off a wide-ranging argument about what Aronson called the "new nonfiction" ("New Knowledge"). The lines—between those who thought there was something categorically new and those who did not—were quickly drawn, and the dispute spread through electronic and print media. In a thoughtful summary of and response to the controversy, Myra Zarnowski and Susan Turkel argue, though, that the important question emerging from that debate is not whether today's nonfiction is new but whether nonfiction should "model the process of inquiry" for its readers ("Creating," 29). Seen from this perspective, the skirmish touched off by Aronson's essay is an early sample of a much more profound disagreement. On one side is the idea that nonfiction should be centered around inquiry and highlight places where bias, a lack of information, or complications to standard narratives make more complex the conclusions that we have drawn based on the evidence that we have. In tension with this

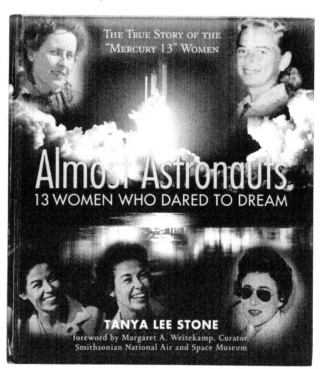

Tanya Lee Stone, *Almost Astronauts: 13 Women Who Dared to Dream* (2009).

idea is the drive to provide authoritative nonfiction that, unlike infamous instances of children's nonfiction of the past, delivers accurate, reliable information.

Tanya Lee Stone's *Almost Astronauts: 13 Women Who Dared to Dream* (2009) provides an eloquent test case for where these theories of nonfiction overlap and conflict. In the years since *Almost Astronauts* first won national recognition, Stone has explained her own theory of the field in astute ways that explore the conflict between the two positions that Zarnowski and Turkel identify, and following the arguments as they surface in her explanations as well as how they resist one another in her best-known book lays bare the compelling reasons behind the two positions. In my first chapter, I explored the growing sense within the field that critical engagement is of primary importance to nonfiction, but in this chapter I want to clarify why the mainstream opinion—that children's nonfiction must be a literature of facts—remains so tenacious. I also want to use Stone's book to demonstrate the consequences of a theory of nonfiction that insists that its books speak with authority. Although noble intentions fuel the argument that children's nonfiction must be authoritative, the pursuit of reliability that this argument requires jeopardizes critical engagement as well as accuracy.

Critical Literacy and the Disappointing History of Children's Nonfiction

The argument that Zarnowski and Turkel see as privileging the modeling of inquiry draws directly from the theoretical base that informs the approach that I have been advocating. Specifically, critical literacy theory, as it has come to be known, descends from Paulo Freire's "problem-posing" education, in which learning is based on inquiry rather than absorption of safely vetted facts. In problem-posing education, teachers invite students to enter into and even guide inquiry. Contemporary theorists and educators working within this tradition do not discount the importance of information, but they prize most highly interactions between learners and texts that foster questions. Kathy Short's essay about the importance of literature in the elementary classroom, for example, offers observations on form and meaning, but it is more invested in the argument that the ideal reading situation is one in which "children learn to problem-pose and question the everyday world" ("Reading," 52). Elsewhere, Katie Van Sluys bases her theory of language literacy on "curricular invitations," in which "participants are decision makers from the start" (*What If,* 2). As she lists the nine properties of such invitations, she states pointedly that curricular invitations "represent our best current understandings," implying a respect for hard-earned information. However, she follows that statement immediately with the argument that good curricular invitations also "embrace opportunities to use multiple ways of knowing to construct and contest meaning," and she ends her list by insisting that curricular invitations "invite further inquiry" (6). The nonfiction that Zarnowski and Turkel see as providing "explicit modeling of the inquiry process" ("Creating," 30) is a nonfiction committed to critical literacy's project of inviting children to the exercise of thinking about information rather than receiving it passively. Critical literacy is the first of the two positions in the debate over children's nonfiction, and although this position respects answers, it insists on questions.

When, as the Aronson debate demonstrates, champions of this position clash with other children's nonfiction professionals, the conflict comes not over the appropriateness of inviting children to inquiry but out of a profound (and, frankly, reasonable) aversion to children's nonfiction's historical habit of prioritizing didacticism at the expense of truthfulness. The history of this practice in the United States goes back to the earliest days of American children's publishing. Consider Mason Locke Weems's early-nineteenth-century blockbuster children's biographies of George Washington and Benjamin Franklin. Weems's Washington biography recounts the story of young Washington and the cherry tree, which Leonard S. Marcus calls "the Washington exemplum against which American children would for generations afterward measure their own moral worth. It mattered not at all to the ebullient [Weems] that the episode rested on little more than hearsay" (*Minders,* 11). Marcus also argues that Weems "deliberately overplayed Franklin's piety with a view to 'correcting' his shortcomings" (12). In both cases, Weems enjoyed financial and professional success because he privileged moral instruction over historical record.

That practice hardly ended with Weems, and the name of one successful series in this vein has become shorthand for a casual massaging of history. The Childhood of Famous Americans (CFA) series proliferated across American libraries in the middle of the twentieth century, and recounting the sins committed between their famously bright orange covers has provided fodder for scholars and critics ever since. Peter C. Kunze, for example, uses the series volume on Helen Keller to illustrate a historically questionable and politically loaded "heroification" ("What," 311–12), and Craig Howes combines a sneer with a shrug when he writes that the conclusion to Shirlee Petkin Newman's biography of Liliuokalani "is as predictable as it is distorted—after all, Newman's biography is part of the *Childhood of Famous Americans* series" ("Hawaii," 70). Nonetheless, new volumes in the series have continued to appear—with similar results, if Marilyn Taniguchi's complaint that the 2006 book on

Jackie Robinson is both "heavily fictionalized" and "saccharine" is any indication ("Review," 136). It is the CFA series that Wendy Lukehart uses to explain the motivation for the formation of contemporary "professional standards" for librarians, specifically those that guard against "invented dialogue and fictional scenarios" ("Brushes," 40). Although Lukehart writes specifically about librarians, the Aronson debate also indicates that the same opinion is widespread among writers of children's nonfiction.[1] Nonfiction written from this perspective is often the product of thoughtful questions, but more important—at least in the finished draft—is the validity of the answers.

When Tanya Lee Stone explains her approach to nonfiction, she demonstrates the vitality of the two positions, which at key points overlap. In the same special issue of *Horn Book* in which Aronson expounds his argument for a new nonfiction, Stone presents her theory of children's nonfiction, a theory characterized by attention to what Stone calls the "fine, fine line" between truth and falsehood. A self-confessed fan of "those orange-covered *Childhood of Famous Americans* biographies," Stone "was furious" upon her later discovery that much of the content of the books was fictionalized. "Do you know," she asks, "how many facts are embedded in my knowledge base that are not, in truth, facts? I don't." The metonym of the CFA series allows Stone to argue the position of the children's literature professional guarding against willfully inaccurate nonfiction. But she also gestures toward critical literacy. On the same page, Stone argues that "the answer to the question—what is the truth?—is such a tricky one," and she explains that she is "continually stressing to students how important it is to remember that every single thing they read and hear, from books to newspaper articles to the evening news, is colored by the perspective of the human being who wrote it" ("Fine," 86). Such a message is primarily one of critical literacy: Stone encourages young people to understand the information they are given as information that comes from a perspective, one that they are allowed to question. At the end of the essay, she contends that writers for children should "indicate intention," should "let the reader in on your secret." She calls on her fellow writers to "confide in [children], and invite them along for the ride" (87). Her point is that writers of nonfiction should make clear to children, in order to be truthful with them, where facts have been bent, and the terms in which she makes that argument sound fundamentally similar to the terms in which Van Sluys calls for curricular invitations through which children can "contest meaning." The bulk of Stone's essay is given to a condemnation of inaccuracy, but it also makes an argument that nonfiction should make plain the places where bias and intention mean that the answers given should be read critically. Although I have claimed that a profound conflict exists between critical literacy and the field's urge to produce authoritative information, Stone's essay indicates that the two forces may *not* be mutually exclusive.

But there is another key word in Stone's essay that hints at an irreconcilability between the two. As she finishes her recollection of the CFA series, Stone concludes that "those books didn't need truthiness to be engaging. I loved them. But ultimately, they let me down. I can't rely on what I learned from them" ("Fine," 87). From the perspective of someone who remembers Weems and the countless other authors of nonfiction who compromised accuracy, "rely" isn't such a problematic word. However, from the perspective of critical literacy, it is anathema. To *rely* on something means, according to the *Oxford English Dictionary,* "to depend on with full trust or confidence." The idea that readers should *trust* nonfiction echoes throughout the essay, as when Stone writes about an obligation to her readers to present nothing but clear facts (84–85) and the importance of readers knowing that she speaks "with authority" (85). Again, in the context of a protest against the sins of earlier nonfiction, Stone's point is understandable: she suspects that the inaccuracies "embedded" in her mind have harmed her, and she naturally objects to similar texts. But if Aronson and others are calling for, as Zarnowski and Turkel claim, a kind of nonfiction that models inquiry, then a nonfiction that encourages its readers to depend upon it "with full trust or confidence" is problematic: to rely on something implies that one accepts it, not questions it. In this view, nonfiction's ability to provide answers is more important than its ability to prompt questions. Stone's essay therefore also implies that the two positions anticipated in the Aronson essay *are* fundamentally incompatible, despite her plea to her fellow writers to "let the reader in on your secret."

Almost Astronauts and Choosing the Questions

That incompatibility provides an important entrée into Stone's most famous book, which, true to the theory of nonfiction her essay illustrates, tends to choose reliability over opportunities for critical engagement. *Almost Astronauts* tells how a group of women proved that they were top contenders for positions in America's early space program, then lost their chance for the stars through a combination of reasons that remain tragic decades later. Randall Lovelace, a prominent medical doctor with a proven track record of thoughtful research with important implications for aviation, decided in the 1950s to use his close relationship with NASA to develop a series of tests designed to demonstrate that women could be excellent astronauts. In the person of Jerrie Cobb, an extraordinarily gifted and driven human being, he found a subject whose test results far exceeded even his own expectations. Stone tells how Lovelace and Cobb selected a group of women, who came to be known as the Mercury 13, to participate in further tests that continued to prove his hypothesis true, but through external prejudice and internal jealousy, the program foundered shortly before key tests, scheduled to take place at naval facilities in Pensacola, Florida, could produce the broad evidence on which Lovelace intended to make his case. In a surprisingly brief series of hearings, a congressional subcommittee looked into the matter and concluded that all parties had operated without prejudice. In a period of less than two years, women learned they could be exceptionally good astronauts, then learned that whatever their qualifications, they would once again be left behind.

Almost Astronauts speaks with impressive authority and, therefore, reliability. In 2010, it won the Robert F. Sibert Informational Book Medal, the American Library Association's highest award for children's nonfiction. The Sibert is granted by the same organization that gives the Newbery and Caldecott Medals, awards that have shaped the buying habits of parents, teachers, and librarians for generations. Indeed, everything about *Almost Astronauts* from its format to its peritexts bespeaks authority: boasting an oversized hardback edition from a selective press, sporting a rave on the back from "the first woman to pilot a space shuttle," and led by a foreword from (as the front cover puts it) "Margaret A. Weitekamp, Curator, Smithsonian National Air and Space Museum," Stone's book is as serious as it is passionate.

The key scene in *Almost Astronauts*'s claim to reliability is an interview that Stone reproduces in her narrative. In May 2007, Stone caught up with many of the remaining Mercury 13 women at a special event in their honor. Among those women was Jerrie Cobb, the woman who played the most public role in support of the project in the early 1960s. Susan Campbell Bartoletti, herself a winner of the Sibert Medal, has praised "Stone's perseverance" in tracking down this interview with Cobb. Bartoletti cites this interview as an example of what an "extreme researcher" will do ("Extreme," 29), and the dust jacket's back-flap copy expresses similar admiration, explaining that "as she did her own original research, [Stone] learned a dark secret about the early space program that had been hidden for forty years," instructing the curious reader to "see page 63" for an example. On that page, Stone recounts part of her interview with Cobb, specifically a section of the interview in which Cobb recalls a conversation with then Vice President Lyndon B. Johnson. Stone explains her own trepidation in asking the famously untalkative Cobb about her conversation with Johnson, then tells this story:

> [Cobb] took a breath and shook her head a little. Then she told me that Johnson had looked at her and said, "Jerrie, if we let you or other women into the space program, we'd have to let blacks in. We'd have to let Mexican Americans in, and Chinese Americans. We'd have to let every minority in, and we just can't do it." (*Almost,* 63)

This statement is extraordinary, especially coming from, as Stone points out, the same man who as president later "signed an affirmative-action plan to make federal agencies actively give women and minorities equal employment opportunities" (62).[2] Stone presents the scene skillfully, recounting her personal amazement at the story and sketching the ramifications that Johnson's statement and the prejudice behind it would have for "women, African Americans, Hispanics, Asians," and so many other Americans (63). Stone goes on to explain how she asked Cobb for permission to use this information in *Almost Astronauts,* and she highlights Cobb's reluctance. "She wasn't sure," Stone writes of Cobb. "She is by nature uncomfortable saying anything negative about anyone" (63).

And there, apparently, the conversation began to stall. It's a lovely moment in a compelling scene, as the researcher is caught between her discovery of an excellent piece of evidence and her reluctance to alienate her source. But at this tense juncture in the narrative of research, Stone catches a break. She writes,

> And then, in the Wisconsin hotel lobby the evening news came on. We watched as the cameras cut to an interview with Cobb. And then I heard it—for the second time: Johnson's comment about having to let minorities into the space program if he let in the women. Cobb slapped me on the leg in surprise—she hadn't remembered she had said that out loud to the reporter. "Well, there you have it—I said it on the air, so go ahead and use it!" I told her I would. (63)

The decisions that *Almost Astronauts* makes in negotiating inquiry and reliability are evident throughout the book, but here they have special consequences. On one hand, the scene is an obvious example of showing the reader the research that the author has done, which is to say that it is modeling inquiry, an idea that I explored in chapter 3. Stone's journey to Wisconsin, her interview with Cobb, and her desperation at being forbidden to use the knowledge that she has won are central, dramatic moments of asking questions, played out for the reader rather than erased in the final draft. Thus it satisfies the call for nonfiction to show its work, to model inquiry.

However, even in this scene about what the dust jacket copy calls "her own original research," Stone's book tends to favor reliability over inquiry. Even though the scene is on its surface a story of research, there is one line of research the narrative does not pursue. That line emerges when Cobb, the seventy-six-year-old woman who gives Stone the information about her interview with Johnson, can't remember that she has already shared the information, probably even quite recently, considering that the interview was still in that day's news cycle. The scene accepts Cobb's version of the story about her visit to Johnson, but Cobb proves herself in this moment to be a text that ought to be questioned, not as one on which we should rely.

Nonetheless, the narrative quickly passes by Cobb's evident unreliability. Cobb's imperfect recollection of her television interview is a fairly obvious reason to question her recollection of her interview with Johnson, but the book doesn't choose to do so. The assumption that Cobb is right is especially strange in light of a recent interview with Stone, in which she asserts that "the primary source interviews that I do are unreliable. I have to do a lot of corroborating research" (qtd. in Bang-Jensen, "Talking," 13). Jane Hart, another Mercury 13 participant, was also present at that interview with Johnson, and she was still alive at the time of Stone's interview with Cobb, but the book does not compare Stone's recollection with Hart's or, for that matter, that of any other source. Such comparison, of course, would be part of a process of inquiry, critical engagement with the source rather than a reliance on its authority, but this scene does not present Cobb as a source to be questioned. Rather, the five paragraphs of the story of Stone's interview with Cobb are set off with block indentation, the margins around the story lengthened as though quoting a source. What the formatting suggests is something that the book as a whole repeatedly implies: questions may be asked, but information from Cobb should be accepted with confidence. Although the story records Cobb's mistake, it does not present that mistake as a place to continue—let alone model—inquiry.

But what if we insist on inquiring anyway? In this signature scene, which the book's jacket copy, pacing, and formatting feature, Stone treats Cobb's testimony as a fact on which to rely. If, however, we treat it now, after the date of the publication of *Almost Astronauts*, as an opening for critical engagement, that testimony leads to a chain of insights that tells us more about the consequences of pursuing reliability. Cobb's claim is probably impossible to verify fully, but at least one other source of information—Martha Ackmann's book *The Mercury 13: The Untold Story of Thirteen American Women and the Dream of Space Flight* (2003)—offers corroboration. Ackmann writes, "Many minority groups were asking for attention from NASA, the Vice President [said]. They wanted to be astronauts, too. If the United States allowed women in space, then blacks, Mexicans, Chinese, and other minorities would want to fly too" (147). Ackmann cites three sources for her version of the scene: a letter from Cobb to Johnson, an interview with Jane Hart, and an e-mail from Cobb to Ackmann. Therefore, although Stone's book discourages us from questioning whether Cobb is right about her interview with Johnson, if we take a cue from the rest of the scene and chase down information on our own, we can find good evidence that Cobb's recollection of that interview is in fact correct.

But in doing so, we come across another problem. In her reported reluctance to grant Stone permission to tell the story of the conversation with Johnson, Cobb implies that she has not told anyone else what Johnson said, certainly not anyone else who might have reported the story more widely. Stone reinforces this implication in her statement that "Cobb knew Johnson's reasons but did not reveal them until 2007," the year of Stone's interview with Cobb (62). But the record shows that Cobb did not keep her conversation with Johnson a secret until 2007, a fact that comes to light in searching for corroboration of Cobb's recollection of her talk with Johnson: Ackmann's book, the book in which we find the same story in almost exactly the same words, was published in 2003, four years before Stone heard the story from Cobb, six years before Stone published it in *Almost Astronauts*. *The Mercury 13* was the first major book published on the subject, and it is a study that Stone's book cites 12 times (out of 109 total citations). *Almost Astronauts* is not only *not* the first book to reveal this information, but it repeatedly cites another book that had already done so. Cobb's story about her interview with Johnson is probably true. The story *Almost Astronauts* tells about when Cobb opened up about that interview is evidently false.

This untruth is important from both of the theoretical positions that I have been exploring in this chapter. Obviously, it is problematic because it threatens, to paraphrase Stone, to lodge in its readers' memories facts that are not facts ("Fine," 86). It is also, though, significant from the position of critical literacy, because this untruth is key to an affirmation of reliability of which critical literacy is skeptical in the first place. After all, the claim that *Almost Astronauts* is the first to reveal Johnson's comments is a claim that is bound up with the book's authority, both announced and assumed: the dust jacket announces the book's authority through its claim to the scene's original research, and Bartoletti's praise of the book hinges on Stone's tenacity in winning that unique interview with Cobb. Stone's interview with Cobb is more than simply evidence of what Johnson said in private; it is also evidence that Stone's book is the result of thorough research on which readers can rely. Too, the account *Almost Astronauts* gives of Stone's talk with Cobb lends reliability to the book because it associates *Almost Astronauts* with Cobb's firsthand authority. In fact, in a 2014 interview, Stone cites her conversation with Cobb as an example of how she gets to the emotional truth of a story, saying that it is on interviews such as this one that she has learned to "rely" (qtd. in Bang-Jensen, "Talking," 13).

In these multiple ways, the untrue claim that the story of Johnson's comments "had been hidden for forty years" is linked to the book's pursuit of reliability. Thus when *Almost Astronauts* claims that it is the first to tell what happened in the interview with Johnson, it violates the rule that children's nonfiction must be accurate and provides further evidence that claims to reliability should be met with skepticism.

I don't know why *Almost Astronauts* makes, indeed advertises, the untruth that Stone was the first to reveal what (Cobb says) Johnson said. It's possible that Stone did not read Ackmann's book carefully, thereby missing the six-page version of the story that Ackmann gives. It's possible that she didn't read Ackmann's book until after she interviewed Cobb, which would mean that she was genuinely surprised when Cobb told the story, though that scenario still doesn't explain why *Almost Astronauts* maintains that Cobb kept the story secret until 2007. There's another possibility, and although it's a stretch, it's the one that I'm going to choose to believe for the simple reason that I like *Almost Astronauts* and want to give its author the benefit of the doubt: Stone did read Ackmann's book, read it carefully, and read it before she interviewed Cobb. But over the long course of her research, during which time she was likely also working on other projects, she forgot that she had first read about the Cobb–Hart–Johnson interview in the pages of Ackmann's book. Then, while she finished writing *Almost Astronauts,* she only revisited the parts of Ackmann's book that were necessary for the rest of her story. Not needing to look up anything about the interview with Johnson, she simply didn't come across Ackmann's version of it again as she looked for the items that she needed for the rest of the book. In the scenario I prefer, then, *Almost Astronauts* is certainly wrong, but only accidentally so.

But let me make something clear: *the reason that Stone's book is wrong does not matter.* It's possible that the explanation for this error in a scene that the book chooses to spotlight is more nefarious than I have decided to believe, but insofar as I am using *Almost Astronauts* as a test case for nonfiction and the tension between reliability and inquiry, the reason for the untruth is unimportant in comparison with the realization that untruths can and do appear even in nonfiction that announces (and has been recognized for) its dedication to truthfulness. *Almost Astronauts* is—and this is part of Stone's point in her essay about the genre—intended to be an example of nonfiction that privileges truthfulness, but even this book, publicly dedicated to being right, is actually wrong. In fact, it is wrong in exactly the scene to which it indicates readers should attend. If *Almost Astronauts* can be wrong in this scene, then the argument that nonfiction must be reliable at all costs begins to sound naive. Indeed, I would go so far as to say that as long as nonfiction is written by human beings, it is always going to be wrong, frequently at equally pivotal moments.

So what do we do next? We have found a mistake in *Almost Astronauts,* a mistake crucial to the authority with which the book tries to speak. According to the accuracy model of children's nonfiction, the book is a disappointment. But that model is, if noble, impossible to satisfy. We have reached what is not only the end of the accuracy approach but the *inevitable* end of the accuracy approach. However, the approach that I have been illustrating in the previous chapters allows a much richer reading. Instead of scanning for the inevitable failures of a book's accuracy, we can search for where the book does and does not invite questions. Such a reading requires asking not, as Stone encourages us to ask, where her book is reliable but where it hides its vulnerabilities, where it chooses to bury inquiry in favor of cultivating an air of reliability.

The Heroine

The scene set in that Wisconsin hotel lobby is one of the places where *Almost Astronauts* deflects questions from its protagonist, and much of the rest of the book's treatment of Cobb uses a similar technique. Bartoletti calls Cobb the "main heroine" of Stone's book ("Extreme," 29), and a look at how *Almost Astronauts* deflects critical engagement from the figure of Cobb bears that opinion out. Stone opens with a moving portrait of several of the Mercury 13 participants gathered to watch the launch of "Eileen Collins, the first woman to command a space shuttle" (*Almost Astronauts,* 3). Most of the women "huddle close like sisters," but one "paces" the scene alone. Although "this is an emotional time for all of them," the narrator confides, it is "perhaps especially [emotional] for her, Jerrie Cobb" (1). Stone artfully opens her story with the rich disappointment that will characterize the climax of the narrative, and she centers the narrative of that disappointment around the character of Cobb. After all, "it was Jerrie who led them in a quest to live their dreams, Jerrie who first believed they had a shot at all this, Jerrie who still, to this day, is fighting for her dream" (1). When an early incarnation of the testing program failed before any significant progress had been made, Stone notes that none of the three central figures, "nor especially Cobb," was ready to quit (15). She uses a motif of paragraphs beginning with the words "the first" to emphasize Cobb's status as a pioneer (16–18). When Stone writes of Cobb's discovery that a necessary battery of tests in Pensacola for the Mercury 13 women had been canceled, Cobb is similarly heroic: "Cobb flew to Washington, D.C. When faced with an obstacle, she always rose to the occasion. She was going to find out what was going on if it took everything she had" (55). In Stone's hands, Cobb is a strong, capable woman who endured terrible prejudice with aplomb.

At this point, the standard rhetorical move of analysis, the move required by the accuracy model of nonfiction, is to make an argument that occupies one of two dichotomous positions: I must argue either that Cobb was in fact the woman Stone portrayed her to be or that she was not. But both positions within that traditional rhetorical mode are logical dead ends. If interrogating the truth of Stone's account reveals that Stone is wrong about Cobb, there is nothing more to observe. And, as I have already stated, because Stone is human, the real shock would be if everything she wrote about her main character were entirely true. If interrogating the truth of Stone's account reveals that Cobb is in fact a strong, capable woman who endured terrible prejudice with aplomb—and it seems to me that one would be a fool to suggest otherwise—again there is nothing more to say. All that is left for the reader to do is submit to the facts of Stone's account. Such an approach to the study of children's nonfiction obstructs rather than expands engagement with the book. Therefore, instead of watching for the factuality of Stone's text, I want to watch for where it skirts around inquiry, where it declines to ask questions, especially where doing so reinforces the authority of Cobb, from which *Almost Astronauts* draws its reliability.

Despite the book's portrait of Cobb, an early letter she sent to the other participants in the program raises questions about the image of Cobb as a quiet, confident leader, questions that Stone's book avoids. These questions do, however, arise in the materials from which Stone drew her information. Although *Almost Astronauts* presents Cobb as a reluctant leader, one who hated even to talk about herself (30), Ackmann hints that Cobb went out of her way to assume and maintain a leadership position within the group. When Lovelace moved a testing date, for example, Lovelace, Cobb, and Jackie Cochran—a woman who looms large elsewhere in the Mercury 13 story—all three wrote to the women participating in the tests to tell them of the change. Cobb, however, got the jump on the other two, and she took a position in the letter that raises questions about the purity of Cobb's motivations. "Cobb wrote first," Ackmann explains, "assuming an authoritative stance," and offered advice on how to prepare for and thrive during the tests. She also, according to Ackmann, "enclosed a release form discharging the

United States of any legal claim that might ensue from the testing and asked that the forms be returned to her home" (*Mercury 13*, 127). Cobb's choice of subject in the letter, coupled with the fact that she wrote her letter first, suggests a much more complicated leader than the one *Almost Astronauts* portrays. The release form included with the letter also calls that version of Cobb into question. As Ackmann explains, "the form Cobb sent had no indication that it had been generated by the U.S. Naval School of Aviation Medicine. In fact, the school is inaccurately referred to as the U.S. Naval Aviation Medical Center. Most likely, Cobb herself crafted the form" (127n). If Ackmann is right, Cobb's letter represents not a self-effacing, reluctant leader but one with careful designs to secure her leadership position in the minds of the other participants. *Almost Astronauts* leaves out Cobb's questionable motives with the effect that Cobb takes on a mythologized sheen as a hardworking, overachieving woman who never wanted the responsibility that fate thrust upon her.

The Foil

Almost Astronauts further protects Cobb against questions by giving her an antagonist whose character is similarly simplified: Jackie Cochran. A quotation from the book's biographical sketch of Cochran gives a good summary of the problems to which *Almost Astronauts* reduces her character:

> The girl born Bessie Pittman . . . claimed not to be part of her biological family and left her true identity behind. When Bessie Pittman moved to New York City in 1929, she became Jacqueline Cochran and never looked back. Jackie Cochran was a person who would do just about anything to make the world fit her sense of what it should be. And she did not think women should go into space unless she figured prominently in the plan. (75)

This sketch presents a Cochran with several significant flaws, such as her underhanded nature. Although children's literature has frequently been skeptical about the link between biological relationships and personal identity,[3] here *Almost Astronauts* easily labels Cochran's earlier identity as Bessie Pittman her "true identity." Cochran's character in Stone's book is therefore fundamentally disingenuous, which leads to her second major flaw: her ruthlessness. The book follows Cochran's betrayal of her "true identity" by highlighting Cochran's callousness, claiming that Cochran "never looked back." Whereas Cobb's determination was a virtue, Cochran's is all but maniacal, as she "would do just about anything to make the world fit her sense of what it should be." And although *Almost Astronauts* removes references to Cobb's questionable machinations to remain at the center of the Mercury 13 program, Cochran's greatest flaw is that she was unwilling to see women in space "unless she figured prominently in the plan."

In the same way that *Almost Astronauts* elides questions about Cobb's reliability in her recollection of her interview with Johnson, the book also secures the authority of Sarah Gorelick, another member of the Mercury 13, when Gorelick's testimony finds fault in Cochran. Stone recounts a story about a conversation between Cochran and Lovelace from early in the program, when Cochran, despite her age, evidently still considered herself a feasible pilot for the mission. According to the version of the story in *Almost Astronauts*, Cochran, in keeping with her shifty, ruthless character, handled Lovelace's rejection of her candidacy badly:

> Furious, she threatened to pull her funding. Sarah Gorelick happened to be at the clinic doing her testing that week and heard Cochran letting loose, screaming and yelling at Lovelace. He held his ground and told her the truth—that her age and previous health conditions prevented her from being a candidate. (72)

Stone does not provide a citation for this evidence, but it's possible that she is drawing from versions of the story provided by two other books on the Mercury 13 program. One, *Right Stuff, Wrong Sex* (2004), is written by Margaret A. Weitekamp, who also provides the foreword to Stone's book. Weitekamp similarly traces Cochran's lack of physical participation in the program to a meeting with Lovelace overheard by Gorelick, but Cochran's reaction—and its opposition to the "truth" maintained by Lovelace—are less pat in Weitekamp's version of the story:

> Sarah Gorelick Ratley remembered having her own appointment with Dr. Lovelace interrupted so that he could talk to Cochran about her test results. As she sat in the office, "Dr. Lovelace looked in her patient folder and remarked that she would not be a candidate for the space program due to a heart problem that had developed." Cochran did not take the news well. Ratley recalled, "The door was closed as I walked down the hall but I was aware of loud voices in the background." (82)

Whereas Stone's version of the story presents a view of the conversation between Cochran and Lovelace as though Gorelick were present, Weitekamp shows her witness moving away from the scene, and Cochran's "screaming and yelling" at a Lovelace who "held his ground and told her the truth" is instead "loud voices" from both Cochran and Lovelace, with no secure handle on what the voices were saying. Ackmann's version of the same story, published before Weitekamp's, is even less authoritative. As a "distressed" Lovelace looked over the results of Cochran's recent physical exam,

> Lovelace unthinkingly muttered to Gorelick, "She's not going to be happy about this." When Cochran appeared at Lovelace's office for the next appointment, Gorelick greeted her respectfully and then quickly disappeared. As she was walking down the hallway, Gorelick heard shouting coming from Randy Lovelace's office. While only Lovelace and Cochran would ever really know what news was being delivered, Gorelick's conversation with Lovelace led her to believe that Jackie Cochran was furious that her medical reports ruled out any possibility of astronaut candidacy. (90–91)

A careful comparison of these three versions of the story looking not for factuality but for authority is revealing. Importantly, all three writers draw the same conclusion, and again, no one suggests that Cochran was patient or compliant. In other words, the distinction that I am making is not precisely a distinction in accuracy. The difference between the three versions of the story is that over the course of the scene, *Almost Astronauts* erases the point of view present in the other two stories, similar to the process that I explored in chapter 2, through which textbooks intent on maintaining their own authority obscure the sense of an author with whom to argue through their use of third-person language. Whereas both Weitekamp and Ackmann emphasize that Gorelick was actively moving away from Lovelace's office during a scene to which she was the sole outside witness, *Almost Astronauts* names Gorelick as a witness, then protects her authority as a source by neglecting to mention that Gorelick herself says that she was not in a position to hear what exactly went on behind Lovelace's closed door. By sidestepping questions about Gorelick's authority, *Almost Astronauts* is able to maintain a caricature of Cochran as a woman who prosecuted her centrality to the Mercury 13 program ruthlessly.

The relationship between Lovelace and Cochran appears, however, to have been crucial to the Mercury 13 program, and a letter that Cochran sent to Lovelace near the beginning of her awareness of the program provides another important contrast in the way that Stone and her sources present Cochran. Stone does not cite the original letter, so her description of the letter and Lovelace's reaction to it are probably adapted from what Ackmann and Weitekamp have written on the subject. As with its treatment of the conflict between Cochran and Lovelace over Cochran's physical preparedness for participation in the program, *Almost Astronauts* frames its explanation of Cochran's four-page letter in ways that simplify Cochran as a character, especially as that character interacts with the project:

> Cochran got involved with the program in November 1960. She assumed that Lovelace was bringing her on in a leadership role and immediately wrote him a long letter detailing suggestions for how the program should be run. Not surprisingly, one of Cochran's recommendations was to change the age requirements for testing, which would have allowed her to be eligible. (71)

Here, *Almost Astronauts* is advancing many of the aspects of the caricature of Cochran that it will use throughout. Cochran's presumptive assumption of the leadership role—which *Almost Astronauts* has been presenting as Cobb's rightful role—comes into play, and as elsewhere, Cochran's leadership is always self-serving. According to this version of the story, Cochran was, true to the book's caricature, underhanded, aggressive, and even proprietary.

But there is little support for this caricature in the letter itself. There, Cochran does urge Lovelace to include—and the phrasing is important—"a few" women who exceeded his original upper limit of thirty-five years of age. However, in that same sentence, she also urges him to include "*at least* a few" women at the lower end of the spectrum, "even though they have not had all the air experience set forth in your original specifications" (emphasis added). She continues by explaining, "In this way you will get a check on the effect of aging which will be valuable. Most particularly would I get some of the youngsters in." This is a strange recommendation if we are to believe that Cochran—at the time she wrote the letter, already in her fifties and in possession of an extraordinary pilot's résumé—was trying to shift the requirements to benefit herself. Cochran also argues for expanding the criteria for entrance to the program because, in her experience with the World War II–era Women Airforce Service Pilots (WASP), "we found . . . that the best material was in the age bracket between 20 and 23" (2–3). Although the origins of the WASP program are complicated, when Cochran's proposal for the squadron that would eventually become the WASPs was accepted on September 15, 1942, Cochran was already thirty-six years old. With that information in mind, and despite the book's argument, Cochran's letter makes the case that the best female pilots in her experience with the WASPs were *other* women, women younger than Cochran was at the time she wrote the letter, younger even than Cochran had been during the WASP program. Therefore, Cochran's letter does not support the simplified characterization that *Almost Astronauts* gives Cochran.[4] There is little doubt that as early as a month after she sent this letter, Cochran began campaigning on her own behalf (see Weitekamp, *Right Stuff*, 80), but the characterization *Almost Astronauts* presents strips any nuance out of the letter. What is left is a simpler piece of evidence that undercuts a version of the Mercury 13 story that might compete with the one in which Cobb is a determined, straight-shooting heroine. *Almost Astronauts* allows—indeed, exaggerates—questions about Cochran's motivation, but it eliminates questions about Cobb's.

Skeptical Reading

The mythologization of Cobb and caricaturization of Cochran work together with how *Almost Astronauts* presents Stone's interview with Cobb. All three advance the book's ambition of reliability. In doing so, they interfere with inquiry in ways very similar to those that I detailed in chapter 3, where I demonstrated the various rhetorical methods by which a book can preserve or crack the authority of its characters. In *Almost Astronauts,* the techniques at play in reducing the complexity of the characters go even further. In places, this characterization obscures Stone's research rather than modeling it; presents a hero whose actions must be admired, not questioned; and provides a villain who, as a foil to Cobb, turns the tale into a monologue in honor of one point of view rather than a dialogue between many. Each case not only deflects inquiry but also presents a vision of the past that is less true. In obscuring opportunities for critical engagement, the book is also less factual.

Stone's book is, therefore, evidence of two important points. The first is that whereas the reliability model of children's nonfiction leads only—and inevitably—to disappointment, paying attention to where a book invites or declines critical engagement can enrich our understanding of that book. The second, though, is that even the principles of critical literacy—the theory that underwrites my own approach to nonfiction—cannot be applied unreflectively. In the early chapters of my study, I laid out multiple rhetorical cues that often signal an openness to critical engagement, but one of them, indeed, the very rhetorical cue that Zarnowski and Turkel single out as the hallmark of nonfiction in the Aronson style, works very differently in Stone's book. The key scene in *Almost Astronauts* that establishes its authority is the scene in which Stone collects information. In this scene, Stone certainly models the process of inquiry, but the result is that Cobb's authority is fused with that of the author, by extension inviting readers to rely on her book rather than question it. Even simply watching for where nonfiction models inquiry, then, is not enough. Although I have produced a list of rhetorical cues that often signal where a book invites inquiry, none of them can be used without careful reflection.

What this list offers is a way to think about how a book is inviting critical engagement, but of course, it can't begin to answer the question of whether children even need such invitations. In the Conclusion to my study, I explore evidence that children frequently engage critically whether or not their books want them to, but in the meantime, I can report that there is some evidence that children will follow the cues given by nonfiction. Zarnowski and Turkel's essay shows that some fifth-grade students who read the kind of nonfiction that Aronson prefers did ask the kinds of questions that Aronson would have them ask: put another way, while reading nonfiction that models inquiry, they inquired ("Creating," 33). Conversely, Sam Wineburg ("On the Reading," 514) and Richard Paxton ("Someone," 239–40) have both demonstrated that students who have grown used to nonfiction written in a style that protects its author's authority are reluctant to engage with evidence critically. We don't know yet whether children *need* books that invite them to read critically. We do, however, see that when adults—writers, teachers, parents, and other grown-ups who want to support children's habitual inquiry—ask children to rely on nonfiction, the chances that children will become part of the conversation plummet.

Critical literacy, in calling for books that open up inquiry, is delighted by the pursuit of accuracy, as long as that pursuit is itself also a subject of study rather than an exercise completed behind the scenes by authoritative adults. Therefore critical literacy should not be understood as incompatible with nonfiction that insists on a "fine line" between truth and untruth. It *is* incompatible with nonfiction that asks its readers to "rely" on its truthfulness, but *Almost Astronauts*—penned by an author devoted to truthful nonfiction—demonstrates that even the best nonfiction should never ask its readers to depend on it with full confidence anyway.

7
THE EMPATHY OF CRITICAL ENGAGEMENT
Emotion and Sentimentality in Children's Nonfiction

I SPENT MUCH OF THE FIRST DECADE of the new millennium working on a project that finally became a book in 2011, and it wasn't until much later that I started finding out what I had gotten wrong. Because of the glacial speed of the reviewing process in the humanities, most reviews of the book began appearing in 2013, and I read them all with a desperate need for affirmation that I hadn't felt since my high school years. The reviewers were almost universally kind, but one criticism struck me immediately as sharp and, unfortunately, true. My book was a study of mid-nineteenth-century sentimental novels and the later girls' novels that followed in their footsteps, and I opened the acknowledgments page with a wink at the reader that I had hoped would be charmingly self-effacing. I warned that for a little while, I needed to write with unabashed emotion about the people who had helped me, though I promised that in the rest of the book, I would "write with intellectual detachment about sentimentality" (*Disciplining Girls,* ix). One reviewer, Lauren Byler, picked up on this comment and wondered, "Why must sentimentality be approached with 'intellectual detachment'?" In opposing "intellectual detachment" and "sentimentality," she argued, I reiterated "a deep-rooted American anxiety about sentimentality's potential to void individuality and to feminize, disempower, and render us incompetent" ("Review," 245). With this opening gesture, Byler complained, I had received, accepted, and magnified an opposition between sentimentality and critical study that was not only inaccurate but harmful. A decade of work, and I hadn't even gotten through the first paragraph without making a mistake.

In many ways, this chapter is a response to Byler's criticism. Conventional wisdom, the sort of wisdom I casually endorsed in that first book, often holds that emotional attachment resists critical engagement, and feminist theory has both rejected and amended that wisdom. As the first part of this chapter demonstrates, feminism has produced a theoretical model that rescues emotion from the dust heap of critical analysis, but as the next part demonstrates, feminism has also warned that emotion—specifically, sentimentality and the immersion that it encourages—exaggerates its claims to critical engagement. If children's nonfiction is, as I have been arguing throughout, a venue with tremendous potential for critical engagement, then this issue of how emotional and critical engagement can interact is crucial. My experience with children's literature leads me to believe that it is a literature deeply invested in emotion, so if my model paints emotion as the enemy of critical engagement, it will render off-limits a great number of the very texts that it hopes to approach.[1] My point is not, as Katrin Pahl puts it, "to simply celebrate emotion" but "to wrest emotionality from its dismissal" ("Logic," 1457). Sentimentality has, this chapter demonstrates, worked at times to "render us incompetent," to echo Byler's summary of my ill-conceived comment. In such cases, sentimentality has indeed served nonfiction poorly by offering an end to inquiry, even by helping to mask ideology that insists on a certain interpretation of information. But feminist theory also offers a strategy by which sentimental engagement can fuel a call to inquiry, can be a requisite component in critical engagement with genuinely progressive consequences. Just as are voice, character, peritexts, and photography, emotion in a work of nonfiction is a possible venue for critical engagement, and careful attention to how a book uses emotion to invite or decline critical engagement reveals a great deal about the critical goals of that book.

Successful Emotional, Critical Engagement

Feminism gives the most pointed explanation of what imagining critical engagement without emotion has cost us. Lissa Paul, for example, writes of her experience as a feminist scholar in an academy that conceived of its value through its disdain for emotion. When she tried to examine Ted Hughes's work for children with and through affection, she encountered resistance that she finally came to think was based on New Criticism's desire to position itself above human emotion and separate itself from political engagement. "I realized," she explains, "that the presence or absence of affection had nothing to do with scholarship or critical ability and that feminist theory, which had fuelled my confidence in my textual pleasures, had other lessons for me to learn" (*Reading*, 15). Feminism has many such "lessons" about how to use emotion to drive critical intervention. As Sara Ahmed reflects, "when I think of my relationship to feminism, for example, I can rewrite my coming into being as a feminist subject in terms of different emotions, or in terms of how my emotions have involved particular readings of the worlds I have inhabited." She then goes on to list anger, pain, love, wonder, joy, and hope as emotions that led directly to what she calls her "politicization" (*Cultural Politics*, 171). In contrast, privileging an intellect free of emotion frequently works to "subordinate" women and everything linked with them. "Emotions are associated with women," she argues, "who are represented as 'closer' to nature, ruled by appetite, and less able to transcend the body through thought, will and judgement" (3), an argument that matches exactly with Paul's experience. The answer that Ahmed proposes is not "to claim that feminism is rational rather than emotional" but "to contest the assumption that 'rational thought' is unemotional, or that it does not involve being moved by others" (170). This intersection between intellectual engagement and emotion, often disavowed, is ripe for rediscovery.

Children's nonfiction has already demonstrated an ability to appeal to emotion while tangling with big ideas. Barbara Bader, for example, demonstrates that nonfiction has a long history of attending to children's curiosity ("Nonfiction"),[2] and Margery Fisher highlights nonfiction books with "the word 'quest' or 'discover' or 'look at'" in their titles, words whose denotation includes inquiry and whose connotation indicates pleasure (*Matters*, 15). Myra Zarnowski, in fact, sees not a gap but a link between joy and the difficulty of research questions. After working with middle-grade students, trade nonfiction, and the children's own research projects, she has determined that students are willing, even eager, to engage with difficult nonfiction for a simple reason:

> Because these questions, like ordinary puzzles, are challenging. It's the same reason that many people read mysteries, do crossword puzzles, watch all sorts of quiz shows trying to outguess the contestants, and even look for Waldo in the crowded pictures of *Where's Waldo?* (1997). It's the puzzling question or challenge that's motivating, whether we're in kindergarten, graduate school, or beyond. (*History*, 106)

It's typical, Zarnowski argues, to think of exploring information and enjoying oneself as activities that are opposed to one another, but her experience is that the two are instead fundamentally connected. And key to that connection are emotions, in this case the feelings of puzzlement and curiosity. Finally, Jeannine Atkins champions curiosity as the chief emotion evoked by good nonfiction, even elevating the ability to generate curiosity above perfect accuracy. "Of course, we get things wrong, too," she concedes, "but how many of us are curious about people and events we knew little about until we were lured by shows 'based on a true story'? We can quibble after watching a film, and we do, but before we raised questions we got to be immersed in a story" ("Did That Really Happen?," 31). For these experts in children's nonfiction, immersion is not an impediment to asking questions but a key step.

When creators of children's nonfiction talk about their work, they frequently do so in terms that make plain the connection, not the conflict, between emotion and inquiry. Sy Montgomery, author of *The Snake Scientist* (1999), mentions love repeatedly: "Sitting in a pit with 18,000 snakes—what's not to love? And I loved meeting so many kids who went to the snake dens on their school field trips. They loved snakes—as we knew our readers would too." She also speaks specifically of writing books with the aim of helping "readers

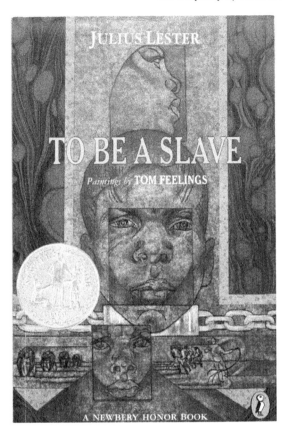

Julius Lester, *To Be a Slave* (1968; reprint, 1998).

experience the thrill of discovering the unknown" (qtd. in Zappy, "Sing," 34). Excitement, passion, joy—all of these emotions run not counter to but underneath the process of grappling with new data. More painful emotions, too, fill the experience of research as writers of nonfiction experience it, as Julius Lester explains in the preface of his Newbery Honor book *To Be a Slave* (1968). Lester reflects on his experience of realizing that the tale of his own family history would end not in a coat of arms but in "a bill of sale." He found himself "overwhelmed by a sense of loss. There was an emptiness within me that could not be filled and I grieved." These emotions did not paralyze him; rather, they drove him to research. He recalls, "I needed to be able to follow the trail of my existence back through time, to hear stories about those whose existence had made mine possible"

(4). As he explored the work of those who came before him, he was filled with a new emotion: rage. "I was angered," he writes, by what he saw in B. A. Botkin's book of interviews with former slaves. The book's portrait of black people looking back on their days of enslavement with deference for their former masters infuriated him, and that anger drove him to the source material. Lester realized "that Botkin had drawn his material from the slave narratives of the Federal Writers' Project, which were housed in the Archive of Folksong at the Library of Congress," so, the preface goes on to explain, he went back to those narratives himself (5). The result was *To Be a Slave*. The entire book is therefore framed as an intellectual, critical encounter with original materials, one driven by emotion. Whether the emotions are comfortable or painful, these authors explain that their emotions are a necessary part of their critical engagement.

A Feminist Critique of Critical Sentimental Identification

Contemporary feminism is not, however, completely convinced of the legitimacy of emotion as part of an intellectual engagement. One emotional connection in particular has been the subject of extensive debate in recent feminist theory: sentimental identification, the emotional coordination that comes from a deep, affectionate connection between two people—or a person and a book. Sentimental identification is not a simple emotion but a process of inhabiting another's perspective through a synchronization of emotions. Various emotions can come together in sentimental identification: grief, love, joy, sympathy, guilt, admiration, affection, and more. This model of emotional engagement relies not on a checklist of emotions but on the loss of one's self in the self of another, and emotion provides the means of that investment in someone else's experience. Glenn Hendler writes of "the erasure of identity that sympathetic identification can enact," referring specifically to the nineteenth-century literary modes that asked readers to feel *with* the characters about whom they were reading (*Public*, 135). Such a process was key to literary and political imaginings of (mostly, but not exclusively) white U.S. feminism of the nineteenth century, during the phase of suffragist, abolitionist, and temperance activism that gave rise to the nation's first best sellers, most famously including Harriet Beecher Stowe's *Uncle Tom's Cabin* (1852). These first-wave feminists hoped that emotion would provide a sentimental experience through which white readers would understand the perspective of, for example, those who had escaped slavery but whom the Fugitive Slave Law required to be returned to their chains. As such, sentimentality was a major political tool of nineteenth-century feminism, a tool for harnessing emotion to drive ideological analysis.

Today's feminism, however, is decidedly more ambivalent about this specific form of emotional engagement. Megan Boler argues powerfully on behalf of reclaiming emotion, especially of reclaiming it from a feminist position, but for Boler, endorsing sentimental identification requires extensive qualification. Boler calls this connection "empathy" at times and "sympathy" at others, but her meaning is consistent. "In popular and philosophical conceptions," she explains, "empathy requires identification. I take up your perspective, and claim that I can know your experience through mine" (*Feeling*, 160). Boler is one of many feminists who have been involved in an extensive project of feminist self-reevaluation that has been taking place since at least the 1990s, and here she hints at the core problem of sentimental identification.[3] The objection most often raised is that it ignores differences between people, differences that ground both the oppression that some people experience in a given situation and the privilege that others enjoy in that same situation. Eliding the difference between people, the argument goes, results in homogenization that tends to benefit the people already in power. As a result, when Boler valorizes emotions, they tend to be emotions associated not with affection but with displeasure. Thus she describes the civil rights movement as "significantly shaped by the moral revolution offered by anger" (7). When writing of the successes of feminism, she declares, "The material changes that have occurred as a result of women's organized anger channeled into collective political action are innumerable" (113). Boler denies that her "pedagogy of discomfort," as she calls it, seeks out anger, and she claims that such a pedagogy is also "likely" to bring about "joy, passion, new hopes and a sense of possibility" (188). Nonetheless, this claim is one of the very few times when "joy" and "hope" appear in her book, and even this claim is followed by eight pages on the importance of fear and anger in feminist pedagogy. Although Boler and other feminists have put tremendous effort into rescuing emotion for critical and civic engagement, she remains highly skeptical of identification through emotion.[4]

Recent scholarship on children's literature has extended that skepticism beyond the adult-oriented texts for which it was first developed, and these arguments, too, are telling. Sara Schwebel, for example, struggles with the powerfully emotional connection that historical fiction encourages between readers and the characters whose imaginary perspectives they adopt:

> Typically, children's historical novels invite reader identification with the protagonist and his or her immediate family. This enables an intimate, visceral connection with the past, but it is also limiting. Throughout the colonial period and early republic, indigenous peoples were forcibly displaced to create "free" western lands for pioneers to settle. These characters—as well as their compulsory removal—have traditionally been minimalized in fictional narratives of western settlement written for children. If a reader empathizes with a frontier protagonist, can she comprehend the experience of that woman's Native contemporaries? (*Child-Size*, 3–4)

Schwebel's objection is that immersion in the perspective of the empowered class may serve to teach broader historical movements that are important in a classroom, but it simultaneously normalizes a perspective that *prevents* identification with the people whom Western history tends to marginalize already. Such sentimental alignment with the oppressor and apart from the oppressed is difficult to resist, she argues, "especially when educators encourage children to become lost in books" (4). In the cases of children's historical fiction, Schwebel finds a pattern that retains the technology of nineteenth-century identification but uses that technology not to provide emotional links to the disenfranchised but to confirm the perspective of history's winners. Anastasia Ulanowicz expresses similar concerns about Lynne Cheney's *America: A Patriotic Primer* (2002), specifically invoking Lauren Berlant's feminist critique of sentimentality. Ulanowicz claims that Cheney's point is the production of what Berlant would call "infant citizens," a process requiring "an exercise in sentimentality" that prevents readers from perceiving their society's "many structural injustices" and that "inhibits their participation in collective action" ("Preemptive," 361).[5] These children's literature scholars not only maintain feminism's distrust of sentimental identification but point out how children's literature has used such emotional connection to distract from the very social inequities that first-wave feminism used it to critique.

Sentimental Identification That Thwarts Critical Engagement

I am not going to argue that sentimental identification is innocent of the potential that contemporary feminist theory marks out. Rather, I note that such identification has worked in exactly these ways in many instances across the history of children's nonfiction. One obvious example is James Janeway's *A Token for Children: Being an Exact Account of the Conversion, Holy and Exemplary Lives, and Joyful Deaths, of Several Young Children* (1811). In this text, emotion and instruction meet powerfully, this time in the invitations to noncritical identification embodied in the passionate models of children too good for this earth. Emotion is written on nearly every page of the book, as when Janeway encourages parents to force their children to learn to "weep by themselves after Christ" (4); when he demands of children, "Did you ever get by yourself, and weep for sin" (5); and when he asks them, "How art thou now affected, poor child, in the reading of this book? Have you shed ever a tear since you began reading?" (7) But emotion is not its own aim in Janeway's book. The point of emotion is to fit oneself into the model of the—also weeping—children who led the "holy and exemplary lives" of the title. In service of this goal Janeway begs parents to "put" their offspring "upon imitating these sweet children" (4), beseeches the child readers to beg "that God would make you like these blessed children" (7), and ends his histrionic introduction with an altar call that would impress any televangelist:

> And now, dear children, I have done; I have written to you, I have prayed for you, but what you will do I can't tell. O children, if you love me, if you love your parents, if you love your souls, if you would escape hell fire, and if you would live in heaven when you die, do you go and do as these good children. And that you may be your parents' joy, your country's honour, and live in God's fear, and die in his love, is the prayer of your dear friend, J. Janeway. (10)

In example after example, Janeway's text lays out the misery and ecstasy of one child after another who renounces wickedness, with, as his introduction explains, the hope that the child reader will become like the fictional child. The rich net of love, terror, remorse, and joy served up by "your dear friend" does not invite reflection or theological speculation but conversion to the model offered by Janeway's beautifully, pathetically dead children. Powerful emotion, Janeway hopes, will pour the reading children into the mold of the children about whom they read, resulting in young people who live the ideology of their faith with no inkling that they might question it.

Other works of nonfiction available in the early republic were, if anything, less subtle about the link between emotion, spiritual training, and the end of inquiry. *Garden Amusements, for Improving the Minds of Little Children* (1814) instructs parents to use children's "desire" for knowledge "to be acquainted, by little and little, with every thing that it is proper for them to know" (*Garden*, 3). *Garden Amusements* relates a botanical conversation with children, and the knowledgeable adult speaker makes a point of turning the children's questions about nature into opportunities for authoritative religious instruction rather than ongoing inquiry. The children eat some sweet fruit, for example, and the adult confides that "while they were thus happy in the enjoyment, I thought it a proper time to mix instruction with it" (10). As he collects the children's observations about nature, he rewards them with metaphysical interpretations. For example, when one child, Henry, remarks that a vine "seems to lie low, towards the ground, as if it were of a very humble nature," the adult answers,

I love you for that, my dear boy, you[r] observation is right; for in hot countries, vines run along on the ground, and never presume to rise themselves upward. And this is the character of all good men; they all lie low in their own esteem, however fruitful and precious in the eyes of others. (11–12)

In these lines, the book models a loving relationship that turns investigation into orthodoxy. The "love" with which the adult rewards the boy yields strong disciplinary fruit later, too, as Henry promises to recite a song about a bird "if you will engage to put me right if I am not perfectly correct" (32). *Garden Amusements* shows that the study of botany may begin with careful observations, but it will always end in loving doctrine, with answers tidily packaged for young learners.

These examples come from the beginning of the nineteenth century, but new nonfiction also sometimes uses emotion in ways that refuse rather than invite critical engagement, and although the consequences are not quite spiritual, they are certainly ideological. Michael O. Tunnell's *Candy Bomber: The Story of the Berlin Airlift's "Chocolate Pilot"* (2010) draws a great deal of its power from its emotional appeal, which is not in itself anticritical. Tunnell tells the story of Lieutenant Gail Halvorsen, who was part of the airlift of vital aid into West Berlin during an eleven-month Soviet blockade against land transportation. Halvorsen began his duty flying to Berlin as one of the many officers responsible for transporting coal, flour, medicine, and other necessities, but a brush with the children of the divided city inspired him to begin parachuting packages of candy and gum down to them before he landed. Halvorsen's idea caught on quickly, and by the time the Soviets eased the blockade, tons of candy had been delivered. It is a story of sincere generosity on the part of Halvorsen as well as people all around the world who joined the effort, and Tunnell can hardly be blamed for making use of the genuine sentimentality of Halvorsen's gesture of sympathy. He uses touching personal stories ranging from grown-ups recalling the joy of the candy that floated down from the sky (1–2) to a letter from a father who was able to give his son a birthday present that year because of the providential candy that landed outside his window (60–61). Tunnell mentions, too, children such as the girl Halvorsen recalled as having "wistful blue eyes" (19) and the children who first inspired him with their "thirty hungry faces" (21). It's a moving story, and it would be less true if Tunnell had chosen not to include the emotions that power it.

Still, there is a central way that the emotion of the story serves to distract from a controversy, from a disagreement over what the airlift signified, a place where questions lie waiting for critical engagement. Halvorsen, not unlike the character of Jerrie Cobb whom I explored in the previous chapter, is almost cartoonish in his wholesome goodness, and the warmth that surrounds him and the needy souls he touches helps to distract from a more complicated backstory. For example, Tunnell describes Halvorsen as an icon of American down-home goodness, writing, "No matter how far the Air Force took Gail Halvorsen from his boyhood home on a farm in Utah, the values he learned from his salt-of-the-earth parents never left him" (41). Against Halvorsen and his homespun kindness, Tunnell poses an equally cartoonish Soviet Union, blustering with Grinchy rage at the kindness of America. The Soviets are bad guys from before the beginning, a vision Tunnell captures when he relates the Soviet outrage over the democratic allies refusing to let Stalin have all of Berlin. "When they didn't leave," Tunnell explains, "the Soviets cried foul by claiming that the Western Allies were forcing their democratic, capitalistic ideals on everyone in Germany" (7). Later, when Halvorsen begins dropping candy for the children in East Berlin as well as West, Tunnell rolls his eyes at the Soviets' reaction: "They lodged a formal complaint with the US State Department, claiming the East Berlin candy drops were a 'capitalist trick to influence the minds of young people'" (36). With the Utah-bred honesty of Halvorsen and wistfully hungry Berlin children on one hand and the paranoid Soviets on the other, Tunnell makes laughable the idea that Halvorsen's candy drops signified anything more than ingenuous American generosity. The position in which readers are encouraged to immerse themselves is defined by the tender generosity of the Americans and the wounded neediness of the Germans, and it is defined against the Soviets' paranoia.

Even a cursory survey of popular reports of the airlifts, though, reveals that Tunnell's sentimentality provides a perspective that is poorly positioned to read the complexity of the ideology at stake in the airdrops. In the United States, the success of the airlift—a stunning achievement of technology, organization, and camaraderie—was widely touted as evidence of the superiority of American ideology to communism. Six months into the effort, John Foster Dulles, soon to be named to the Senate and later to become secretary of state, praised the airlift for reminding "some, who seem to have forgotten, that freedom has moral and material reserves that are unpredictable and immeasurable" (Middleton, "Dulles," 3). General Lucius D. Clay, the U.S. military governor, concurred, saying, "I am convinced that the people of Berlin have learned from their experience under one totalitarian government to withstand almost any hardship rather than to accept another totalitarian regime" (Morrow, "Berlin," 12). Comments such as these give strong indication that the airlift was seen as a test of American ideology against Soviet. The candy drops did not receive as much coverage as did the airlift in general, but one article appearing in *Time* did make a point of mentioning the candy along with the more traditional supplies, and that article ended with an explicitly nationalist, even threatening, summary:

> The triumph of organization and improvisation that made it possible is what [Major General William H.] Tunner means by "using airplanes in a manner hitherto unknown." For strategists the airlift has a meaning far beyond its immediate goal of feeding blockaded Berlin. The U.S. Army has never fought a major foreign campaign more than 300 miles from salt water. Suppose it had to fight in the heart of a continent? An airlift like Berlin's might be the answer.
>
> U.S. Airmen have considered this possibility since the China Hump operation and the airborne Burma jungle campaign. Perhaps Russian strategists, who have consistently underestimated air power, are beginning to get the point. (32)

Stalin, then, was hardly alone in perceiving ideological, even imperialist urges behind the airlifts, including the candy drops. Indeed, one might go so far as to say that making Stalin nervous was part of, as the article from *Time* puts it, "the point." Tunnell's sentimental portrait of a kind Halvorsen and the smudged-but-resilient faces of German children distracts from this more complicated story. The narrative that Tunnell shapes uses sentimentality to offer readers the opportunity to immerse themselves in a story that shrugs off accusations of nationalism, accusations that, periodicals of the time indicate, are likely valid. That immersion works in ways very similar to the visible author in Maud and Miska Petersham's *Story Book of Houses,* which I analyzed in chapter 2. There I argued that the Petershams invited readers to join a perspective that normalized a teleological ethnocentrism. The sentimental identification of Tunnell's book likewise offers a comfortable position from which to read history, and in taking up that position, readers are given a perspective that makes perceiving the underlying ideology of the historical facts more difficult.

A Feminist Theory of Critical Sentimental Identification

In many examples, then, sentimental identification gives rise to the same anticritical problems of which feminism has found it guilty in adult literature. However, Megan Boler, who earlier voiced a core piece of feminism's concerns about sentimental identification, also offers a possible revision through which it might be rescued. Boler's revision dodges some key pitfalls, many of which were earlier articulated by Freire.[6] The kind of sentimentality that Boler rejects most firmly is what she calls "passive empathy," which, she writes, "signifies a privilege: allowing oneself to inhabit a position of distance and separation, to remain in the 'anonymous' spectating crowd and abdicate any possible responsibility" (*Feeling,* 184). Freire would agree, as much of his book is given over to warning would-be teachers and activist leaders, people who often come from the moneyed and educated classes, against the temptations of this mode of empathy with the oppressed people in search of liberation. He writes,

> The oppressor is solidary with the oppressed only when he stops regarding the oppressed as an abstract category and sees them as persons who have been unjustly dealt with, deprived

of their voice, cheated in the sale of their labor—when he stops making pious, sentimental, and individualistic gestures and risks an act of love, in its existentiality, in its praxis. To affirm that men are persons and as persons should be free, and yet to do nothing tangible to make this affirmation a reality, is a farce. (*Pedagogy,* 34–35)

Note, though, that Freire rejects the notion that in avoiding the "sentimental," one must also avoid love, just as Boler reveals that excluding "passive empathy" does not mean excluding all empathy. An empathy between people that is ethically sound, according to Boler, is one that insists on recognizing "the responsibility borne by the reader. Instead of a consumptive focus on the other, the reader accepts a commitment to rethink her own assumptions, and to confront the internal obstacles encountered as one's views are challenged" (*Feeling,* 164). Explicit in this statement is the periodic retesting of one's ideas that I have called punctuated plurality and that I placed at the center of my definition of critical engagement. Similarly explicit—and implicit in Freire's warning—is the "responsibility" to recognize not simply connections but injustice, even if that injustice affects only one of the parties joined by empathy. Elsewhere, Freire explains that an "adherence" will come into being between students and the leaders who once "belonged to the social strata of the dominators" but who now "join the oppressed, in an act of true solidarity . . . an act of love and true commitment" (*Pedagogy,* 162). Valid empathy for Boler and genuine love for Freire are thus characterized by a self-reflective emotional connection that works for good outside of oneself, following on the sentimental realignment of one's emotional interiority.

Therefore, although it is a structure of feelings that I myself have shown to have anticritical impulses, I want to argue that sentimental identification invites critical engagement under one condition: when it calls for external action. The reflection that defines critical engagement is required by sentimental identification when empathy is not passive but active. Karin Westman anticipates this argument in an essay on the Harry Potter series wherein she proposes that Rowling's "compelling narrative . . . prompts both sympathetic engagement and critical reflection" ("Blending," 94). Westman rests her argument on the term *sympathy,* a term frequently linked with sentimentality and immersion in the subjective experience of another person. Because Harry is rich (in the wizarding world) as well as poor (in the mundane world), he is better able to understand the creatures and people he meets across the class spectrum. As a result of his ability to sympathize with—to enter into sentimental relationships with—the other characters, Harry is able to observe "the construction and persistence of class prejudice as well as ways to mitigate its debilitating consequences" (97). Thus it is *because* of Harry's sentimental identification with the people around him that he and his friends are driven to "formulate research questions, identify likely sources, and assess the results," a process Westman calls "critical thinking based on inquiry and informed speculation" (98). Westman even goes so far as to propose that Rowling's strategy "encourages readers to view the adult world with skepticism as well as sympathy" (97), a combination that repudiates the common wisdom that sentimentality and intellectual engagement are mutually exclusive.

A great deal of recent children's nonfiction uses its characters in a way that simultaneously invites identification and critical engagement, and Sy Montgomery's *The Snake Scientist* is an eloquent example. Montgomery's book focuses on Robert "Bob" Mason, a scientist pursuing the mystery of the red-sided garter snakes of Manitoba, where thousands of snakes emerge each spring. Mason is a prominent figure in the book, which delves into his research as well as his personal biography, including photographs from his own childhood. Montgomery foregrounds how snakes "have delighted and intrigued" Mason for years (41) and highlights Mason's "curiosity," quoting him as saying that "humans have a thirst for knowledge." The narrator seems to agree with Mason, claiming that "learning about the animals with whom we share this planet offers one way to satisfy our thirst to know" (43). Montgomery's is the same book about which I earlier noted the author's "love" for the subject, and that love shines through on every page. Mason's clearly defined character, powered by strong emotions and clear motivation, provides the centerpiece for the book's invitation to emotional engagement, the locus for identification. As with any robust char-

The Empathy of Critical Engagement ◫ 215

Sy Montgomery, *The Snake Scientist* (1999).

acterization, the character in this book makes mistakes, grows, and refuses to fit into any stock stereotypes. There is no telling whether children actually identify with Mason, but the book goes out of its way to encourage them to do so. Mason is a sentimental figure with whom identification is encouraged.

The part that identification in this book plays in critical engagement is conflicted. To some extent, it is collusive. After all, the book always takes for granted certain premises that this identification cannot but support. For instance, the book is never interested in questioning whether science itself is a valid enterprise. Too, it never troubles the human-gazing-at-animal perspective that characterizes Mason's own work. There are, in other words, many ways that this sentimental identification normalizes, which is to say that it protects from investigation, ideology that serves its own ends. But there are also other places where the book uses the sentimental figure of Mason to encourage inquiry. Perhaps the most extraordinary sentimental work performed by the book is that of encouraging identification between people and snakes through the character of Mason. It might even be fair to say that one of the main points of the book is to assuage the fear that people commonly feel for snakes. Fear is a serious impediment to sentimental identification, so by spending so much energy to remove fear between the reader and snakes, Montgomery's book is pointedly pursuing a sentimental agenda. "Some people fear snakes because they are afraid of what they don't understand," argues Montgomery, but, she writes, "One reason Bob likes to study snakes is *because* we know so little about them" (16, emphasis original). Here Montgomery reverses the standard aversion to snakes and links a drive to inquiry, a drive to studying snakes, with the undoing of fear.

As the book spends chapters further sketching the sentimental character of Mason and the snakes he studies, it builds a case for seeing similarities between snakes and humans, and it is when the book encourages an active rather than a passive empathy that critical engagement is at its richest. Montgomery quotes Mason as saying, "We're actually more similar to snakes than dissimilar. They have all the same organs we do. They have blood. They have lungs. They have hormones" (41). The book first introduces these physical similarities to point out that Mason's "studies of snakes might one day help people," and such self-serving identification might lead to accusations of what Boler calls "passive empathy," a fleeting empathy that persists only so long as it provides pleasure to the empathizer. When Montgomery explains that "Bob and his colleagues might learn something about snakes that could help us come up with a cure for human disease" (41), the identification is all but appropriative, as humans learn to stop fearing snakes so they can get close enough to them to cut out the body parts that might be useful. Montgomery, however, immediately subordinates that empathy to another. "But what *really* keeps Bob interested in the snakes of Narcisse," she writes, "isn't just the hope of helping humans, though that would be nice. It's something more" (42, emphasis original). Montgomery goes on to describe the intellectual satisfaction described earlier and then explains "an even deeper need," one that does not serve simply to cure or please humans but, to recall Boler, one that faces up to "the responsibility borne by the reader." Montgomery quotes Mason as saying, "The average human feels a shared heritage with other creatures on the earth . . . and feels a pain when a species vanishes" (43). Elsewhere, too, Montgomery makes this point. After explaining how "many people fear snakes so much they try to kill every one they see" and how "others don't hate snakes, but they don't try to protect them, either," Montgomery presents what she feels to be the shared responsibility of her readers, as "we build malls or highways on land that snakes need" and "rob them of their homes," activities that destroy snakes "as surely as a bullet or a shovel. Today 200 different species of snakes are in danger of extinction" (39). As the book works to erase fear, its ultimate aim is not a passive empathy but a link between human reader and snake subject that reveals previously unconsidered culpability on the part of the sympathizer. In these ways, the sentimental identification through Mason with the snakes insists on a reading situation in which, as Boler puts it, "the reader accepts a commitment to rethink her own assumptions" (*Feeling*, 164), along the way discovering personal responsibility for the snakes with whom the reader is asked to identify.

A great deal of contemporary children's nonfiction makes use of characters similar to Mason to structure identification that lends itself to critical engagement. *The Snake Scientist* is part of the Scientists in the Field series, and the books in that series routinely feature characters comparable to Mason, such as Tyrone Hayes in Pamela S. Turner's *The Frog Scientist* (2011). Through biography and photographs from Hayes's life before he became a scientist, Turner develops the character of the researcher, humanizing him by focusing on his mistakes and oddities. In one scene, Hayes recalls his joy in the rather messy outdoors when he was a very young child. After describing Hayes's delight at wading, Turner quotes him as saying, "My neighborhood was near a swamp full of frogs, snapping turtles, and snakes. . . . My interest in them started when I was four or five. I tell kids, if there is something you like doing, stick with it!" (9). Turner therefore links joy with inquiry, inviting children to examine what gives them pleasure and to find a way to turn it into a subject of investigation, as Hayes has done. The research that Turner's book describes focuses on an international mystery of amphibians slipping toward extinction all over the world, and the joy of Hayes's childhood transforms into a path of study dedicated to helping threatened animals, creatures that most of the children reading the book will never see. As in Montgomery's book, the point of identification is not selfish but intent on examining the responsibility of the readers to a problem in which they might well be implicated. The Scientists in the Field series is a treasure trove of nonfiction that uses emotion to set up sentimental identification pointed at effecting change, and in case after case, that change requires a sense that children are significant participants in the production and testing of knowledge. Erica Zappy describes Loree Griffin Burns's *Tracking Trash: Flotsam, Jetsam, and the Science of Ocean Motion* (2010) as "an environmental story about plastic in our oceans, ghost nets that trap sea life, and the things a young person could do to help make the situation better." In the next sentence, she connects what young people can do with photographs "that could make anyone a bit sad: a seal trapped in netting, a dead bird with a stomach full of plastic" (35–36). Burns, like so many of the authors in the series, uses a specific scientist working on the problem as the locus of identification, positioning the reader within the scientist's exploration of information and experience of grief, joy, wonder, and all of the other emotions inevitable to the task of researching such a powerful subject. In Burns's own comments on the book and series, she makes explicit her invitation to children to be part of the inquiry and the push for active rather than passive empathy. "These books move beyond environmental disaster stories," she says, "and into the realm of *what are we going to do about it?* Personally this is my favorite aspect of this series . . . kids can begin to see science not only as a potential career, but as a tool with which they can approach the difficult environmental issues of our times" (qtd. in Zappy, "Sing," 36). The inquiry and responsibility that Erica Zappy, the editor of the Scientists in the Field series, sees in such books is part and parcel of the active empathy driven by emotion.

Neither is this profoundly sentimental and critical process limited to the Scientists in the Field series. Cheryl Bardoe's *Mammoths and Mastodons* (2010), for example, concentrates on Daniel Fisher, a paleontologist. As the book details his struggles with evidence, it frames that research within the sentimental longing to help elephants of today:

> With data from so many sources, scientists know more about mammoths and mastodons than about most other prehistoric creatures. Yet we don't know why these animals died out. Solving this mystery becomes even more urgent as elephants struggle to survive today.
>
> Dr. Fisher hopes his research can help save elephants. "This is part of why I do this work," he says. "Part of me looks backward and tries to understand the past. And part of me looks around and tries to understand the animals of the present." (8)

Fisher's research, his passion, his sentimental desire to understand that which is different from him, and his drive to help the elephants of today all dovetail in this passage. Julius Lester, in the same preface whose grief and anger I cited earlier, points to a similar identification shot through with emotion, and he offers that identification as a crucial corrective to injustice. "My object in writing the book," he explains, "was to enable the reader to experience slaves as human beings." He continues, "If a child could experience slaves as human beings, then it might be possible for that same child to look at the descendants of slaves and also see another human being, no more, no less." What Lester is describing is *precisely* sentimental identification, and his purpose in structuring his work of nonfiction around this identification is the rewriting of the fundamental dehumanization of marginalized people that validates discrimination. "History is not just facts and events," he argues. "History is also a pain in the heart and we repeat history until we are able to make another's pain in the heart our own" (*To Be a Slave*, 8). Empathy that pushes for action to improve the lot of the object of empathy is empathy that requires self-examination. Such identification is made possible by emotion, and it is inevitably critical.

One of the most prolific and influential writers of American children's nonfiction, Milton Meltzer, put this revised vision of sentimental identification to work in many of his books. In his 1976 study of the Holocaust, he even promotes immersion through emotional stories as *better* than purely factual approaches to historical events:

> No one of us can know the whole truth. It is not made up merely of facts and figures. We have an abundance of that kind of evidence now, for the hell of Nazi Europe has become one of the most fully documented crimes in history. One can read the cold record for endless hours. The better path to the truth is through the eyewitness accounts—the letters, diaries, journals, and memoirs of those who experienced the terror and grief. (*Never to Forget,* xvi)

Meltzer argues in these lines that a nonfiction account of the Holocaust *must* rely on emotion to be true, that dispassionate facts will *fail* to paint the picture fully and fairly. The best path to understanding, he argues, is not through the "cold record" but by inhabiting the perspective of people whose experiences are defined by emotion. Meltzer's extensive writings about racial injustice take a similar strategy, as in his 1980 book on slavery across world history. "Imagine yourself as a slave," he writes near the beginning, taking a page directly from mid-nineteenth-century sentimental novels. "You have no rights. The law doesn't protect you. . . . You are his property, and the law says he can do almost anything he likes with you. . . . You work as long and hard as he wishes you to, at whatever job he wants done—and for nothing more than the food you need to stay alive" (*All Times,* 2). He continues by asking the reader to imagine being a slave whose choice of mate is determined by the slave owner, then whose children's future is, too (3). He closes the book by insisting that "slavery could be abolished in all such places—if the governments would decide to do it." But he does not leave the enactment of such reform to adults. "We must encourage, aid or shame governments into taking action," he writes. "If the people in countries where slavery does not exist were to put pressure on such governments, it might help. If poorer nations were helped by the richer nations, that could make a difference, too" (60). Meltzer invites readers to immerse themselves in the positions of slaves around the world and then immediately outlines how readers can act upon their empathy. The result is more powerful—and more critical—than reading the cold record.

Nonfiction and Empathy

Sentimental identification also addresses a problem that, according to one recent study, lies at the heart of nonfiction. P. Matthijs Bal and Martijn Veltkamp compare people who read fiction and others who read nonfiction, and they conclude that reading fiction results in sustained empathy, whereas reading nonfiction results in empathy that is, at best, temporary. The study has serious problems—its idea of nonfiction does not extend beyond newspaper reports, its notions of suspension of disbelief are bizarrely out of step with the notions developed by literary theory, it fails to account for what participants read other than their assigned passages during the test period, and it relies on the notoriously fickle tool of self-reporting—but it does produce some relevant insights on nonfiction and empathy. Readers of fiction reported a sustained increase in empathy a week after reading their assigned passages, but readers of nonfiction—as these researchers define it—did not. Bal and Veltkamp further conclude that whether readers felt themselves immersed in their reading material had no outcome on whether their empathy was sustained a week later, meaning that sentimental identification in itself was not enough to provoke lasting empathy. Bal and Veltkamp's study, the goal of which is to document the lasting effects of fiction, cannot offer a solid explanation for this problem, but it does hazard one guess. "High involvement and sympathy for people [encountered] in non-fiction stories," they propose, "may create felt obligations to do something while not possible, which consequently leads to lower empathy" ("How Does Fiction," 9). Nonfiction itself may not be anathema to sustained empathy, then. Rather, nonfiction such as that found in newspaper accounts, nonfiction that provides emotional stories but fails to provide a means to follow up personally, thwarts sustained empathy. The kind of empathy in these stories is essentially the kind of empathy that Boler rejects when she warns against "allowing oneself to inhabit a position of distance and separation, to remain in the 'anonymous' spectating crowd and abdicate any possible responsibility" (*Feeling*, 184). In the sort of nonfiction that Bal and Veltkamp study, one not only abdicates responsibility, one feels that responsibility is not possible.

In other words, the question of whether critical and sentimental engagement can coexist is more complicated than it first appears. Yes, critical engagement can survive sentimental engagement; indeed, as this chapter shows, it can thrive. But as Bal and Veltkamp's study explains, sentimental engagement can only endure if readers perceive an opportunity to act on the urge prompted by identification, for what Freire would call praxis. If we define, as I have been, an invitation to critical engagement as a move that a text makes by which it shows itself as incomplete, then children's nonfiction that invites critical engagement offers exactly the direction for praxis required for the sustained effects of empathy.[7] When nonfiction points to things we don't know, it provides such direction. When it points to the work left to do, it provides such direction. When it animates the debate behind knowledge, it provides such direction. When, as in the cases of *The Snake Scientist, The Frog Scientist, Tracking Trash, Mammoths and Mastodons, To Be a Slave,* and works by Milton Meltzer, nonfiction explains the personal responsibility that sympathetic readers bear, it provides such direction. Can sentimental engagement support critical engagement? Yes. What's more, sustaining sentimental engagement requires critical engagement. The two are not exclusive. Rather, they crave one another.

CONCLUSION
Critical Engagement's Moral Imperative

THE ARGUMENT OF THIS BOOK may have been counterintuitive, but it has not been complicated. Although children's nonfiction has traditionally been valued most highly for its factuality, investigating the accuracy of nonfiction with no other goal than coming to the conclusion that a book is right or wrong can only result in an end to inquiry. Such an investigation will reveal either that the book under analysis is perfectly right—an outcome that I can't imagine to be possible—or that it is flawed in some way, grand or small. The first (non)possibility requires an end to inquiry because the one legitimate reaction to a perfectly accurate text is passive absorption of its burnished knowledge. The second (inevitable) possibility leads directly to condemnation of a book for being what it was always destined to be. Both of the outcomes from such an approach to nonfiction, therefore, are disappointing, but even the premise of that approach—that answers are more valuable than questions—is dangerous. This premise takes for granted the unparalleled value of information that is ready for easy transmission from the source of knowledge to its waiting, dehumanized vessel.

As we struggle to develop a theoretical approach to children's nonfiction, it is more important, I have been arguing, to pay attention to where a book makes itself vulnerable to critical engagement and where it deflects such engagement. Especially useful for such an approach is attention to the voices and characters of nonfiction, and although no aspect of voice or character is a simple indicator of how and where a book invites critical engagement, the hallmarks described in chapters 2 and 3 signal conventional places to investigate. Although the term *critical engagement* overlaps with a great many other terms, for me it means a process of what my Introduction calls "punctuated plurality," a testing and retesting of knowledge and conclusions in which text and reader explore questions and the spaces remaining in human knowledge in a relationship that Bakhtin might call dialogical. It is possible to misread my argument as one in favor of unending questions or opposed to the stability of answers. However, the "punctuated" nature of the plurality for which I argue imagines periods in which questions yield answers, though those answers are held with humility, with an eye already toward the next round in which they will be tested in the context of the new knowledge produced by other questions. In short, there is nothing wrong with facts. Furthermore, there is nothing inherently wrong with emotions, with analyzing things about which one is passionate, especially when emotion forms a connection between subjects pointed toward an outward-looking activism. Such emotional engagement requires self-reflection; it requires critical engagement.

But a question remains that I myself have been avoiding throughout. If I've succeeded in showing that children's nonfiction can and frequently has invited critical engagement, the question still remains whether that is an invitation that matters. Is this an invitation that children can accept? Can children engage with a text critically? This is not the sort of question with which literature scholars usually tangle, but I suspect that it's a question some of my readers have been asking all along.

The main reason that I haven't yet acknowledged the question is that it's a question that annoys me. It's a question that takes as eternal a perception that adults have critical abilities and children do not. Sam Wineburg, however, argues that this idea is historically bound. "In sum," he writes, "we can locate entire epochs of history ... when pre-critical notions of historiography were embraced by adolescent and adult alike. The notion that such beliefs are naturally abandoned as students enter adulthood has neither data nor history on its side" (*Historical Thinking,* 78–79). Like Wineburg, I cannot take seriously the premise of the question, the assumption that adults are critical by nature and children are not. But of course, the real point Wineburg is making is not that children can think critically but that becoming an adult does not guarantee such an ability. So even if Wineburg is right, his claim still doesn't quite answer the question of whether children can perform the kind of thinking that I am struggling to show nonfiction inviting. Therefore, annoyed or not, I do need to answer this question on my own.

The evidence we have so far, fortunately, indicates that the answer is affirmative: yes, children can and do engage critically with information. Bruce VanSledright, whose work follows enthusiastically in Wineburg's footsteps, surveyed the data published on this question at the turn of the millennium. He found that

> the assumption that, say, 10- and 11-year-olds cannot think historically and practice history because they lack the necessary intellectual ability has been challenged repeatedly in recent research studies. These studies—based on interviews with children, their performances on tasks that ask them to do history instead of simply recall it, and observations of them in classroom contexts—suggest that American youngsters are being shortchanged by this assumption. (*In Search,* 17)

Indeed, a bevy of results published at around the time of VanSledright's survey suggests the same thing. Some of the results are essentially anecdotal, such as JoAnn Portalupi and Ralph Fletcher's comment that "we have worked with these kids all over the country, and seen up close their intense desire to question, research, understand, and explain the world around them" (*Nonfiction,* xi). Scholars have also developed more formal case studies in which children can and do engage critically with their materials. Anne Haas Dyson's study of a classroom in which students selected a popular text, unearthed the power disparity encoded within it, and rewrote the story in a way that addressed that disparity, a study that I examine at length in my Introduction, is an obvious example ("Relational"). Bronwyn Mellor and Annette Patterson, too, respond in their 2001 case study of an Australian classroom to exactly the question of children's critical capabilities. "In the vast majority of Australian schools," they explain, "analysis is not usually seen as part of the game for younger students." But when the students of their study were provided with texts that spoke to the children's interests, the "students showed themselves to be confident about even quite complex textual theorizing" ("Teaching Readings?," 134). Even what I consider the driest subjects with which my own study has dealt—the peritexts that I examined in chapter 4—have provided, according to research, fodder for thoughtful critical engagement in the elementary classroom (Portalupi and Fletcher, *Nonfiction*, 29). Can children engage critically? Evidently so.

Jennifer O'Brien's work with children between the ages of five and eight confirms this conclusion, and it also suggests that children are so good at engaging critically that their engagement sometimes goes further than the teacher expects. One exercise asked students to examine "a collection of junk mail catalogs produced for Mothers' Day" ("Children Reading," 41), and O'Brien found that the students were very good at identifying the rules, obligations, and expectations placed upon mothers and taken for granted by the advertisements under analysis. The exercise resulted in questions that allowed students to identify the cracks in the polished surface of society's authoritative face on its normalized ideology, "to use these same resources to question the representations of mothers, to identify gaps, and to suggest possible changes" (52). As such, these early elementary children were able to perform readings that put them in dialogue with their culture, sharing authority in exactly the ways that I have been imagining that authority might be shared between a text and a reader who is critically engaged. What O'Brien found is that "children are not passive readers" but are instead "inventive and skeptical" (52). But it is important to note that this critical engagement was not tidy, was not restricted to the texts or even the subject at which the teacher's exercise was aimed. As the term progressed and the students sharpened their skills, O'Brien writes,

> it became apparent to me that what I was up to was risky if not dangerous in a number of ways. It was at times disruptive to the usual classroom order, interrupting parent, child, and

teacher expectations about what school reading, writing, and talk were for; it encouraged discordant points of view to be expressed; from time to time it involved children in questioning the rules by which they and their families and communities lived out their lives. (52)

For me, these results are extremely encouraging. O'Brien demonstrates first that children can engage critically, and then she demonstrates that the children whom she taught were so enthusiastic about and skilled at critical thinking that they could do it on their own, often to the frustration of the adults around them. Considering the long history of adults using informational texts to keep children in line—a history I touch on in chapter 6—reports of children tangling with information and then frustrating adults do a great deal to cheer me.

And O'Brien's work leads us to another encouraging realization: not only *can* children read critically, but they often do so even when the adults around them do not invite them. For my study, what this means is that it is reasonable not only to expect children to be able to take up a text's invitation to critical engagement but also to anticipate that children will engage critically whether adults encourage them to or not. Dyson's example of children identifying the gender politics taken for granted within a popular film and rewriting its story to provide more equity is an obvious piece of evidence, and Dyson has written elsewhere of what she calls "the dialogic process through which children use known stories and story characters to mediate community conversations about ideological matters" ("Rewriting," 275). Another example comes from a case study by Angel Mei Yi Lin, in which she examines how Cantonese schoolchildren learning English "subverted an English reading lesson that had a focus on practicing skills of factual information extraction from texts" and "negotiated their own preferred comic-style narratives" ("Resistance," 83). Although the subject matter was extremely dry and better suited for a banking-model classroom than for the sort of critical, humanizing classroom for which Freire agitated, the students engaged critically; even though that subject matter centered around a language in which students must have felt a decided lack of expertise, they created a dialogue. And, considering the earnest tone of the text, the dialogue the students created was clearly not one intent on obeying the authority of the text. In one example, Lin finds that "the student has exploited the Response slot to do something playful, to slip in a contribution that will turn the whole story into a comic-strip type of story" (94). In an observation with great importance for a study of texts that might seek to engage their readers, Lin argues that

> school children, however, might seize whatever opportunities they can find in the classroom to negotiate their own sense of the text, for instance, text not as an information-holder, but as a source of enjoyment. When the prescribed school text proves to be unimaginative or unengaging, they exercise their own creativity to recreate a new plot, to negotiate a comic type of story, which suits their taste. It seems that they are negotiating their own kind of literacy for their own purposes, despite the illegitimacy of their own literacy and their own purposes in the school context. (95)

Lin's "negotiation" is directly relevant to the argument that I have been making throughout this study. Can students engage critically when a text invites them to do so? Yes. In fact, it appears that children frequently do so, whether their texts want them to or not. So although children's nonfiction has a long history of treating readers as dehumanized vessels who should sit passively while waiting to receive polished information, Lin's study "shows the students' playful and artful verbal practices despite the alienating school reading curriculum that seems to serve to produce an uncritical labor" (83). The implications for critical engagement with children's nonfiction are profound.

The realization that children can engage critically and frequently do so whether adults invite them to or not opens a different question: why, then, do adults need to get involved at all? Why prioritize the teaching or modeling of critical engagement? I find two answers to this question most compelling. The first is that although children do think critically without prompting, evidence shows that we *can* help. As Leonie Arthur has argued, "educator modelling and scaffolding of critical literacy practices" does indeed show a potential to "encourage children to play with, critique and reconstruct texts" ("Young Children," 185). In describing his own research, VanSledright has argued that, despite their significant potential for critical thinking, unless they are encouraged to practice such thinking, "students showed only some inclination" to do so. As a result, he recommends "that students be given more opportunities to practice historical investigation themselves as a way of building their historical thinking capabilities and enhancing their understanding of both the past and the nature of history as subject matter and academic discipline" (*In Search,* 17–18).[1] Another study "observed that high school and college students who were asked to read multiple documents did not spontaneously attend to source information," techniques that overlap with the rhetorical devices that I explored in chapter 2, again indicating that without adult encouragement, young people are less likely to perform the kinds of readings that I have been imagining (Britt and Aglinskas, "Improving"). However, the same study found that when using "a computer-based tutorial and practice environment for teaching students to source and corroborate while reading history texts," those students produced papers "that were more integrated, cited more sources, and referenced more information from primary and secondary sources" (485). Finally, the place of children's literature and children's schoolteachers becomes even more important in the face of a study of how children learn (or don't learn) to read electronic texts such as television and computer games critically. This study found that parents are "unlikely" to take up the task of encouraging such skills. These researchers argued that "enabling the young to become critical consumers in the face of adult apathy, indifference or antipathy, and to develop control over the technology and authorship within it should be at the heart of education" (Sanger, *Young Children,* 172). Children can perform this sort of engagement on their own, but they're much more likely to do so with adult encouragement, and the books that children read play a key role in that process.

My first argument is that adults should actively invite children to critical engagement because it's good for children when we do. My second argument, though, is that we should do so because it's good for *us* when we do. Adults—librarians, teachers, parents, writers, aunts, voters, crossing guards, literature faculty—have power over children, and although it's power that can be challenged, we have a moral obligation to share the power, especially if we are dedicated to a democratic society. To an extent, my argument here overlaps with arguments others have made. When Patricia J. Cianciolo, for example, argues that "it is the responsibility of teachers and librarians to teach children, *even in the early elementary grades,* how to engage in critical reading of informational books" (*Informational Picture Books,* 11, emphasis original), she is building up to the point that "children need to be taught how to recognize the persuasive techniques used" (13) in nonfiction. This skill is important because it makes the students better readers and therefore better citizens, and of course I agree that this reason is excellent motivation for adults to foster children's critical engagement with what they read. I also agree with Michele Knobel, who argues that teaching "critical literacy practices" can prompt young readers to better analysis not only of texts and of themselves but also of teachers. Specifically, teaching students to engage critically fosters an environment in which the "teachers themselves" must "examine their own ideologies and agendas" ("Simon Says," 69).[2] Cianciolo argues that we must foster critical engagement for social reasons, and Knobel would not disagree, but she also indicates that there are personal reasons for such teaching: if critical engagement is good, then teaching in such a way that requires the teacher to engage in the sort of punctuated plurality for which I have been arguing is also good for the teacher.

I find both of these arguments very convincing, and when they are combined, they are even more powerful. We—especially professionals who specialize in the culture, literature, and education of children—should invite critical engagement and foster it where we can because doing so is democratic, respectful, and humanizing. Wineburg finds that the kinds of invitations to critical engagement that I outlined in chapter 2 are "common in the writing historians do for one another" but "edited out of the writing they do for schoolchildren" (*Historical Thinking,* 12). That pattern shows respect and even a willingness to make ourselves vulnerable to and share power with other adults, but its lack in materials for children demonstrates an attitude that is patronizing, fearful, and, frankly, disgraceful. I have been very careful in this study to avoid arguing that a book is good or bad because of its use or avoidance of invitations to critical engagement, and I want to maintain that position here. However, my strong preference is for relationships (and, as my chapter on emotion hints, I have no qualms about using that word to describe the transaction between readers and books) in which the strong are willing to share power. In children's nonfiction, such a philosophy means highlighting rather than obscuring the cracks in authority. As chapter 6 argues, doing so also has the potential to create a more accurate nonfiction, but my main interest in nonfiction that invites critical engagement is its democratic potential. By decentralizing authority, we foster the conditions not just for the kinds of students we want and for whom we can become the kinds of teachers (parents, friends, neighbors) we would like to be but also for the cultivation of a better democracy.

ACKNOWLEDGMENTS

THIS BOOK would have died a quiet death long ago without the help of many people and organizations. The National Endowment for the Humanities provided a Teaching Development Fellowship during which I performed the broad research on which the book rests, and I reached the crucial point at which the emerging manuscript took its current shape and focus during a summer of research funded by an Arts and Sciences Enhancement Grant from Kansas State University (Jim Machor filled the thankless but requisite role of mentor for this grant). I am very grateful for these awards, which supported the work financially and gave me a word of encouragement when I badly needed one.

Many people at Kansas State University supported the book over the years, sometimes providing key resources without which the book could not have been completed. I taught a course on children's nonfiction in fall 2013, and the students who joined me for that experiment were vital to my emerging thinking on the subject. Mark Crosby, Jim Machor, and Lisa Tatonetti read repeated drafts of grant proposals to fund the work of the book and, through their advice, affected the entire project. Hale librarians helped scan illustrations for the book, and the Interlibrary Loan Office provided enthusiastic, indispensable support throughout my research. All of the children's literature faculty at K-State contributed to this project, but two of my colleagues there deserve specific mention. Phil Nel drew my attention to key work by Paulo Freire and Elizabeth

Partridge; he also helped revise the book proposal and advised me throughout press negotiations. Anne K. Phillips gave me her copy of the March/April 2011 issue of *The Horn Book Magazine* and got materials to me while I was out of the country; she was also the first person who told me that this project was a book and that I should stop pretending otherwise. Other colleagues at K-State helped in specific ways. Mary Kohn, rock-star linguist, confirmed my nervous and decidedly uninformed opinion about verb tense. Jeremy Walker, again at Hale library, helped me find contemporaneous responses to the Candy Bomber. Jim Machor told me where to look for the heart of reader-response and reception theory and let me watch basketball on his TV. Finally, K-State provided a University Small Research Grant to pay for the indexing, resulting in a much more useable book than it would have been if I had created the index myself.

My current home is the Faculty of Education at the University of Cambridge, and I am indebted to my colleagues there for their kindness and camaraderie as the book reached its conclusion. Geoff Hayward and Pauline Mason were particularly supportive, and I am also especially grateful to Georgina Horell, Zoe Jaques, Maria Nikolajeva, David Whitley, and indeed all of the members of the Centre for Children's Literature.

Colleagues across the United States provided significant help. Corey Dunn, Pat Murphy, Karen Sands-O'Connor, Joseph T. Thomas Jr., and Sherryl Vint deserve thanks for so many reasons that even attempting the list would ensure embarrassing failure. Christopher Abraham, archivist at the Eisenhower Presidential Library, found Jackie Cochran's letter to Randy Lovelace. Myra Zarnowski has been an unbelievable source of support ever since I first started working in a field that she and her coauthor Susan Turkel, frankly, own. San Diego State University Library welcomed me for weeks of valuable research in their world-class children's literature archives. Jim Kincaid, whose work models how to criticize power in his choice of both topic and style, has been far more generous than I ever deserved, and much of the writing of this book was drafted with an eye toward his example. Michelle Ann Abate offered sincere friendship and knowledgeable support over the many years I spent writing the book. She is such a true friend that she never once pointed out that she would have written it faster.

This book has enjoyed the attentions of six (!) different anonymous readers, and chapter 6 had two more in its previous life as an article at *Children's Literature in Education,* edited by Annette Wannamaker. I took advice from all of these readers. They candidly expressed their misgivings (and occasional praise) for the work and offered ideas for how to address the book's shortcomings, repeatedly saving me from embarrassment. Who could fail to take advice from such generous colleagues?

Mike Stoffel, Erin Warholm-Wohlenhaus, and Jason Weidemann at the University of Minnesota Press have proactively looked for ways to be helpful throughout this process, and I have continually been surprised by their professionalism and kindness. Kate Mertes provided the index in the sensitive, timely way that is typical of her work.

Friends around the world have played parts in helping this book, often without even knowing that they did so. Netta and Shaun Baker provided childcare that enabled the writing of chapter 2 and revision of chapter 6. Seely Heck provided childcare during the early stages of revision for the book manuscript. Amy and Will Hageman made everything better, where "everything" spans the range from childcare to giving me tickets to a concert my wife really wanted to see. Alicia Sutliff-Benusis helped with revisions that turned chapter 6 into a stand-alone article, and Patricia and Willis Sutliff provided housing and cookies during the same period. Shaun Baker scanned and uploaded pages upon pages of material while I was enjoying a Fulbright semester. Marek, Basia, Jeremy, and Teo Oziewicz hosted my family for a month when things got crazy, and I will never be able to repay them. Karin Kokorski tricked me into letting her host me and gave me a home with a true colleague while I did my work.

The Manhattan Public Library in Manhattan, Kansas, found a book for me when all other resources failed. It also inspired the book's opening, though I must confess that they have replaced the carpet since I wrote those pages.

Melendra Sutliff Sanders listened, advised, and enabled. The first time that I was excited about this book was when she was excited about it.

Finally, I want to take a moment to thank the colleagues I have had at several institutions who have taken on the burden of faculty self-governance and administration. I'm increasingly aware of how important it is for faculty to be active in those exercises, I'm similarly aware of how very much I have to learn before I could do any of those jobs well, and I'm painfully aware of how much research time these colleagues sacrifice month after month to make sure that our departments run smoothly. They somehow continue to manage to produce quality scholarship, a feat that I'm fairly certain I couldn't achieve while bearing significant service burdens. If they didn't do that work, I couldn't do this work, but their work is almost by definition invisible, while mine only counts when it becomes visible. So thank you, colleagues, for the invisible work that you do.

NOTES

Introduction

1. I explore Freedman's book at great length in chapter 5, where I also provide more information about the growth of the field around and after the time of the book's publication.

2. Doreen Rappaport reflects on the influence of Common Core on nonfiction in her 2013 conversation with *Horn Book,* "Doreen Rappaport Talks with Roger."

3. One might even say that this pedagogical strategy out-Freires Freire, who generally chose the codification himself and provided it to his students. In the example that Dyson provides, the students were in charge not only of interpreting, resisting, and reinventing the codification and the ideology that it represented but also of selecting the cultural moment that they felt most provocatively intersected with their own experiences of the world.

4. I see the dichotomy of trapped or liberated in many places throughout Stephens's argument, too many places to list here, but for one of many examples: "The reader is thus offered a number of possible subject positions from which to view characters and events, and the narrator–narratee relationship constructs at least a double role for the reader: a subject position as one of the feasters, and a subject position which shares the narrator's contempt for the feasters and sympathy for the child" (26). If my reading of moments such as this one is right, then the CDA-inflected argument is that a book creates an illusion of choice—a reader can join at least two subject positions defined by the text—but the only real choice is to dwell within the trap of the proffered positions or reject them entirely, thereby achieving freedom.

5. I see Dyson's connection to Freire throughout her essay, but I see it especially in these lines from *Pedagogy of the Oppressed*: "Those who use the banking approach, knowingly or unknowingly (for there are innumerable well-intentioned bank-clerk teachers who do not realize that they are serving only to dehumanize), fail to perceive that the deposits themselves contain contradictions about reality. But, sooner or later, these contradictions may lead formerly passive students to turn against their domestication and the attempt to domesticate reality. They may discover through existential experience that their present way of life is irreconcilable with their vocation to become fully human. They may perceive through their relations with reality that reality is really a *process*, undergoing constant transformation. If men are searchers and their ontological vocation is humanization, sooner or later they may perceive the contradiction in which banking education seeks to maintain them, and then engage themselves in the struggle for their liberation" (61–62). Freire is deeply concerned about the many modes of oppression, but human beings always contain the ability to escape the hegemony of their culture long enough to perceive and even attack that which oppresses them. Significantly, although Freire was an educator and his thoughts have proved crucial to contemporary education theory (including that of the excellent teacher whose classroom Dyson visits), here it appears that for Freire, although teachers may aid and accelerate the liberation of the oppressed, even bad teachers and other members of ideological state apparatuses cannot fully prevent students from perceiving the oppression that envelopes them. The inclination to self-liberation that Freire champions here finds expression in the classroom activities that Dyson documents.

6. Eagleton, I should note, is also opposed to any theoretical model that calls upon readers to "put our beliefs into question and allow them to be transformed," so although I am offering this combination of different strains of Marxism as a solution to a limitation of Eagleton's Marxism, he would likely reject it (*Literary*, 79).

7. Eagleton, only partly joking, calls Barthes a "hedonist" and compares his reading venue to "a boudoir" (*Literary*, 82–83).

8. Neither is this word choice an accident of translation. The original reads as follows: "Il y faut une opération seconde, conséquente à l'évaluation qui a départagé une première fois les textes, plus fine qu'elle, fondée sur l'appréciation d'une certain quantité, du *plus ou moins* que peut mobiliser chaque texte. Cette nouvelle opération est l'*interprétation* (au sens que Nietzsche donnait à ce mot). Interpréter un texte, ce n'est pas lui donner un

sens (plus ou moins fondé, plus ou moins libre), c'est au contraire apprécier de quel pluriel il est fait" (*S/Z* 1970, 11).

1. Beyond Authority

1. And the trend continues to blossom. At the time of the writing of this chapter, the Young Adult Library Services Association, a branch of the American Library Association and a sister committee to that headed by Isaacs, is developing a new award for nonfiction for young adults. A draft of that manual repeatedly defines the field as a literature of facts. The manual draft praises excellent works in the field for providing "a trail for readers to further explore content" (5) and an account of how the authors "document their sources, their research process, and their thought process," but even these dialogic spaces are routinely praised because they will increase "the trust the readers can place in the author as an authority." Although the manual concedes that "there is virtually no such thing as a perfect book," it worries that "nothing erodes authority so much as inaccuracy" (12). Taken as a whole, this draft seems to represent a struggle within the developing award committee to reward nonfiction that makes itself vulnerable to critical engagement—but not at the expense of authority.

2. Ivy Linton Stabell notes how children's biographies were often "meant to be studied and repeated back to adult authorities who should oversee the child's education to reinforce adult dominance, a practice which underscores the public and private power hierarchies in a young child's life" ("Model Patriots," 98). Therefore, children's nonfiction has actively played a role in the banking model of education, with, if Stabell is right, exactly the negative consequences that Freire anticipates.

3. This is not to say that students are the only guilty parties. Kincheloe calls "literal-mindedness . . . the path of least resistance for the teacher" (*Getting* 1989, 336), and he hypothesizes a scenario between teacher and administrator that is all too familiar, one in which "supervisors . . . hold the specter of the test above teachers' heads, asking them if they want to be responsible for students' poor performance on it" (*Getting* 2001, 179).

2. Voice and the Seamless Narrative of Knowledge

1. "In other published works, such elements are also occasionally called weakeners (Brown and Levinson, 1978), downtoners (Holmes, 1932; Quirk, Greenbaum, Leech, and Svartvik, 1972), detensifiers (Huebler, 1983), and understatements (Huebler, 1983)" (Crismore and Vande Kopple, "Readers' Learning," 184–85).

2. See p. 101 of Gregory's text for an example.

3. Nonfiction's Unfinished Characters

1. Abate documents how and where Cheney makes such claims, for example. See p. 106.

2. New work by Dawn Heinecken also offers another direction that nonfiction might follow, though her article and my own research indicate that currently, nonfiction that takes such an approach is rare at best. Heinecken complains about how one subgenre of nonfiction, sports advice books for girls, "operates to support ideologies that do more to limit, than liberate, girls" ("Empowering," 327). She is especially frustrated with how such books emphasize subjectivity that is individualistic, focusing on "individual transformation and personal responsibility rather than structural inequities" (340). Heinecken's insight strikes me as refreshingly unique: neoliberal individualism is, it seems to me, one of the aspects of ideology left unquestioned even in the work that is the friendliest to critical engagement, and narratives of individuals rising despite adversity are certainly one of the aspects of neoliberalism most widely embraced. What Heinecken is offering is another aspect of ideology that nonfiction might trouble, but none of the work she examines does so.

3. My perception at the moment is that science nonfiction seems to be especially well suited to demonstrations of characters in the long middle of discovery, or if other subgenres are equally suited to it, then authors working in those genres have rarely taken advantage of the trope. That said, nonfiction about history increasingly makes a display of the long middle of discovery that its *authors* endure. Chapter 4 of my study, which considers the peritexts of nonfiction, offers many such examples, but James Cross Giblin's *The Rise and Fall of Senator Joe McCarthy* (2009) is one example that deserves attention now: Giblin's section on his "Bibliography and Source Notes" gives a lengthy account of his own path through the research, and it does so in the first person, effectively making Giblin himself both a visible author, as I explained in chapter 2, and a character of sorts involved in the long middle of discovery.

4. Inquiry at and in the Margins

1. See, just for the most prominent and recent example, Nathalie op de Beeck's *Suspended Animation*, p. xiii.

2. For the essays arguing with Rose, see Karen Sánchez-Eppler's essay "Marks of Possession," which uses reception theory to argue that there are certainly books that can be said to be for children; Marah Gubar's essay

"On Not Defining Children's Literature," which draws a similar conclusion through Wittgenstein's "family resemblance"; and Robin Bernstein's essay "Children's Books, Dolls, and the Performance of Race," which examines how children have used dolls "to reconfigure the stories" they read (163). Kenneth Kidd's essay "Queer Theory's Child and Children's Literature Studies" argues that queer theory hasn't paid enough attention to Rose's destabilizing of the child.

3. See my "Chaperoning Words."

4. See p. 20 for an example of a page with twenty-eight lines per page and p. 14 for an example with thirty.

5. The most obvious reason to distrust a theory of peritexts that identifies smaller font as unsuited to the readers of the main text is that, in books for younger readers as well as adults, the captions of illustrations are almost always in a smaller font and with smaller line spacing than the main text they accompany, but no one would suggest that captions are somehow not to be read by the same person reading the rest of the page. Furthermore, I'm reluctant to deny myself the pleasure of looking for critical invitations in peritexts with stingier spacing because Bolden's other peritexts in these books are such a delight. The book designer has restricted all of the entries in the notes section, for example, to thin, cramped font, but treasures there abound. Bolden frequently uses this space to comment on mistakes in primary texts corrected upon consultation with other texts, claims she has discovered for which she can find no evidence, and other seams in the continuity of knowledge. My favorite such moment comes when Bolden explains how she inferred the date of Frederick Douglass's visit to the home of Maritcha's grandmother: "Maritcha indicated that her parents were married at the time of the visit. They married in 1840, so the visit had to have been between 1840 and 1848. According to the chronology in *Douglass: Autobiographies* (New York: The Library of America, 1994), p. 1055, Douglass first met Charles Rémond in 1842. Douglass lectured in New York State several times during the 1840s" (44). Again, my broader point is that although I do think that increasing the font of peritexts indicates an anticipation of children as the audience, I don't think that reducing the font necessarily indicates the reverse. My narrower point, of course, is that I don't want to think that a smaller font indicates a rejection of children as readers because Bolden provides such terrific examples of peritexts that I'd love to see under the scrutiny of children.

6. The main text for *Sarah Rector* has approximately twenty-six vertical lines per page (see, e.g., pp. 3, 37, and 49), and although no page in the prologue or author's note has a full top-to-bottom page of text, the spacing

and font appear to be identical. The acknowledgments, which do have a full page of text (p. 69), have exactly twenty-six lines, matching the main text.

7. The subject of award committees' preferences is important but often frustrating for researchers hoping to advance evidence-based arguments about those preferences: many award committees, including those under the auspices of the American Library Association, are often pledged to secrecy about the conversations had during nominating discussions, so there is very little direct evidence to use in such an analysis. Furthermore, award committees usually revise their membership each year, meaning that any preferences evident in one group of award winners cannot be assumed to apply to a group from any other year. However, some of my students and I recently completed a study using an inferential methodology in which we looked across books honored by the two major awards of children's nonfiction over many years and drew some broad conclusions about tendencies in those awards. See Joe Sutliff Sanders, Katlyn M. Buckley, Kynsey M. Creel, and Charlie C. Lynn, "Legitimate Humanity."

5. Seeing Photographs

1. Not every photograph is unary, and even when it is, any given viewer of that photograph still has the ability to push back against its authority. When we study a painting, we frequently consider the color palette chosen or trace the brush strokes that remain in the paint, and in these ways a painting is, to rephrase Barthes, the "it that we see." Viewers of photographs can also "see" the medium and its artistic choices—a picture's use of the rule of thirds, its use of natural lighting, its location of a focal point—despite the medium's insistence that it is a transparent window to the truth. Furthermore, we sometimes seek out and happily find details included in photographs despite the intentions of the photographer, thus allowing us to create a meaning in a photograph that escapes, indeed that is irrelevant to, the photographer's message in the photograph as a whole (*Camera Lucida*, 47). Barthes calls such a detail a "punctum," and we can get a sense of its rebellious nature in Barthes's phrase that the punctum allows him to "dismiss all knowledge, all culture. I refuse to inherit anything from another eye than my own" (51). Barthes's punctum is inevitably too personal to provide the basis for a theory of photography in children's nonfiction—never mind the fact that I can't help but wonder what unexamined network of privileges enables (and limits) Barthes's avowed ability to dismiss knowledge and culture—but it is a good reminder that readers can and do resist images, can and do push back against the authority of photographs. Still, my interest in this chapter is not how human beings read a photograph rigorously even

when that photograph asks to be taken as transparent. Rather, my interest is in how a work of nonfiction can present a photograph in a way that invites or discourages rigorous readings.

2. Mickenberg also examines Selsam's book. As I observed in my Introduction, Mickenberg's approach is historical, especially in comparison with my aesthetic approach, but she, too, is interested in how the book "encourages [readers] to look beyond the obvious, to probe beneath the surface, to question, and to conceive of possible explanations" (*Learning*, 195).

3. Freedman's hedge—"*is believed to be* the only actual battle picture of the entire war"—may also be his strategy for skirting around a controversy associated with the photograph. In 1963, well before Freedman wrote his book and likely before he began his research, Frederic Ray published an essay in *Civil War Times Illustrated* questioning whether the photograph was indeed taken during a battle scene. Later researchers, including William A. Frassanito (*Antietam*, 71), have taken the matter to be settled in favor of Ray's pessimism, but the original title for the photograph, "View of Battlefield of Antietam, on day of battle, Sept. 17, 1862," certainly provides a more compelling context for the photograph than a more accurate title, such as "Man a Safe Distance from Battle Looks through Binoculars." I don't know what Freedman knew about the photograph or the debate of its veracity, but his hedge here allows him to provide a more compelling caption without being untruthful.

4. Frassanito has made relevant arguments about the photographer who oversaw the capture of this photograph, Alexander Gardner. First, he joins with most scholars of Civil War photography in positing that both this picture and the "terrible" photograph were taken by Gardner and his team, although Mathew B. Brady was originally credited with the photograph (*Antietam*, 71). If Frassanito is right, which seems all but certain, then the contrast between the two pictures is especially striking. Second, he claims—again convincingly—that Gardner and his team manipulated the position of corpses in at least one other famous Civil War photograph to improve the composition (*Gettysburg*, 187–92). If Frassanito is right, then there is even more reason to consider this photograph as carefully framed to increase the chances of viewers looking through the photograph rather than at it and detecting its artificiality.

5. Loewen makes a parallel point in chapter 11 of *Lies My Teacher Told Me*.

6. Higonnet's book on representations of children across the history of Western representational art follows Kincaid's theory. Because her main focus is on high art, she touches on Hine only very briefly. She mentions him

in passing in a paragraph on protest photography, concluding that "photography has always included pictures of children whose realism is supposed to lead beyond bodies toward social conditions, and whose conscious intention, at least, is hardly to abuse real children, but, on the contrary, to use photographs of their bodies to achieve reforms in children's favor" (*Pictures*, 117). This use of a disembodied image of children to allow adults to make social arguments to other adults is probably the most explicit link between her argument and Kincaid's over the subject of photography, but she anticipates these points in very provocative language, especially where she writes about how, "in late twentieth-century western societies, pictures of children scare us more than any others" (*Pictures*, 11).

6. The Pursuit of Reliability in *Almost Astronauts*

1. This is not to say that such writers of children's nonfiction are only or even chiefly concerned with accuracy. Since the rise of awards for nonfiction by the American Library Association and the National Council of Teachers of English, "literary" attributes such as theme and style have become increasingly important aspects of highly regarded nonfiction for children. Nonetheless, as the example of Stone's book demonstrates, it is the authoritative aspect of nonfiction that tends to come into conflict with the call for nonfiction to model inquiry.

2. Stone probably means Executive Order 11246, which Johnson signed on September 24, 1965. The term "affirmative action" had already been used in a 1961 executive order signed by John F. Kennedy in March 1961, but Johnson's signature on the 1965 order was a crucial piece of law, even going so far as to extend requirements of the Civil Rights Act of 1964.

3. Think of Frances Hodgson Burnett's *The Secret Garden* (1911) (in which a girl becomes unlike her mother in order to thrive), Katherine Paterson's *The Great Gilly Hopkins* (1978) (in which a foster child must redefine what a "real" family is), or Justin Richardson and Peter Parnell's *And Tango Makes Three* (2005) (a picture book based on a true story in which two male penguins form a new family defined by something other than biology).

4. And neither do the two books from which Stone draws much of her research. Weitekamp argues that "although changing the requirements in these ways meant that Cochran herself qualified as a candidate," at least in this letter, Cochran "did not address that possibility directly" (*Right Stuff*, 79–80). Too, Ackmann notes exactly the lines about "women between the ages of twenty and twenty-three" (*Mercury 13*, 81), though she does not make the comparison with Cochran's age during the WASP program.

7. The Empathy of Critical Engagement

1. Although serious literary study counterincentivizes any claim by children's literature scholars that the field is marked by emotion, various commentators have already alluded to just this point. As Alison Waller has argued, when adults return to children's literature, that return is routinely marked by joy *(Constructing)*. Similarly, Yung-Hsing Wu's work on sentimentality and print culture surrounding Harry Potter, "Magical Matter," suggests that profound emotional connections between children's books and their readers are the norm. Consider, too, the advice of Robert Lawson, still the only person to have won both the Caldecott Medal and the Newbery Medal. In his acceptance of the 1941 Caldecott, he argues that writers, illustrators, publishers, and librarians have a specific duty to children regarding their books, a duty described by emotion: "We must not give them just a splendid or an intriguing Juvenile List. We must give them BOOKS. Books that will become tattered and grimy from use, not books too handsome to grovel with. Books that will make them weep, books that will rack them with hearty laughter. Books that absorb them so that they have to be shaken loose from them. Books that they will put under their pillows at night. Books that give them gooseflesh and glimpses of glory" ("Caldecott," 283–84). Children's books certainly show a dedication to artistry and other aspects of excellence, but one of the hallmarks of children's literature is, I think, a dedication to emotion.

2. Milton Meltzer, she explains, wrote to "satisfy" curiosity, whereas Susan Campbell Bartoletti "writes to kindle and deepen interest" (45).

3. The most pointed of these feminist critiques has come from Lauren Berlant, whose prolific career summarizes beautifully how many contemporary feminists have come to distrust the ideology of first-wave feminism. See especially *The Female Complaint*.

4. Similar objections to the possible overlap between emotional and critical engagement abound, including James A. Anderson's objection to calls for "critical" viewing of television: "Coupling immersion and acceptance with active reflection seems difficult at best. Is the critical viewer to watch but not enjoy?" ("Television," 314). John Stephens's work, which, as I explain in the Introduction, anticipates my own, praises interrogative texts, writing that "the most notable effect of these strategies is to discourage unquestioning empathy or identification with the main characters as subjects and to situate the reader as a separately constructed subject firmly outside the text, sometimes as a subject position in opposition to society's official structures of authority" (Stephens, *Language,* 156). It is probably not fair

to suggest that Stephens is opposed to emotion or even necessarily sentimentality in literature, but here he warns against an identification that is "unquestioning," which of course would make such identification the opposite of critical engagement as I have been defining it.

5. Katharine Capshaw, too, though not from an explicitly feminist perspective, warns against "immersion" in children's books, pointing with approval to the photobook's metatextual capability of startling readers out of their complacent identification with narrative perspectives (*Civil Rights,* xiii–iv).

6. Boler's theory has a very complicated relationship with Freire's. One of Boler's main points is that when scholars talk about emotion, they decline to mention their debt to feminism. At one point, Boler expresses frustration at the elevated position Freire occupies, a position she feels costs second-wave consciousness raising some of the credit it is due. She argues, further, that the reason Freire's interest in emotion has been able to escape condemnation is that he "isn't a feminist, and doesn't analyze gender" (*Feeling,* 111–12). Nonetheless, Boler is clearly aware of Freire's ideas, and much of her "pedagogy of discomfort" highlights the overlap between consciousness-raising exercises and Freire's "problem-posing" education detailed in *Pedagogy of the Oppressed.*

7. Capshaw argues that the photobooks of the civil rights movement do exactly what I am saying nonfiction can do, despite Bal and Veltkamp's claims: "The best photobooks about civil rights use the form's metatextual status in order to permit the child to recognize that meaning is constructed, that knowledge and history are, to use June Jordan's words, 'the business of choose and show,' and that the reader can actively make sense of how the ideas in the book connect to experience outside the book. This is the reason a children's photobook about civil rights can both reflect and provoke, both envision movement experience and aim to shape a response to the events of the book" (*Civil Rights,* xiv).

Conclusion

1. These quotations come from VanSledright's summary of the work he published with Christine Kelly, "Reading American History."

2. Knobel's point brushes up against Immanuel Kant's famous argument that human beings should treat nonhuman animals kindly because doing so helps us become the kind of people we ought to be.

BIBLIOGRAPHY

Abate, Michelle Ann. *Raising Your Kids Right: Children's Literature and American Political Conservatism.* New Brunswick, N.J.: Rutgers University Press, 2010.

Abbott, John Stevens Cabot. *The Adventures of the Chevalier de La Salle and His Companions, in Their Explorations of the Prairies, Forests, Lakes, and Rivers, of the New World, and Their Interviews with the Savage Tribes, Two Hundred Years Ago.* New York: Dodd and Mead, 1875.

Ackmann, Martha. *The Mercury 13: The Untold Story of Thirteen American Women and the Dream of Space Flight.* New York: Random House, 2003.

Agamben, Giorgio. *State of Exception.* Translated by Kevin Atell. Chicago: University of Chicago Press, 2005.

Ahmed, Sara. *The Cultural Politics of Emotion.* New York: Routledge, 2004.

Aliki. *William Shakespeare and the Globe.* New York: HarperCollins, 1999.

Anderson, James A. "Television Literacy and the Critical Viewer." In *Children's Understanding of Television: Research on Attention and Comprehension,* edited by Jennings Bryant and Daniel R. Anderson, 297–330. New York: Academic Press, 1983.

Aoki, Elaine M. "The Significance of Topics of Orbis Pictus Award-Winning Books." In *History Makers: A Questioning Approach to Reading and Writing Biographies,* edited by Myra Zarnowski, 42–56. Portsmouth, N.H.: Heinemann, 2003.

Aronson, Marc. *If Stones Could Speak: Unlocking the Secrets of Stonehenge.* Washington, D.C.: National Geographic, 2010.

———. "New Knowledge." *The Horn Book Magazine,* March/April 2011, 57–62.

Aronson, Marc, and Marina Budhos. *Sugar Changed the World: A Story of Magic, Spice, Slavery, Freedom, and Science.* Boston: Clarion Books, 2010.

Arthur, Leonie. "Young Children as Critical Consumers." *The Australian Journal of Language and Literacy* 24, no. 3 (2001): 182–94.

Atkins, Jeannine. "Did That Really Happen? Blurring the Boundary between Fiction and Fact." *Book Links* 11, no. 6 (2002): 30–31.

Bader, Barbara. "Nonfiction: What's Really New and Different—and What Isn't." *The Horn Book Magazine,* November/December 2011, 41–46.

Bakhtin, Mikhail Mikhaïlovich. "Discourse in the Novel." 1934–35. In *The Dialogic Imagination: Four Essays by M. M. Bakhtin,* edited by Michael Holquist, translated by Caryl Emerson and Michael Holquist, 259–422. Austin: University of Texas Press, 1981.

Bal, P. Matthijs, and Martijn Veltkamp. "How Does Fiction Reading Influence Empathy? An Experimental Investigation on the Role of Emotional Transportation." *PLoS ONE* 8, no. 1 (2013): 1–12.

Bang-Jensen, Valerie. "Talking with Tanya Lee Stone." *Book Links* 24, no. 1 (2014): 11–13.

Bardoe, Cheryl. *Mammoths and Mastodons: Titans of the Ice Age.* New York: Abrams Books for Young Readers, 2010.

Barthes, Roland. *Camera Lucida: Reflections on Photography.* 1980. Translated by Richard Howard. New York: Hill and Wang, 2010.

———. "The Death of the Author." 1968. Translated by Stephen Heath. In *Image, Music, Text,* 142–48. New York: Hill and Wang, 1977.

———. *S/Z.* Paris: Éditions du Seuil, 1970.

———. *S/Z.* 1970. Translated by Richard Miller. New York: Hill and Wang, 1974.

Bartoletti, Susan Campbell. "The Extreme Sport of Research." *The Horn Book Magazine,* March/April 2011, 24–30.

———. *Growing Up in Coal Country.* Boston: Houghton Mifflin, 1996.

———. *They Called Themselves the KKK: The Birth of an American Terrorist Group.* Boston: Houghton Mifflin, 2010.

Berlant, Lauren. *The Female Complaint: The Unfinished Business of Sentimentality in American Culture.* Durham, N.C.: Duke University Press, 2008.

Bernstein, Robin. "Children's Books, Dolls, and the Performance of Race; or, the Possibility of Children's Literature." *PMLA* 126, no. 1 (2011): 160–69.

Bill, Victoria L., and Idorenyin Jamar. "Disciplinary Literacy in the Mathematics Classroom." In *Content Matters: A Disciplinary Literacy Approach to Improving Student Learning,* edited by Stephanie M. McConachie and Anthony R. Petrosky, 63–85. San Francisco: Jossey-Bass, 2009.

Bolden, Tonya. *Maritcha: A Nineteenth-Century American Girl.* New York: Harry N. Abrams, 2005.

———. *Searching for Sarah Rector, the Richest Black Girl in America.* New York: Abrams Books for Young Readers, 2014.

Boler, Megan. *Feeling Power: Emotions and Education.* New York: Routledge, 1999.

Brimner, Larry Dane. *Birmingham Sunday.* Honesdale, Pa.: Calkins Creek, 2010.

Britt, M. Anne, and Cindy Aglinskas. "Improving Students' Ability to Identify and Source Information." *Cognition and Instruction* 20, no. 4 (2002): 485–522.

Burnett, Frances Hodgson. *The Secret Garden.* 1911. New York: W. W. Norton, 2006.

Burns, Loree Griffin. *Tracking Trash: Flotsam, Jetsam, and the Science of Ocean Motion.* Boston: Houghton Mifflin, 2010.

Byler, Lauren. Review of *Disciplining Girls: Understanding the Origins of the Classic Orphan Girl Story,* by Joe Sutliff Sanders. *Children's Literature* 41 (2013): 245–51.

Capshaw, Katharine. *Civil Rights Childhood: Picturing Liberation in African American Photobooks.* Minneapolis: University of Minnesota Press, 2014.

Carlson, James R. "Songs That Teach: Using Song-Poems to Teach Critically." *English Journal* 99, no. 4 (2010): 65–71.

Carter, Betty. "What Makes a Good Preschool Science Book?" In *A Family of Readers: The Book Lover's Guide to Children's and Young Adult Literature,* edited by Roger Sutton and Martha V. Parravano, 83–86. Somerville, Mass.: Candlewick Press, 2010.

Cheney, Lynne. *America: A Patriotic Primer.* New York: Simon and Schuster Books for Young Readers, 2002.

Christensen, Nina. "Rupture: Ideological, Aesthetic, and Educational Transformations in Danish Picturebooks around 1933." In *Children's Literature and the Avant-Garde,* edited by Elina Druker and Bettina Kümmerling-Meibauer, 171–87. Amsterdam: John Benjamins, 2015.

Cianciolo, Patricia J. *Informational Picture Books for Children.* Chicago: American Library Association, 2000.

Cochran, Jacqueline. Letter to W. Randolph Lovelace II. November 28, 1960. Eisenhower Presidential Library, Abilene, Kans.

Comber, Barbara. "Critical Literacies and Local Action: Teacher Knowledge and a 'New' Research Agenda." In *Negotiating Critical Literacies in Classrooms,* edited by Barbara Comber and Anne Simpson, 271–82. Mahwah, N.J.: Lawrence Erlbaum Associates, 2001.

Crismore, Avon. "The Rhetoric of Textbooks: Metadiscourse." *Journal of Curriculum Studies* 16, no. 3 (1984): 279–96.

Crismore, Avon, and William J. Vande Kopple. "Readers' Learning from Prose: The Effects of Hedges." *Written Communication* 5, no. 2 (1988): 184–202.

Curtis, Verna Posever. "Lewis Hine's Child Labor Photographs." In *Photog-

raphy and Reform: Lewis Hine and the National Child Labor Committee, edited by Verna Posever Curtis and Stanley Mallach, 31–47. Milwaukee, Wis.: Milwaukee Art Museum, 1994.

Desai, Christina M. "The Columbus Myth: Power and Ideology in Picturebooks about Christopher Columbus." *Children's Literature in Education* 45 (2014): 179–96.

Doherty, Jonathan L., comp. *Lewis Wickes Hine's Interpretive Photography: The Six Early Projects.* Chicago: University of Chicago Press, 1978.

Dyson, Anne Haas. "Relational Sense and Textual Sense in a U.S. Urban Classroom: The Contested Case of Emily, Girl Friend of a Ninja." In *Negotiating Critical Literacies in Classrooms,* edited by Barbara Comber and Anne Simpson, 3–18. Mahwah, N.J.: Lawrence Erlbaum Associates, 2001.

———. "Rewriting for, and by, the Children: The Social and Ideological Fate of a Media Miss in an Urban Classroom." *Written Communication* 14, no. 3 (1997): 275–312.

Eagleton, Terry. *Literary Theory: An Introduction.* Oxford: Basil Blackwell, 1983.

———. "The Subject of Literature." *Cultural Critique* 2 (Winter 1985–86): 95–104.

Edinger, Monica. "After 'The End.'" *The Horn Book Magazine,* March/April 2011, 79–82.

Ennis, Robert H. "Goals for a Critical Thinking Curriculum." In *Developing Minds: A Resource Book for Teaching Thinking,* edited by Arthur L. Costa, 54–57. Alexandria, Va.: Association for Supervision and Curriculum Development, 1985.

Fisher, Margery. *Matters of Fact: Aspects of Non-fiction for Children.* Leicester, U.K.: Brockhampton Press, 1972.

Fleischman, John. *Phineas Gage: A Gruesome but True Story about Brain Science.* Boston: Houghton Mifflin, 2002.

Ford, Danielle J. "More than Just the Facts." In *A Family of Readers: The Book Lover's Guide to Children's and Young Adult Literature,* edited by Roger Sutton and Martha V. Parravano, 211–16. Somerville, Mass.: Candlewick Press, 2012.

Frassanito, William A. *Antietam: The Photographic Legacy of America's Bloodiest Day.* New York: Charles Scribner's Sons, 1978.

———. *Gettysburg: A Journey in Time.* New York: Charles Scribner's Sons, 1975.

Freedman, Janet L. *Reclaiming the Feminist Vision: Consciousness-Raising and Small Group Practice.* Jefferson, N.C.: McFarland, 2014.

Freedman, Russell. *Kids at Work: Lewis Hine and the Crusade against Child Labor.* New York: Clarion, 1994.

———. *Lincoln: A Photobiography.* New York: Clarion Books, 1987.

Freeman, Evelyn B., and Diane Goetz Person. *Connecting Informational Children's Books with Content Area Learning.* Boston: Allyn and Bacon, 1998.

Freire, Paulo. *Pedagogy of the Oppressed.* 1968. Translated by Myra Bergman Ramos. New York: Herder and Herder, 1970.

Garden Amusements, for Improving the Minds of Little Children. New York: Samuel Wood, 1814.

Genette, Gérard. *Paratexts: Thresholds of Interpretation.* 1987. Translated by Jane E. Lewin. Cambridge: Cambridge University Press, 1997.

Giberne, Agnes. *Radiant Suns: A Sequel to Sun, Moon and Stars.* New York: Macmillan, 1894.

Giblin, James Cross. *The Rise and Fall of Senator Joe McCarthy.* Boston: Houghton Mifflin Harcourt, 2009.

Goldberg, Vicki. *The Power of Photography: How Photographs Changes Our Lives.* New York: Abbeville, 1991.

Gregory, John. *A Father's Legacy to His Daughters.* Edinburgh: A. Strahan, T. Cadell, and W. Creech, 1788.

Gubar, Marah. *Artful Dodgers: Reconceiving the Golden Age of Children's Literature.* New York: Oxford University Press, 2009.

———. "On Not Defining Children's Literature." *PMLA* 126, no. 1 (2011): 209–16.

Gutman, Judith Mara. *Lewis W. Hine, 1874–1940: Two Perspectives.* New York: Grossman, 1974.

Haskins, Jim. "The Triumph of the Spirit in Nonfiction for Black Children." In *Triumphs of the Spirit in Children's Literature,* edited by Francelia Butler and Richard Rotert, 88–96. Hamden, Conn.: Library Professional Publications, 1986.

Heinecken, Dawn. "Empowering Girls through Sport? Sports Advice Books for Young Female Readers." *Children's Literature in Education* 47, no. 4 (2016): 325–42.

Hendler, Glenn. *Public Sentiments: Structures of Feeling in Nineteenth-Century American Literature.* Chapel Hill: University of North Carolina Press, 2001.

Higonnet, Anne. *Pictures of Innocence: The History and Crisis of Ideal Childhood.* London: Thames and Hudson, 1998.

Hollindale, Peter. "Ideology and the Children's Book." *Signal* 55 (January 1988): 3–22.

Holmes, Thom. *Fossil Feud: The Rivalry of the First American Dinosaur Hunters.* Parsippany, N.J.: J. Messner, 1998.

Horn Book. "Dorreen Rappaport Talks with Roger." March 1, 2013.

Horning, Kathleen T. *From Cover to Cover: Evaluating and Reviewing Children's Books.* New York: HarperCollins, 1997.

Howes, Craig. "Hawaii through Western Eyes: Orientalism and Historical Fiction for Children." *The Lion and the Unicorn* 11, no. 1 (1987): 68–87.

Isaacs, Kathleen T. "The Facts of the Matter: Children's Nonfiction, from Then to Now." *The Horn Book Magazine*, March/April 2011, 10–18.

Janeway, James. *A Token for Children: Being an Exact Account of the Conversion, Holy and Exemplary Lives, and Joyful Deaths, of Several Young Children*. Boston: Lincoln and Edwards, 1811.

Jenkins, Steve. "The Importance of Being Wrong." *The Horn Book Magazine*, March/April 2011, 64–68.

Jenks, Tudor. *The Century World's Fair Book for Boys and Girls; Being the Adventures of Harry and Philip with Their Tutor, Mr. Douglass, at the World's Columbian Exposition*. New York: The Century, 1893.

Jetton, Tamara L. "Information-Driven versus Story-Driven: What Children Remember When They Are Read Informational Stories." *Reading Psychology: An International Quarterly* 15 (1994): 109–30.

Johnson, Rebecca L. *Journey into the Deep: Discovering New Ocean Creatures*. Minneapolis, Minn.: Millbrook Press, 2011.

[Joyce, Jeremiah]. *The Wonders of the Telescope; or, A Display of the Starry Heavens and of the System of the Universe: Calculated to Promote and Simplify the Study of Astronomy*. 1805. Reprint, London: Richard Phillips, 1809.

Jurmain, Suzanne. *Forbidden Schoolhouse: The True and Dramatic Story of Prudence Crandall and Her Students*. Boston: Houghton Mifflin, 2005.

Kemp, John R. *Lewis Hine: Photographs of Child Labor in the New South*. Jackson: University Press of Mississippi, 1986.

Kidd, Kenneth. "Queer Theory's Child and Children's Literature Studies." *PMLA* 126, no. 1 (2011): 182–88.

Kincaid, James R. *Child-Loving: The Erotic Child and Victorian Culture*. New York: Routledge, 1992.

———. *Erotic Innocence: The Culture of Child Molesting*. Durham, N.C.: Duke University Press, 1998.

Kincheloe, Joe L. *Getting beyond the Facts: Teaching Social Studies in the Late Twentieth Century*. New York: Peter Lang, 1989.

———. *Getting beyond the Facts: Teaching Social Studies/Social Sciences in the Twenty-First Century*. 2nd ed. New York: Peter Lang, 2001.

Knobel, Michele. "Simon Says See What I Say: Reader Response and the Teacher as Meaning-Maker." 1993. In *Literacies: Social, Cultural and Historical Perspectives*, edited by Colin Lankshear and Michele Knobel, 61–72. New York: Peter Lang, 2011.

Kunze, Peter C. "What We Talk about When We Talk about Helen Keller: Disabilities in Children's Biographies." *Children's Literature Association Quarterly* 38, no. 3 (2013): 304–18.

Lankshear, Colin, and Michele Knobel. "Critical Literacy and Active Citizenship." In *Literacies: Social, Cultural, and Historical Perspectives,* edited by Colin Lankshear and Michele Knobel, 75–101. New York: Peter Lang, 2011.

Lasky, Kathryn. *John Muir: America's First Environmentalist.* Cambridge, Mass.: Candlewick, 2006.

———. *Vision of Beauty: The Story of Sarah Breedlove Walker.* Cambridge, Mass.: Candlewick, 2000.

Latrobe, Kathy H., and Judy Drury. *Critical Approaches to Young Adult Literature.* Drury, N.Y.: Neal-Schuman, 2009.

Lauber, Patricia. *Volcano: The Eruption and Healing of Mount St. Helens.* New York: Bradbury Press, 1986.

Lawson, Robert. "The Caldecott Medal Acceptance." *The Horn Book* 17 (July–August 1941): 273–84.

Leland, Christine H., and Jerome C. Harste. "That's Not Fair! Critical Literacy as Unlimited Semiosis." *The Australian Journal of Language and Literacy* 24, no. 3 (2001): 208–19.

Leland, Christine, Mitzi Lewison, and Jerome Harste. *Teaching Children's Literature: It's Critical!* New York: Taylor and Francis, 2013.

Lester, Julius. *To Be a Slave.* 1968. Reprint, New York: Dial Books, 1998.

Lin, Angel Mei Yi. "Resistance and Creativity in English Reading Lessons in Hong Kong." In *Negotiating Critical Literacies in Classrooms,* edited by Barbara Comber and Anne Simpson, 83–99. Mahwah, N.J.: Lawrence Erlbaum Associates, 2001.

Loewen, James W. *Lies My Teacher Told Me: Everything Your American History Textbook Got Wrong.* New York: Simon and Schuster, 1995.

Lukehart, Wendy. "Brushes with Greatness." *School Library Journal* 60, no. 1 (2014): 40–46.

Macy, Sue. *Bull's-Eye: A Photobiography of Annie Oakley.* Washington, D.C.: National Geographic Society, 2001.

Mallach, Stanley. Introduction to *Photography and Reform: Lewis Hine and the National Child Labor Committee.* Edited by Verna Posever Curtis and Stanley Mallach. Milwaukee, Wis.: Milwaukee Art Museum, 1994.

Marcus, Leonard S. *Minders of Make-Believe: Idealists, Entrepreneurs, and the Shaping of American Children's Literature.* Boston: Houghton Mifflin, 2008.

Martello, Julie. "Drama: Ways into Critical Literacy in the Early Childhood Years." *The Australian Journal of Language and Literacy* 24, no. 3 (2001): 195–207.

Martin, Jacqueline Briggs. *Snowflake Bentley.* Boston: Houghton Mifflin, 1998.

McCully, Emily Arnold. *Marvelous Mattie: How Margaret E. Knight Became an Inventor.* New York: Farrar, Straus, and Giroux, 2006.

Mellor, Bronwyn, and Annette Patterson. "Teaching Readings?" In *Negotiating Critical Literacies in Classrooms,* edited by Barbara Comber and Anne Simpson, 119–34. Mahwah, N.J.: Lawrence Erlbaum Associates, 2001.

Meltzer, Milton. *All Times, All Peoples: A World History of Slavery.* New York: Harper and Row, 1980.

———. *Never to Forget: The Jews of the Holocaust.* New York: Harper and Row, 1976.

———. "Where Do All the Prizes Go? The Case for Nonfiction." *Horn Book* 52 (1976): 17–23.

Mickenberg, Julia L. *Learning from the Left: Children's Literature, the Cold War, and Radical Politics in the United States.* New York: Oxford University Press, 2006.

Middleton, Drew. "Dulles in Berlin Declares Airlift beyond Politics." *New York Times,* October 18, 1948, 1, 3.

Montgomery, Sy. *Quest for the Tree Kangaroo.* Boston: Houghton Mifflin, 2006.

———. *The Snake Scientist.* Boston: Houghton Mifflin, 1999.

Moore, J. Hamilton. *The Young Gentleman and Lady's Monitor, and English Teacher's Assistant.* London: Samuel Green, 1794.

Morrow, Edward A. "Berlin Airlift on Big Holiday Job; Clay Sees It Winning Winter Test." *New York Times,* December 27, 1948, 12.

Müller, Anja. *Framing Childhood in Eighteenth-Century English Periodicals and Prints, 1689–1789.* Burlington, Vt.: Ashgate, 2009.

Murphy, Jim. *An American Plague: The True and Terrifying Story of the Yellow Fever Epidemic of 1793.* New York: Clarion Books, 2003.

Nelson, Kadir. *We Are the Ship: The Story of Negro League Baseball.* New York: Jump at the Sun, 2008.

Nelson, Scott Reynolds. *Ain't Nothing but a Man: My Quest to Find the Real John Henry.* With Marc Aronson. Washington, D.C.: National Geographic, 2008.

Nodelman, Perry. *The Hidden Adult: Defining Children's Literature.* Baltimore: Johns Hopkins University Press, 2008.

Nolen, Susan Bobbitt. "Effects of a Visible Author in Statistical Texts." *Journal of Educational Psychology* 87, no. 1 (1995): 47–65.

Norcia, Megan A. *X Marks the Spot: Women Writers Map the Empire for British Children, 1790–1895.* Athens: Ohio University Press, 2010.

O'Brien, Jennifer. "Children Reading Critically: A Local History." In *Negotiating Critical Literacies in Classrooms,* edited by Barbara Comber and Anne Simpson, 37–54. Mahwah, N.J.: Lawrence Erlbaum Associates, 2001.

Onion, Rebecca. "Writing a 'Wonderland' of Science: Child-Authored Periodicals at the Brooklyn Children's Museum, 1936–1946." *American Periodicals: A Journal of History and Criticism* 23, no. 1 (2013): 1–21.

Op de Beeck, Nathalie. *Suspended Animation: Children's Picture Books and the Fairy Tale of Modernity.* Minneapolis: University of Minnesota Press, 2010.

Pahl, Katrin. "The Logic of Emotionality." *PMLA* 130, no. 5 (2015): 1457–66.

Partridge, Elizabeth. "Narrative Nonfiction: Kicking Ass at Last." *The Horn Book Magazine,* April 23, 2013.

Paterson, Katherine. *The Great Gilly Hopkins.* New York: Crowell, 1978.

Paul, Lissa. *Reading Otherways.* Portsmouth, N.H.: Boynton/Cook, 1998.

Paxton, Richard. "'Someone with Like a Life Wrote It': The Effects of a Visible Author on High School History Students." *Journal of Educational Psychology* 89, no. 2 (1997): 235–50.

Peck, Penny. *Readers' Advisory for Children and 'Tweens.* Santa Barbara, Calif.: Libraries Unlimited, 2010.

Peel, Katie R. "'Strange Fruit': Representations of Julius and Ethel Rosenberg in Children's and Young Adult Nonfiction." *Children's Literature Association Quarterly* 36, no. 2 (2011): 190–213.

Perini, Rebecca L. "The Pearl in the Shell: Author's Notes in Multicultural Children's Literature." *The Reading Teacher* 55, no. 5 (2002): 428–31.

Petersham, Maud, and Miska Petersham. *The Story Book of Houses.* Chicago: John C. Winston Company, 1933.

———. *The Story Book of Iron and Steel.* Chicago: John C. Winston Company, 1935.

———. *The Story Book of the Things We Wear.* Chicago: John C. Winston Company, 1939.

Portalupi, JoAnn, and Ralph Fletcher. *Nonfiction Craft Lessons: Teaching Information Writing K–8.* Portland, Maine: Stenhouse, 2001.

Porzio, Allison. "Absolute Critical Literacy for Part-Time Critical Readers: Sherman Alexie's *The Absolute[ly] True Diary of a Part-Time Indian* and Cultural Studies." *The English Record* 58, no. 1 (2008): 31–39.

Publishers Weekly. Unsigned review of *Kids at Work: Lewis Hine and the Crusade against Child Labor,* by Russell Freedman. 1994.

Ray, Frederic. "No Finer Picture of an Engagement?" *Civil War Times Illustrated* 1 (February 1963): 10–13.

Reynolds, Kimberley. *Left Out: The Forgotten Tradition of Radical Publishing for Children in Britain 1910–1949.* London: Oxford University Press, 2016.

———. *Radical Children's Literature: Future Visions and Aesthetic Transformations in Juvenile Fiction.* New York: Palgrave Macmillan, 2007.

Richardson, Justin, and Peter Parnell. *And Tango Makes Three.* New York: Simon and Schuster Books for Young Readers, 2005.

Rose, Jacqueline. *The Case of Peter Pan, or, the Impossibility of Children's Fiction.* London: Macmillan, 1984.

Russell-Brown, Katheryn. *Little Melba and Her Big Trombone.* Illustrated by Frank Morrison. New York: Lee and Low Books, 2014.

Sampsell-Willmann, Kate. *Lewis Hine as Social Critic.* Jackson: University Press of Mississippi, 2009.

Sánchez-Eppler, Karen. "Marks of Possession: Methods for an Impossible Subject." *PMLA* 126, no. 1 (2011): 151–59.

Sanders, Joe Sutliff. "Chaperoning Words: Meaning-Making in Comics and Picture Books." *Children's Literature* 41 (2013): 57–90.

———. *Disciplining Girls: Understanding the Origins of the Classic Orphan Girl Story.* Baltimore: Johns Hopkins University Press, 2011.

Sanders, Joe Sutliff, Katlyn M. Buckley, Kynsey M. Creel, and Charlie C. Lynn. "Legitimate Humanity: How Award-Winning Children's Nonfiction Complicates Stereotypes." In *Prizing Children's Literature: The Cultural Politics of Children's Book Awards,* edited by Kenneth B. Kidd and Joseph T. Thomas Jr., 58–72. New York: Routledge, 2016.

Sanger, Jack, with Jane Wilson, Bryn Davies, and Roger Whitakker. *Young Children, Videos and Computer Games: Issues for Teachers and Parents.* London: Falmer Press, 1997.

Schwebel, Sara L. *Child-Size History: Fictions of the Past in U.S. Classrooms.* Nashville, Tenn.: Vanderbilt University Press, 2011.

Selsam, Millicent E. *Hidden Animals.* New York: Harper and Row, 1947.

Short, Kathy L. "Reading Literature in Elementary Classrooms." In *Handbook of Research on Children's and Young Adult Literature,* edited by Shelby Wolf, Karen Coats, Patricia Enciso, and Christine Jenkins, 48–62. New York: Routledge, 2011.

Shteir, Ann B. "Wakefield, Priscilla." In *Oxford Dictionary of National Biography,* edited by Lawrence Goldman. New York: Oxford University Press, 2014.

Smith, Karen Patricia. "Acknowledging, Citing, Going Beyond: Issues of Documentation in Nonfiction Literature." In *The Best in Children's Nonfiction: Reading, Writing, and Teaching Orbis Pictus Award Books,* edited by Myra Zarnowski, Richard M. Kerper, and Julie M. Jensen, 32–41. Urbana, Ill.: National Council of Teachers of English, 2001.

Sontag, Susan. *On Photography.* New York: Farrar, Straus, and Giroux, 1977.

Stabell, Ivy Linton. "Model Patriots: The First Children's Biographies of George Washington and Benjamin Franklin." *Children's Literature* 41 (2013): 91–114.

Stanley, Diane, and Peter Vennema. *Bard of Avon: The Story of William Shakespeare.* New York: Morrow Junior Books, 1992.

Stephens, John. *Language and Ideology in Children's Fiction.* Language in Social Life Series. London: Longman, 1992.

Stone, Tanya Lee. *Almost Astronauts: 13 Women Who Dared to Dream.* Somerville, Mass.: Candlewick Press, 2009.

———. "A Fine, Fine Line: Truth in Nonfiction." *The Horn Book Magazine,* March/April 2011, 84–87.

Stowe, Harriet Beecher. *Uncle Tom's Cabin; or, Life among the Lowly.* Boston: John P. Jewett, 1852.

Strong, Frances L. *All the Year Round, a Nature Reader, Part 1: Autumn.* Boston: Ginn, 1896.

Sturtevant, Katherine. *A True and Faithful Narrative.* New York: Farrar, Straus, and Giroux, 2006.

Sutton, Roger. "An Interview with Russell Freedman." *The Horn Book Magazine,* November/December 2002, 695–704.

———. "It Won't Be on the Test." *The Horn Book Magazine,* March/April 2011, 7–8.

Tanaka, Shelley. *Amelia Earhart: The Legend of the Lost Aviator.* New York: Abrams Books for Young Readers, 2008.

Taniguchi, Marilyn. Review of *Jackie Robinson and the Big Game,* by Dan Gutman. *School Library Journal,* June 2006, 136.

Taylor, Ann. *City Scenes, or a Peep into London for Good Children.* London: Harvey and Darton, 1828.

Time. "Precision Operation." 52, no. 16 (1948): 32.

Todorov, Tzvetan. *Mikhail Bakhtin: The Dialogical Principle.* Translated by Wlad Godzich. Minneapolis: University of Minnesota Press, 1984.

Tomlinson, Carl M., Michael O. Tunnell, and Donald J. Richgels. "The Content and Writing of History in Textbooks and Trade Books." In *The Story of Ourselves: Teaching History through Children's Literature,* edited by Michael O. Tunnell and Richard Ammon, 51–62. New York: Heineman.

Trachtenberg, Alan. "Ever—the Human Document." In *America and Lewis Hine: Photographs 1904–1940,* 118–37. New York: Aperture, 1977.

Trusler, John. *Principles of Politeness, and of Knowing the World; by the Late Lord Chesterfield. Methodized and Digested under Distinct Heads, with Additions, by the Reverend Dr. John Trusler: Containing Every Instruction Necessary to Complete the Gentleman and Man of Fashion, to Teach Him a Knowledge of Life, and Make Him Well Received in All Companies. For the Improvement of Youth; Yet Not beneath the Attention of Any.* London: John Bell, 1775.

Tunnell, Michael O. *Candy Bomber: The Story of the Berlin Airlift's "Chocolate Pilot."* Watertown, Mass.: Charlesbridge, 2010.

Turner, Pamela S. *The Frog Scientist.* Boston: Houghton Mifflin Books for Children, 2009.

Ulanowicz, Anastasia. "Preemptive Education: Lynne Cheney's *America: A Patriotic Primer* and the Ends of History." *Children's Literature Association Quarterly* 33, no. 4 (2008): 341–70.

VanSledright, Bruce. *In Search of America's Past: Learning to Read History in Elementary School.* New York: Teachers College Press, 2002.

VanSledright, Bruce, and Christine Kelly. "Reading American History: The Influence of Multiple Sources on Six Fifth Graders." *The Elementary School Journal* 98, no. 3 (1998): 239–65.

Van Sluys, Katie. *What If and Why? Literacy Invitations for Multilingual Classrooms.* Portsmouth, N.H.: Heinemann, 2005.

Vardell, Sylvia. "A New 'Picture of the World': The NCTE Orbis Pictus Award for Outstanding Nonfiction for Children." *Language Arts* 68 (October 1991): 474–79.

Vološinov, V. N. *Marxism and the Philosophy of Language.* 1929. Translated by Ladislave Matejka and I. R. Titunik. Cambridge, Mass.: Harvard University Press, 1986.

Wakefield, Priscilla. *An Introduction to Botany, in a Series of Familiar Letters, with Illustrative Engravings.* 1796. 3rd ed. Philadelphia: Solomon W. Conrad, 1818.

———. *The Juvenile Travellers, Containing the Remarks of a Family during a Tour through the Principal States and Kingdoms of Europe with an Account of Their Inhabitants, Natural Productions, and Curiosities.* 1801. London: Darton and Harvey, 1808.

———. *Perambulations in London, and Its Environs: Comprehending an Historical Sketch of the Ancient State, and Progress, of the British Metropolis; A Concise Description of Its Present State, Notices of Eminent Persons, and a Short Account of the Surrounding Villages. In Letters. Designed for Young Persons.* 2nd ed. London: Darton, Harvey, and Darton, 1814.

Waller, Alison. *Constructing Adolescence in Fantastic Realism.* New York: Routledge, 2009.

Watson, J. Madison. *Independent Third Reader: Containing a Simple, Illustrated Treatise on Elocution; Choice and Classified Readings; with Full Notes and a Complete Index.* 1870. Reprint, New York: A. S. Barnes, 1876.

Weikle-Mills, Courtney. *Imaginary Citizens: Child Readers and the Limits of American Independence, 1640–1868.* Baltimore: Johns Hopkins University Press, 2013.

Weitekamp, Margaret A. *Right Stuff, Wrong Sex: America's First Women in Space Program.* Baltimore: Johns Hopkins University Press, 2004.

Westman, Karin. "Blending Genres and Crossing Audiences: *Harry Potter* and the Future of Literary Fiction." In *The Oxford Handbook of Children's Literature*, edited by Julia L. Mickenberg and Lynne Vallone, 93–112. Oxford: Oxford University Press, 2011.

Wineburg, Samuel S. "Historical Problem Solving: A Study of the Cognitive Processes Used in the Evaluation of Documentary and Pictorial Evidence." *Journal of Educational Psychology* 83, no. 1 (1991): 73–87.

———. "Historical Thinking and Other Unnatural Acts." *Phi Delta Kappan* 80, no. 7 (1999): 488–99.

———. *Historical Thinking and Other Unnatural Acts: Charting the Future of Teaching the Past*. Philadelphia: Temple University Press, 2001.

———. "On the Reading of Historical Texts: Notes on the Breach between School and Academy." *American Educational Research Journal* 28, no. 3 (1991): 495–519.

Wollstonecraft, Mary. *A Vindication of the Rights of Woman: With Strictures on Political and Moral Subjects*. 1792. Reprint, London: J. Johnson, 1796.

Woodbury, Ronald. "From the Traditional Lecture toward Dialogical Learning: Changing Patterns in the Teaching of History." In *Ideas That Work in College Teaching,* edited by Robert L. Badger, 85–91. New York: State University of New York Press, 2008.

Wu, Yung-Hsing. "The Magical Matter of Books: Amazon.com and The Tales of Beedle the Bard." *ChLAQ* 35, no. 2 (2010): 190–207.

YALSA. "Award for Excellence in Nonfiction for Young Adults Chair's Manual." Draft 1. 2012.

Zappy, Erica. "Sing a Song of Science: Scientists in the Field." *The Horn Book Magazine,* March/April 2011, 33–38.

Zarnowski, Myra. *History Makers: A Questioning Approach to Reading and Writing Biographies*. Portsmouth, N.H.: Heinemann, 2003.

———. "Reading for the Mystery in the Nonfiction Science Books." *Journal of Children's Literature* 39, no. 2 (2013): 14–21.

Zarnowski, Myra, and Susan Turkel. "Creating New Knowledge: Books That Demystify the Process." *Journal of Children's Literature* 38, no. 1 (2012): 28–34.

———. "Nonfiction Literature That Highlights Inquiry: How *Real* People Solve *Real* Problems." *Journal of Children's Literature* 37, no. 1 (2011): 30–37.

INDEX

Page numbers in *italics* indicate illustrations.

Abate, Michelle Ann, 80
Abbott, John Stevens Cabot: *The Adventures of the Chevalier de La Salle and His Companions* (1875), 78–80, 82–83, 90
Ackmann, Martha: *The Mercury 13: The Untold Story of Thirteen American Women and the Dream of Space Flight* (2003), 186–89, 191–92, 194–95, 244n4
active empathy, 213, 216, 218
affirmative action, 244n2
Agamben, Giorgio: *State of Exception* (2005), 162
Ahmed, Sarah, 201
Ain't Nothing but a Man: My Quest to Find the Real John Henry (Scott Reynolds Nelson, with Marc Aronson, 2008), 121–22, *121,* 125, 140, 147–50, *148*
Aliki [Liacouras Brandenberg]: *William Shakespeare and the Globe* (1999), 51
All the Year Round, a Nature Reader, Part 1: Autumn (Strong, late nineteenth century), 117, 124
Almost Astronauts: 13 Women Who Dared to Dream (Tanya Lee Stone, 2009), 30–31, 177–98, *178;* antagonist, Cochran cast as, 192–97; awards and critical reception, 183–84; critical literacy theory and, 179–83, 198; heroine, Cobb cast as, 190–92; interview with Cobb, questions about reliability of, 184–90, 193, 197; narrative framework of, 183; reliability over critical engagement, choosing, 178–79, 181–84, 197–98
Althusser, Louis, 16
America: A Patriotic Primer (Cheney, 2002), 80, 206–7
American Library Association, 10, 30, 33, 131, 183, 239n1, 242n7, 244n1
American Plague, An: The True and Terrifying Story of the Yellow

Fever Epidemic of 1793 (Murphy, 2003), 69–70
Anderson, James A., 11, 245n4
And Tango Makes Three (Richardson and Parnell, 2005), 244n3
Antietam Battlefield (1862), photos of, 154–56, *154, 156,* 160, 243nn3–4
Aristotle, 103
Aronson, Marc, 57, 177, 180, 181, 182, 197, 198; *Ain't Nothing but a Man: My Quest to Find the Real John Henry* (with Scott Reynolds Nelson, 2008), 121–22, *121,* 125; *If Stones Could Speak: Unlocking the Secrets of Stonehenge* (2010), 51–53, *52,* 94–95, 96–97, 138–39, 140–41; *Sugar Changed the World: A Story of Magic, Spice, Slavery, Freedom, and Science* (with Marina Budhos, 2010), 124–25
Arthur, Leonie, 228–29
Association for Library Service to Children, Committee on Notable Children's Books, 33
Atkins, Jeannine, 202
Atkinson, Richard, 95, 141
audience: for children's literature in general, 122–25; font size and line spacing affecting, 123–27, 128, 241–42nn5–6; for peritexts, 119–25; reading levels, 26–28
authority-based view of children's nonfiction. *See* fact-based view of children's nonfiction
award committee preferences, 242n7

Bader, Barbara, 201
Bakhtin, Mikhail, 14–17, 18, 50, 65, 90–91, 173, 224
Bal, P. Matthijs, 221, 246n7
"banking" concept of education, 12, 19, 36–37, 39–40, 227, 238n5, 239n2
Bardoe, Cheryl: *Mammoths and Mastodons* (2010), 94, 98–99, 218–19
Bard of Avon (Stanley and Vennema, 1992), 51
Barthes, Roland: negotiating theories of critical engagement with, 19–21, 22, 24, 238–39nn7–8; on photographs *(Camera Lucida,* 1980), 134, 135, 136, 155, 160, 161, 173, 242n1; *S/Z* (1970), 19–21, 24; on voice, 64
Bartoletti, Susan Campbell, 184, 188, 245n2; *Growing Up in Coal Country* (1996), 54, 65–66; *They Called Themselves the KKK: The Birth of an American Terrorist Group* (2010), 70–71, 138, 141
Bentley, Wilson, 87
Berlant, Lauren, 207, 245n3
Bernstein, Robin, 241n2
Bill, Victoria L., 42
Birmingham Sunday (Brimner, 2010), 111, 113
Bolden, Tonya, 97, 98, 126–31, 241n5; *Maritcha: A Nineteenth-Century American Girl* (2005), 126–28, *126,* 138, 140, 241n5; *Searching for Sarah Rector, the Richest Black Girl in America* (2014), 128–30, *129,* 139, 142, 143–44, 241–42n6
Boler, Megan, 205, 212–13, 216–17, 246n6
Botkins, B. A., 204
Brady, Mathew B., *154,* 243n4

Brimner, Larry Dane: *Birmingham Sunday* (2010), 111, 113
Budhos, Marina, and Marc Aronson: *Sugar Changed the World: A Story of Magic, Spice, Slavery, Freedom, and Science* (2010), 124–25
Burnett, Frances Hodgson: *The Secret Garden* (1911), 244n3
Burns, Loree Griffin: *Tracking Trash: Flotsam, Jetsam, and the Science of Ocean Motion* (2010), 218
Byler, Lauren, 199–200

Caldecott Medal, 183, 245n1
Camera Lucida (Barthes, 1980), 134, 135, 136, 155, 160, 161, 173, 242n1
Candy Bomber: The Story of the Berlin Airlift's "Chocolate Pilot" (Tunnell, 2010), 209–12
capacity of children for critical engagement, 31, 198, 224–28
Capshaw, Katharine: *Civil Rights Childhood* (2014), 80–81, 136–37, 151, 246n5, 246n7
captions. *See* photographs
Carlson, James R., 12–13
carnivalesque text, 18–19
Carter, Betty, 83
Case of Peter Pan, or, the Impossibility of Children's Fiction, The (Rose, 1984), 122–23, 240–41n2
CDA (critical discourse analysis), 14, 16, 24, 237n4
CFA (Childhood of Famous Americans) series, 180–81
characters, 29–30, 77–105, 224; defined, 77–78; dialogue, critical engagement as, 86, 100–101; flawed characters, 78–83; Fleischman's *Phineas Gage*, case study of, 99–105, *100*; Freedman's *Kids at Work*, case study of, 163–64; Freedman's *Lincoln: A Photobiography*, case study of, 156–58; heroification of, 78–80, 82–83, 180–81, 190–92, 210; humanization of, 85, 92, 152, 217; "in the light of becoming," 90–92; mistakes of, 86–90; photographs and, 138–41, 152; in process of inquiry, 92–99, 240n3; voice and character, intersection of, 101–5; vulnerability of, 83–86
Cheney, Lynne: *America: A Patriotic Primer* (2002), 80, 206–7
Childhood of Famous Americans (CFA) series, 180–81
child labor, Hines's photographs of, 162–75, *165*
Children's Literature Association Quarterly, 122–23
children's nonfiction. *See* critical engagement with children's nonfiction
Christmas cards, 139
Cianciolo, Patricia J., 28, 29, 67, 95, 96, 99, 230
City Scenes, or a Peep into London for Good Children (Taylor, 1828), 118
Civil Rights Act of 1964, 244n2
Civil Rights Childhood (Capshaw, 2014), 80–81, 136–37, 151, 246n5, 246n7
Clay, Lucius D., 211
Cobb, Jerrie, 183, 184–93, 196–97, 210
Cochran, Jackie (Bessie Pitman), 191, 192–97, 244n4

codifications, 4–5, 143–44, 150, 237n3
Collins, Eileen, 190
Columbus, Christopher, 74, 80
Comber, Barbara, 12, 13
Common Core State Standards, 9
conclusions, ability to draw, 21–22, 70–71, 145
Cope, Edward Drinker, 88–90, *88*
Coretta Scott King Author Award, 1
Crandall, Prudence, 111–13
Crismore, Avon, 29, 39, 40, 50–51, 55–56, 113
critical discourse analysis (CDA), 14, 16, 24, 237n4
critical engagement with children's nonfiction, 1–32, 223–31; as adult priority, 228–31; capabilities of children regarding, 31, 198, 224–28; characters, 29–30, 77–105, 224 (*see also* characters); conclusions, ability to draw, 21–22, 70–71, 145; defining critical engagement, 7, 11–14; as dialogue, 12–15, 31 (*see also* dialogue, critical engagement as); emotional engagement and, 31, 199–222 (*see also* emotion and sentimentality); fact-based view, 29, 33–45 (*see also* fact-based view of children's nonfiction); format, significance of, 107; humility, as characteristic of, 29, 30, 31–32, 40, 47, 224; inquiry-based view, 29, 40–45 (*see also* inquiry-based view of children's nonfiction); methodology, limitations, and parameters, 7–10; negotiating theoretical approaches to, 15–22; nonhistorical approach to, 2–3, 5–6, 10; nonlinear reading, 107–8; peritexts, 30, 107–32 (*see also* peritexts); photographs, 30, 133–75 (*see also* photographs); popularity of genre with children, 1–2; punctuated plurality and, 7, 22, 43, 213, 224, 230; reading levels, ignoring, 26–28; scholarship on, 2–6; sections or moments rather than whole books, focus on, 22–26; terms for children's nonfiction, 7–8; textbooks differentiated, 7–9; voice, 29, 47–75, 224 (*see also* voice). *See also specific texts and authors*
critical literacy theory, 179–83, 198
critical sentimental identification. *See* emotion and sentimentality
Currie, William, 69
Curtis, Verna Posever, 167

Desai, Christina M., 80
dialogue, critical engagement as, 12–15, 31; characters and, 86, 100–101; children's capability for critical engagement, 227; negotiation of theory and, 21; peritexts and, 110; in photographs, 169–70, 171; punctuated plurality and, 224; questions rather than answers, nonfiction viewed as literature of, 44; voice and, 64, 65–67, 69, 71–73, 75
didacticism prioritized at expense of truthfulness, 180–83
Disciplining Girls: Understanding the Origins of the Classic Orphan Girl Story (Sanders, 2011), 199
Doherty, Jonathan L., 171
Douglas, Stephen, 157–58
Douglass, Frederick, 158, 241n5
Du Bois, W. E. B., 97, 135
Dulles, John Foster, 211

Dylan, Bob, 13
Dyson, Anne Haas, 14–15, 17, 225, 227, 237n3, 238n5

Eagleton, Terry, 16, 17, 238nn6–7
Earhart, Amelia, 87
Edinger, Monica, 120
Egg to Chick (Selsam, 1946), 5
Elting, Mary: *We Are the Government* (1946), 9
emotion and sentimentality, 31, 199–222; conventional wisdom regarding critical engagement and, 199–200, 245–46n4; critical sentimental identification, feminist critique of, 204–7; critical sentimental identification, feminist theory of, 212–20; feminist theory on, 31, 200, 201, 204–7, 212–20, 245n3, 246nn5–6; fiction versus nonfiction, empathy elicited by, 221; grief in Freedman's *Lincoln* and *Kids at Work*, 160–62, 175; passive empathy, dangers of, 212–13, 216, 217; profound emotional connections between children's books and their readers, 245n1; sentimental identification thwarting critical engagement, 207–12; as venue for critical engagement, 200, 201–4, 221–22
Engels, Friedrich, 5
Enni, Robert H., 13
epitexts, 109
Executive Order 11246, 244n2

fact-based view of children's nonfiction, 29, 33–45; ability of nonfiction to transfer facts to children, 34–35; critical engagement threatened by, 34, 35–40; inquiry-based view versus, 40–45, 223; Stone's *Almost Astronauts* choosing reliability over critical engagement, 178–79, 181–84, 197–98; transmission of facts, nonfiction viewed primarily as means of, 33–34
Father's Legacy to His Daughters, A (Gregory, 1761/1773), 57–59
fear: in feminist pedagogy, 206; La Salle credited with not experiencing, 78; of snakes, 216–17
Federal Writers' Project, 204
feminist theory: consciousness raising in, 143; critique of critical sentimental identification, 204–7; on emotion and intellect, 31, 200, 201, 204–7, 212–20, 245n3, 246nn5–6; on imperialist role of children's nonfiction, 2
fiction versus nonfiction, empathy elicited by, 221
first-person narration, 29, 49, 55, 57, 60–62, 73, 95, 97, 127, 149, 240n3
Fisher, Daniel, 218–19
Fisher, Margery, 6, 29, 95, 201–2
flawed characters, 78–83
Fleischman, John: *Phineas Gage: A Gruesome but True Story about Brain Science* (2002), 99–105, *100*, 140, 142–44, 145
Fletcher, Ralph, 11, 28, 107, 225
font size and line spacing, 123–27, 128, 241–42nn5–6
Forbidden Schoolhouse: The True and Dramatic Story of Prudence Crandall and Her Students (Jurmain, 2005), 111–13
Ford, Danielle J., 40–41, 42
Forrest, Nathan Bedford, 70–71
Fort Sumter, 157

Fossil Feud: The Rivalry of the First American Dinosaur Hunters (Holmes, 1998), 88–90, *89*, 94
Foster, Rube, 62, 63
Franklin, Benjamin, 67, 180
Frassanito, William A., 243nn3–4
Freedman, Janet L., 143
Freedman, Russell: *Kids at Work* (1994), 162–75, *165*; *Lincoln: A Photobiography* (1987), 9, 26–27, 30, 150–62, *154*, *156*, 173–75, 243n3
Freeman, Evelyn B., 3, 4, 7, 35, 42–43, 95, 96
Freire, Paolo: "banking" concept of education and, 12, 19, 36, 37, 227, 238n5, 239n2; characters and, 81, 83, 86, 87, 91, 95–96, 98, 99, 103; on codifications, 4–5, 143–44, 150, 237n3; critical literacy theory and, 179; defining critical engagement and, 11–14; dialogue of critical engagement and, 14–15, 31; on emotion and sentimentality, 212–13, 246n6; fact-based teaching style rejected by, 35–36, 37–38, 40; negotiating educational theory of, 15–17, 19
Frog Scientist, The (Turner, 2009), 54, 68–69, *68*, 84, 85, 93, 217–18, 222
Fugitive Slave Law, 205

Gadsden, Walter, 111
Gage, Phineas, 99–105, *100*
Garden Amusements, for Improving the Minds of Little Children (1814), 208–9
Gardner, Alexander, 153, *154*, *156*, 243n4
Genette, Gérard, 30, 108, 109

Gettysburg Address, 152
Giberne, Agnes, 97–98
Giblin, James Cross: *The Rise and Fall of Senator Joe McCarthy* (2009), 240n3
Goldberg, Vicki, 135, 167
Gorelick, Sarah, 193–95
Great Gilly Hopkins, The (Paterson, 1978), 244n3
Gregory, John: *A Father's Legacy to His Daughters* (1761/1773), 57–59
grief, in Freedman's *Lincoln* and *Kids at Work*, 160–62, 175
Growing Up in Coal Country (Bartoletti, 1996), 54, 65–66
Gubar, Marah, 240–41n2

Halvorsen, Gail, 209–12
Harlow, John, 102
Harry Potter series (Rowling), 214–15, 245n1
Harste, Jerome C., 3–4, 13
Hart, Jane, 186, 187, 189
Hayes, Tyrone, *68*, 69, 84, 85, 93, 217–18
hedges, 29, 49, 50–55, 74, 138, 239n1, 243n3
Heinecken, Dawn, 240n2
Hendler, Glenn, 204
Henry, John, 121–22, *121*, 140, 147–50
heroification of characters, 78–80, 82–83, 180–81, 190–92, 210
Hidden Animals (Selsam, 1947), 146–47, 150, 243n2
Higonnet, Anne, 135, 243–44n6
Hines, Lewis, 163–75, *165*, 243–44n6
Hollindale, Peter, 4
Holmes, Thom: *Fossil Feud: The*

Rivalry of the First American Dinosaur Hunters (1998), 88–90, *89*, 94
Horn Book, The, 83, 131, 181
Horning, Kathleen T., 123–24
Howes, Craig, 180
Hudson, Bill, 111
Hughes, Ted, 201
humanization of characters, 85, 92, 152, 217
humility, as characteristic of critically engaging nonfiction, 29, 30, 31–32, 40, 47, 224

identification, sentimental. *See* emotion and sentimentality
If Stones Could Speak: Unlocking the Secrets of Stonehenge (Aronson, 2010), 51–53, *52*, 94–95, 96–97, 138–39, 140–41
individualism, neoliberal, 240n2
inquiry-based view of children's nonfiction, 29, 40–45; critical literature theory, 179–83; fact-based view versus, 40–45, 223; "new nonfiction" debate and, 177–78; Stone's *Almost Astronauts* choosing reliability over inquiry, 178–79, 181–84, 197–98; Young Adult Library Services Association award criteria, 239n1
Introduction to Botany (Wakefield, 1796), 95, 118–19
irony, 31, 60–63, 141
Isaacs, Kathleen T., 33, 150

Jackson, Amy, 142
Jamar, Idorenyin, 42
Janeway, Jane: *A Token for Children: Being an Exact Account of the Conversion, Holy and Exemplary Lives, and Joyful Deaths, of Several Young Children* (1811), 207–8
Jefferson, Thomas, 80
Jenkins, Steve, 41–42, 43
Jennison, Edwin, 159, 161
Jetton, Tamara L., 34–35, 44
John Muir: America's First Environmentalist (Lasky, 2006), 71–72, 101
Johnson, Lyndon B., 184–88, 193, 244n2
Johnson, Rebecca L.: *Journey into the Deep* (2011), 99
Jones, Bernard Bryan "B.B.," Robert E. Lee, and Montfort, 139
Jordan, June, 246n7
Journey into the Deep (Johnson, 2011), 99
Joyce, Jeremiah: *The Wonders of the Telescope* (1805), 67–68
Jurmain, Susan: *Forbidden Schoolhouse: The True and Dramatic Story of Prudence Crandall and Her Students* (2005), 111–13
Juvenile Travelers, The (Wakefield, 1801), 61

Kant, Immanuel, 246n2
Keller, Helen, 180
Kemp, John R., 168
Kennedy, John F., 244n2
Kidd, Kenneth, 241n2
Kids at Work (Freedman, 1994), 162–75, *165*
Kincaid, James R., 166, 243–44n6
Kincheloe, Joe L.: on fact-based view of nonfiction, 33, 36–39, 40, 239n3; on voice, 47–48, 59, 67, 74
King, Martin Luther, Jr., 111

Knight, Margaret E., 114–16, *114*
Knobel, Michele, 75, 230, 246n2
Ku Klux Klan (KKK), 70–71, 138, 141
Kunze, Peter C., 180

Lankshear, Colin, 75
La Salle, Robert de, 78–80, 82–83, 90
Lasky, Kathryn: *John Muir: America's First Environmentalist* (2006), 71–72, 101; *Vision of Beauty: The Story of Sarah Breedlove Walker* (2000), 23, 24
Lauber, Patricia: *Volcano: The Eruption and Healing of Mount St. Helens* (1986), 145–46, *146*, 150, 151
Laurence, Sir John, 55
Lawson, Robert, 245n1
Leland, Christine H., 3–4, 13
Lester, Julius: *To Be a Slave* (1968), 54, 203–4, *203*, 219, 222
Lewison, Mitzi, 13
Life on the Mississippi (Twain, 1883), 66
"light of becoming," characters in, 90–92
Liliuokalani, 180
Lin, Angel Mei Yi, 227–28
Lincoln, Mary Todd, 153, 157, 159
Lincoln, Thomas (Tad), 153, 159, 161
Lincoln, William Wallace (Willie), 159–60, 161
Lincoln: A Photobiography (Freedman, 1987), 9, 26–27, 30, 150–62, *154*, *156*, 173–75, 243n3
line spacing and font size, 123–27, 128, 241–42nn5–6
Liston, Melba Doretta, 83–84, 86–87, 91–92

Little Melba and Her Big Trombone (Russell-Brown; 2014), 83–84, 86–87, 91–92
Localizers and Whole Brainers, in Fleischman's *Phineas Gage* (2002), 100–102, 104
Loewen, James W., 158, 243n5
Los Angeles Times Book Award, 1
Lovelace, Randall, 183, 191, 193–96
Lukehart, Wendy, 181
Lyons, Maritcha Rémond, 126–28, *126*, 138, 140, 241n5

Macy, Sue, 68, 139, 140
Mallach, Stanley, 169
Mammoths and Mastodons (Bardoe, 2010), 94, 98–99, 218–19
Marcus, Leonard S., 150–51, 180
Margaret A. Edwards Award, 1
Maritcha: A Nineteenth-Century American Girl (Bolden, 2005), 126–28, *126*, 138, 140, 241n5
Marsh, Charles Othniel, 88–90, *88*
Martello, Julie, 3
Martin, Jacqueline Briggs, 87
Marvelous Mattie: How Margaret E. Knight Became an Inventor (McCully, 2006), 114–16, *114*
Marx, Karl: and Marxism, 16, 238n6
Mason, Robert (Bob), 93–94, 214–17
McCarthy, Joe, 240n3
McCully, Emily Arnold: *Marvelous Mattie: How Margaret E. Knight Became an Inventor* (2006), 114–16, *114*
Mellor, Bronwyn, 225–26
Meltzer, Milton, 219–20, 222, 245n2
Mercury 13 women: Martha Ack-

mann, *The Mercury 13* (2003), 186–89, 191–92, 194–95, 244n4; Weitekamp, *Right Stuff, Wrong Sex* (2004), 193–95, 196, 244n4. See also *Almost Astronauts: 13 Women Who Dared to Dream*
metadiscourse, 56
metatextual status of photobooks, 246n5, 246n7
Mickenberg, Julia L., 5, 9, 243n2
mistakes of characters, 86–90
Montgomery, Sy, 202–3; *Quest for the Tree Kangaroo* (2006), 85, 92–93, 99; *The Snake Scientist* (1999), 93–94, 97, 98, 202, 214–17, *215*, 222
Moore, J. Hamilton: *The Young Gentleman and Lady's Monitor, and English Teacher's Assistant* (late 18th century), 117
moral positions taken by photographs, 162, 163, 164–67, *165*, 169, 175
moral relativism, 70–71
Moses, Susan, 139
Moss, Barbara, 34
Muir, John, 71–72, 101
Murphy, Jim: *An American Plague: The True and Terrifying Story of the Yellow Fever Epidemic of 1793* (2003), 69–70

National Book Award for Young People's Literature, 1
National Child Labor Committee (NCLC), 163–64, 167, 168
National Council of Teachers of English, 10, 131, 244n1
NCLC (National Child Labor Committee), 163–64, 167, 168
necromancers, 49, 64–70, 74, 139

Negro League baseball, 61–64, *62*, 73
Nelson, Kadir: *We Are the Ship: The Story of Negro League Baseball* (2008), 61–64, *62*, 73
Nelson, Scott Reynolds, with Marc Aronson: *Ain't Nothing but a Man: My Quest to Find the Real John Henry* (2008), 121–22, *121*, 125, 140, 147–50, *148*
Newbery Awards, 1, 150–51, 163, 183, 203, 245n1
New Criticism, 201
Newman, Shirlee Petkin, 180
"new nonfiction" debate, 177–79, 181
Nolen, Susan Bobbitt, 55–56, 61
nonfiction for children. See critical engagement with children's nonfiction
nonlinear reading, 107–8

Oakley, Annie, 68, 139, 140
O'Brien, Jennifer, 226–27
op de Beeck, Nathalie, 27–28
Orbis Pictus, 131

Pahl, Katrin, 200
paratexts, 109
Parnell, Peter, and Justin Richardson: *And Tango Makes Three* (2005), 244n3
Partridge, Elizabeth, 1–2
passive empathy, 212–13, 216, 217
Paterson, Katherine: *The Great Gilly Hopkins* (1978), 244n3
Patterson, Annette, 225–26
Paul, Lissa, 201
Paxton, Richard, 56, 64, 198
Peck, Penny, 33
Peel, Katie R., 65

Perambulations in London, and Its Environs (Wakefield, 1809), 53, 54–55, 59–61, 62

Perini, Rebecca L., 119–20

peritexts, 30, 107–32; in Bolden's work, 126–31; defined, 109; font size and line spacing, 123–27, 128, 241–42nn5–6; historical roots of, 117–19; intended audience for, 119–25; nonlinear reading of nonfiction and, 107–8; potential for critical engagement offered by, 113–17; sequestration of opportunities for critical engagement in, 109–13

Person, Diane Goetz, 3, 4, 7, 35, 42–43, 95, 96

Petersham, Maud and Miska: *Story Book of Houses* (1933), 73–74, 212; *Story Book of Iron and Steel* (1935), 73; *Story Book of the Things We Wear* (1939), 73

Phineas Gage: A Gruesome but True Story about Brain Science (Fleischman, 2002), 99–105, *100*, 140, 142–44, 145

photographs, 30, 133–75; codifications and, 143–44, 150; dialogue, critical engagement as, 169–70, 171; Freedman's *Kids at Work*, case study of, 162–75, *165*; Freedman's *Lincoln: A Photobiography*, case study of, 30, 150–62, *154*, *156*, 173–75; grief in Freedman's work, suspension of critical engagement due to, 160–62, 175; invitations to study and compare, 145–50, 151–52; metatextual status of, 246n5, 246n7; moral positions taken by, 162, 163, 164–67, *165*, 169, 175;

peritexts, captions as, 30, 107, 109, 110, 111, 131; techniques used/not used in, 154–55, *154*, *156*, 242–43n1; threats to critical engagement from, 133–37, 141–44, 152, 242–43n1; truthfulness of, questioning or accepting, 135, 137, 139–41, 152–53, 159–60, 163–64, 167–69; unary, 136, 141, 160, 173, 174, 242n1; use in children's nonfiction, 133, 150–51; voice and character used to encourage critical interpretation of, 138–41

Pitman, Bessie (Jackie Cochran), 191, 192–97, 244n4

Pittsburgh Survey, 169–70

plurality, punctuated, 7, 22, 43, 213, 224, 230

plural narrator, 62, 73

Portalupi, JoAnn, 11, 28, 107, 225

Porter, T. J., 129–30

Porzio, Allison, 11

professional approach to disciplines, pedagogy based on, 42–43, 92–99, 108

punctuated plurality, 7, 22, 43, 213, 224, 230

punctum, 242n1

Quest for the Tree Kangaroo (Montgomery, 2006), 85, 92–93, 99

questions, children's nonfiction as literature of. *See* inquiry-based view of children's nonfiction

Ray, Frederic, 243n3

reading levels, 26–28

Rector, Sarah, 128–30, *129*, 139, 142, 143

Rémond, Charles, 241n5

Reynolds, Kimberley, 5–6, 81
Richardson, Justin, and Peter Parnell: *And Tango Makes Three* (2005), 244n3
Richgels, Donald J., 8
Right Stuff, Wrong Sex (Weitekamp, 2004), 193–95, 196, 244n4
Rise and Fall of Senator Joe McCarthy, The (Giblin, 2009), 240n3
Robinson, Jackie, 181
Roosevelt, Eleanor, 163
Roosevelt, Teddy, 72
Rose, Jacqueline: *The Case of Peter Pan, or, the Impossibility of Children's Fiction* (1984), 122–23, 240–41n2
Rosenberg, Ethel and Julius, 65
Rowling, J. K.: Harry Potter series, 214–15, 245n1
Rush, Benjamin, 69–70
Russell-Brown, Katheryn: *Little Melba and Her Big Trombone* (2014), 83–84, 86–87, 91–92
Russian formalism, 16

Sampsell-Willman, Kate, 134–35, 168, 169, 170–71
Sánchez-Eppler, Karen, 240n2
Sanders, Joe Sutliff: *Disciplining Girls: Understanding the Origins of the Classic Orphan Girl Story* (2011), 199
Sanger, Jack, 229
Schomburg Center for Research in Black Culture, 128
Schwebel, Sara L., 8, 206
Scientists in the Field series, 217–18
seamless narrative, problem of, 47–49, 74
Searching for Sarah Rector, the Richest Black Girl in America (Bolden, 2014), 128–30, *129*, 139, 142, 143–44, 242–42n6
second-person narration, 99
Secret Garden, The (Burnett, 1911), 244n3
Selsam, Millicent Ellis: *Egg to Chick* (1946), 5; *Hidden Animals* (1947), 146–47, 150, 243n2
sentiment. *See* emotion and sentimentality
Shakespeare, William, 51
Shaw, Matilda, 139
Sibert Medal, 183, 184
Simon, Seymour, 150
slavery: Marc Aronson and Marina Badhos, *Sugar Changed the World: A Story of Magic, Spice, Slavery, Freedom, and Science* (2010), 124–25; Julius Lester, *To Be a Slave* (1968), 54, *203*, 203–4, 219, 222; Lincoln's position on, 157–58; Meltzer on, 220; sentimental identification as means of combating, 205; Harriet Beecher Stowe, *Uncle Tom's Cabin* (1852), 205
Smith, Karen Patricia, 131
Smith, Rachel, 155
Smith, Vicky, 66
Snake Scientist, The (Montgomery, 1999), 93–94, 97, 98, 202, 214–17, *215*, 222
Sontag, Susan: *On Photography* (1977), 133–34, 135, 144, 155, 161, 162
sourcing heuristic, 108
Stabell, Ivy Linton, 239n2
Stalin, Joseph, 210, 211
Stanhope, Philip, 81–83
Stanley, Diane, and Peter Vennema: *Bard of Avon* (1992), 51

"starters" versus "stoppers," 95, 99
Stephens, John, 16, 17–19, 22, 24, 237n4, 245–46n4
Stone, Tanya Lee: *Almost Astronauts: 13 Women Who Dared to Dream* (2009), 30–31, 177–98, 178. See also *Almost Astronauts: 13 Women Who Dared to Dream*
Stonehenge, 51–53, 52, 94–95, 96–97, 138–39, 140–41
"stoppers" versus "starters," 95, 99
Story Book of Houses (Petersham, 1933), 73–74, 212
Story Book of Iron and Steel (Petersham, 1935), 73
Story Book of the Things We Wear (Petersham, 1939), 73
Stowe, Harriet Beecher: *Uncle Tom's Cabin* (1852), 205
Strong, Frances L.: *All the Year Round, a Nature Reader, Part 1: Autumn* (late 19th century), 117, 124
Sturtevant, Katherine: *A True and Faithful Narrative* (2006), 120
Sugar Changed the World: A Story of Magic, Spice, Slavery, Freedom, and Science (Marc Aronson and Marina Budhos, 2010), 124–25
suspension of disbelief, 221
Sutton, Roger, 131
S/Z (Barthes; 1970), 19–21, 24

Tanaka, Shelley, 87
Taniguchi, Marilyn, 180–81
Taylor, Ann: *City Scenes, or a Peep into London for Good Children* (1828), 118
television, critical viewing of, 245n4
textbooks, differentiated from children's nonfiction, 7–9

They Called Themselves the KKK: The Birth of an American Terrorist Group (Bartoletti, 2010), 70–71, 138, 141
third-person narration, 29, 97, 195
Time magazine, 211–12
To Be a Slave (Lester, 1968), 54, 203–4, 203, 219, 222
Todorov, Tzvetan, 50
Token for Children, A: Being an Exact Account of the Conversion, Holy and Exemplary Lives, and Joyful Deaths, of Several Young Children (Janeway, 1811), 207–8
Tomlinson, Carl M., 8
tone, 49, 54, 72, 73, 98, 102, 145, 151, 159, 227
Trachtenberg, Alan, 168–70, 174
Tracking Trash: Flotsam, Jetsam, and the Science of Ocean Motion (Burns, 2010), 218
True and Faithful Narrative, A (Sturtevant, 2006), 120
Trusler, John, 81
truthfulness: children's nonfiction prioritizing didacticism at expense of, 180–83; of photographs, 135, 137, 139–41, 152–53, 159–60, 163–64, 167–69
Tunnell, Michael O., 8; *Candy Bomber: The Story of the Berlin Airlift's "Chocolate Pilot"* (2010), 209–12
Tunner, William H., 211
Turkel, Susan, 57, 92, 177, 179, 182, 197, 198
Turner, Pamela S.: *The Frog Scientist* (2009), 54, 68–69, 68, 84, 85, 93, 217–18, 222
Twain, Mark: *Life on the Mississippi* (1883), 66

Ulanowicz, Anastasia, 206–7
unary photographs, 136, 141, 160, 173, 174, 242n1
Uncle Tom's Cabin (Stowe, 1852), 205

Vande Kopple, William J., 50–51
VanSledright, Bruce, 225, 229
Van Sluys, Katie, 179, 182
Vardell, Sylvia, 25–26
Veltkamp, Martijn, 221, 246n7
Vindication of the Rights of Woman, A (Wollstonecraft, 1792), 58
visible narrators/authors, 23, 29, 49, 55–64, 73–74, 163, 240n3
Vision of Beauty: The Story of Sarah Breedlove Walker (Lasky, 2000), 23, 24
voice, 29, 47–75, 224; character and voice, intersection of, 101–5; dialogue, critical engagement as, 64, 65–67, 69, 71–73, 75; first-person narration, 29, 49, 55, 57, 60–62, 73, 95, 97, 127, 149, 240n3; hallmarks of critical engagement in, 70–75; hedges, 29, 49, 50–55, 74, 138, 239n1, 243n3; necromancers, 49, 64–70, 74, 139; photographs and, 138–41; plural narrator, 62, 73; seamless narrative, problem of, 47–49, 74; second-person narration, 99; third-person narration, 29, 97, 195; tone, 49, 54, 72, 73, 98, 102, 145, 151, 159, 227; visible narrators/authors, 23, 29, 49, 55–64, 73–74, 163, 240n3
Volcano: The Eruption and Healing of Mount St. Helens (Lauber, 1986), 145–46, *146*, 150, 151
Vološinov, V., 16
vulnerability of characters, 83–86

Wakefield, Priscilla, 118; *Introduction to Botany* (1796), 95, 118–19; *The Juvenile Travelers* (1801), 61; *Perambulations in London, and Its Environs* (1809), 53, 54–55, 59–61, 62
Walker, Sarah Breedlove, 23, 24
Waller, Alison, 245n1
Washington, George, 180
WASPs (Women Airforce Service Pilots), 196, 244n4
Watson, J. Madison, 117–18
We Are the Government (Elting, 1946), 9
We Are the Ship: The Story of Negro League Baseball (Nelson, 2008), 61–64, *62*, 73
Weems, Mason Locke, 180, 182
Weitekamp, Margaret A., 184; *Right Stuff, Wrong Sex* (2004), 193–95, 196, 244n4
Werhan, E. T., 130
Westman, Karin, 213–14
Whole Brainers and Localizers, in Fleischman's *Phineas Gage* (2002), 100–102, 104
William Shakespeare and the Globe (Aliki, 1999), 51
Wineburg, Sam: on children's capacity for critical engagement, 198, 224–25; on fact-based view of nonfiction, 36–40, 43–44; on humility in nonfiction, 29, 40, 47; on peritexts, 110–11, 113–14, 116–17, 118, 130–31; on sourcing heuristic, 108; on voice, 47, 59, 64, 65, 67, 74–75, 139
Wittgenstein, Ludwig, 241n2
Wollstonecraft, Mary: *A Vindication of the Rights of Woman* (1792), 58
Women Airforce Service Pilots (WASPs), 196, 244n4

Wonders of the Telescope, The (Joyce, 1805), 67–68
Woodbury, Ronald, 42
Wright brothers, 163
Wu, Yung-Hsing, 245n1

yellow fever epidemic (1793), 69–70
Young Adult Library Services Association, 131, 239n1
Young Gentleman and Lady's Monitor, and English Teacher's Assistant, The (Moore, late 18th century), 117

Zappy, Erica, 218
Zarnowski, Myra: on characters, 90, 92, 94, 95, 96; on emotion and sentimentality, 202; inquiry-based view of non-fiction, advocacy of, 33, 177, 179, 182, 197, 198; negotiation of theory and, 22–23, 24; on peritexts, 107, 108, 110, 131; on photographs, 142–43, 144, 145, 147, 149; on voice, 51, 56–59, 66–67

Joe Sutliff Sanders is author of *Disciplining Girls: Understanding the Origins of the Classic Orphan Girl Story*, editor of *The Comics of Hergé: When the Lines Are Not So Clear*, and coeditor of *Good Grief! Children's Comics, Past and Present* and *Frances Hodgson Burnett's* The Secret Garden*: A Children's Classic at 100*. He is a university lecturer in English and children's literature in the Faculty of Education at the University of Cambridge.